MANAGING PEOPLE FOR THE FIRST TIME

Gaining commitment
and improving performance

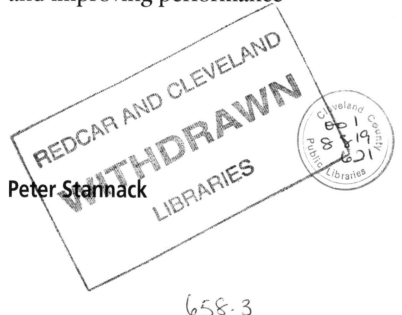

Peter Stannack

PITMAN PUBLISHING
128 Long Acre, London WC2E 9AN

A Division of Longman Group UK Ltd

© Livewire 1993

First published in Great Britain 1993

British Library Cataloguing in Publication Data
A CIP catalogue record for this book can be obtained from the British Library.

ISBN 0 273 60355 8

Typeset by PanTek Arts, Maidstone, Kent
Printed and bound in Great Britain by
Clays Ltd, St Ives plc

CONTENTS

FOREWORD

As Small Firms' Minister I act as champion for 96 per cent of British businesses. These employ less than 20 people and if you count the businesses with less than 100 people the figure rises to 99 per cent. The future success of this country depends on companies in this sector.

Small firms are increasingly becoming the principal job generators and are likely to remain so in the coming decade, as large companies focus on core activities and chase productivity in order to be globally competitive. Helping small firms to plan ahead and to recognise the issues associated with growth is very important. It is not necessary for small firms to re-invent the wheel, there is an enormous amount of experience to call on.

The DTI policy is to keep and grow the companies we have whilst creating a climate for others to start up and grow. This book has been written to help the owner, ready to grow, to understand and deal with the issues involved in moving from a small operation where every decision can be taken by one person, to the next stage where ideas and plans need to be executed by other people in order for the company to grow successfully. Livewire makes a wonderful midwife to business so I'm certain it will be an ideal friend for the exit from the nursery.

Denton of Wakefield

BARONESS DENTON OF WAKEFIELD
Parliamentary Under-Secretary of State for Consumer Affairs and Small Firms.

Acknowledgements

I am grateful to Sean Blair, Samantha Gemmell and Nick Oliver, all owner managers of young businesses, for reading early drafts and for their helpful comments and suggestions. I must also thank all my colleagues at Project North East and Livewire and, in particular, Sandy Ogilvie and David Irwin, for their patience, guidance and support.

1 SETTING THE SCENE

'If you think the way you've always thought, you'll get
what you've always got. Is it enough?'
ANON.

This book has been designed to help you develop your skills or ability – the way that you practise as a manager in a small organisation.

The first section of this book offers some of the 'tools' which a manager can use to work more effectively with people.

The second section looks at some of the contexts in which these 'tools' can and should be employed and introduces the idea of the 'job contract' – the contract between manager and employee which begins on the day that the manager places a recruitment advert or the employee sends off a CV. The informal job contract is about the expectations created between the manager and the employee. The formal job contract is a written symbol of this relationship.

Although this book refers to managing people, that might be misleading. Managing people is a problematic task. This book is about managing the relationship between the manager and his or her employees. Successful managers, and successful managers as leaders, do not manage people they manage their relationships with people. The final section of the book looks at integrating this in practice.

SALLY Ann Thorn generally hadn't the time to look in bookshops these days. They'd been having so many problems at the Norham Road site that it was looking as though they might have to close it. It had taken them two years to open it, and it looked like it was going to close after less than nine months. Sally couldn't understand why, but the staff seemed to be doing what they liked.

Anyway, Sally had been stuck waiting after offering to take her Mum Christmas shopping and had wandered into the local bookstore because it had been near her meeting place. Sally had been amazed at the number of books on the shelves offering advice on management and running a business. Picking up one after another, she briefly looked through them before putting them back.

'Are you looking for anything in particular, Miss?'

A salesperson had come up behind her.

'No, no thanks, I was just browsing. A lot of titles, aren't there?'

'Oh yes, business is our fastest growing section.'

'I wish that we could say the same,' said Sally. 'Still, it looks like a lot of ways to say the same thing.'

The salesperson looked alarmed. He wasn't going to get into arguments with loony customers.

'Well Madam, I suppose you could say that. These books are very popular.'

Because she was bored, and feeling mischievous, Sally replied, 'They don't change anything though, do they?

The salesperson was backing away rapidly now.

'I suppose not, Madam, not if you don't want to.'

As Sally turned back to the shelves she thought about what he'd said.

☐   ☐   ☐

Objectives

In this sense, managing people is both an easy and a difficult matter. It is easy because it means using skills that we've developed all our lives. It is difficult because we fail to recognise the complexity of the situations in which we find ourselves, and often apparently simple situations involving two people can be incredibly complex – just think about a marriage or relationship. Each of these skills is a tool in the toolbox which we call experience. The problem with our toolbox is that we often don't realise the range of tools which we already have available to manage people. We tend to stick with a comfortable few tools that we've used for years. We've got a hammer in there and a screwdriver, maybe a couple of chisels. Unfortunately, using the same tools again and again without maintenance tends to blunt them. And of course, when our tools don't work we either smash the machine, call in a specialist engineer, or simply walk away with the job half-finished.

Being an effective manager means taking stock of your toolbox, bringing out tools that you've not used for a while, or that you may have used in the wrong way, and sharpening the tools that you have been using. That is what this book is about.

No book will change anything in any major way unless you want it to. This book is intended to help you consider some of the issues involved in managing people in a small organisation. It is different from other books in that it is designed to help you realise how much you already know, rather than wasting your time with irrelevant information.

It is aimed at people working in small manufacturing, retail or service organisations which employ up to fifty people. It may be useful to you if you want to look at new, more effective ways of managing people in small organisations. It will be useful to you if you are managing people for the first time. This book defines an organisation as something in which people act together for a common purpose. They can pursue profit-related activities or non-profit activities. As entrepreneurial skills come to be more highly regarded in many organisational environments, it may also be useful to managers who work in small units within larger organisations. It offers a framework which states that in order to manage people effectively, you need to manage relationships effectively. This may involve considering:

1. the 'rules' of the relationship;

2. the support or maintenance given to the relationship;

3. the way in which the relationship develops and is developed.

Relationships are much easier to manage in the context of this framework. Considering the management of relationships rather than the management of people will also offer you a more flexible way of managing because it gives you more things to manage, manager–employee relationship, employee–employee relationships? Managing people will only give us one way of looking at the person problem: 'Told him what to do and he wouldn't do it' – there must be something wrong with him 'Managing the relationship gives a more accurate way of looking at the problem. 'I told him what to do and he wouldn't do it – there must be something wrong with the relationship.'

How this book proposes to achieve these objectives

This book is designed to help you manage people more effectively. It takes as its starting point a number of assumptions. The first, as we've noted, is that effective managers manage their relationships with employees rather than trying to manage their employees directly.

The second of these is that managing relationships is something that we all do from an early age. Management skills – negotiation, communication, learning and setting goals – are essential parts of growth and development for human beings. You already use a considerable number of management techniques without actively considering how they work. This book tries to help you examine the ways in which you use these techniques, examine them and improve them where necessary.

The third assumption is that management can be learned more effectively if it is relevant to the needs of the learner. Wholesale learning – learning which is offered because someone else thinks that it would be good for you to know – will not help you learn effectively.

The fourth is that each of the skill areas which is addressed in the first section of this book is unique to you as an individual. No two people learn in the same way. No two people manage stress or time in the same way and no two people communicate in quite the same way. Each of these skills is unique to you as a person.

This book will enable you to assess your own approach to issues such as time management, management of pressure, communication and its functions. Once you know where you are, you can adapt the broad approaches which it contains to suit your style. Effectively, this book is a tailored book designed to fit your individual needs.

FUNCTIONS OF THEORIES

Theories are a distillation of other people's experience. They help us borrow that experience and develop solutions to problems which we may face. They are not something which should be held in reverence or as being any more useful than your own experience. If a theory does not work, you should not bother with it.

Theories should be flexible and adaptable to the needs of the people who use them. This means that this book does not offer you one right answer. When you are working with people there are no right answers; there are only answers which are appropriate to the particular time and conditions in which you are working.

Theories are also about survival. They help you make sense of reality and help you manipulate and control it. This means that they act as a map which will get us around the world in comparative safety. Since all theories must leave things out, it is important not to confuse the map with the landscape. Theories are a tool to help you deal with both your personal world and your world of work.

Finally, remember that theories are only powerful because they enable us to feel comfortable. Remember that you control the theory that you use, the theory does not control you. You can chop bits off a theory, add bits to it or combine two theories together. If it works for you when you do this, congratulations: you've just invented a new theory.

The reason that I have said so much about theories is because this book does not offer you one best way or one 'right' answer. When we work with people there is no one best way or right answer. Each of the following chapters will offer you a number of theories about some elements of management. Let's say, for instance, that you want to look at teambuilding. The chapter on teambuilding will offer you a variety of different ways of looking at the process of building a team. None of these theories will offer you a complete picture of what team-building is about. You may, and will, probably find that putting the theories to work means that you will borrow bits from each of the theories offered in order to build something that works for you.

The 'Government Health Warning' on this book is that you can regard all the viewpoints it offers as being equally valid. If you feel that one particular theory has all the answers, you should stop and look again. Teambuilding is not just about Belbin's team types, nor is leadership just about team, task and individual. All of these theories are one way of looking at the way in which you can manage people effectively. The more ways of looking at management you have, the more tools you will be able to bring to bear in actually doing it. The fact that there can be more than one valid way of looking at the world is shown by the illustration of the Necker cube in Fig. 1.1. Look at the Necker cube. You will see after a while

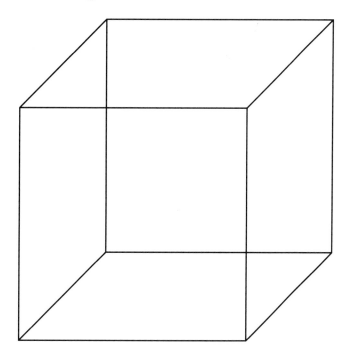

Fig. 1.1 The Necker cube

that it changes from being a left (or a right) facing cube to being a right (or a left) facing cube. This is because your brain is equally comfortable interpreting the information it receives in either way. Seeing the Necker cube as only a right facing cube or a left facing cube would be wrong. It is both. In order to develop an effective way of managing people we need multiple views of looking at the world. You may wish to order or prioritise these multiple viewpoints and one way in which you can do this is through a systems' viewpoint.

A SYSTEMS' VIEWPOINT

When working in any organisation, it is often very easy to make a quick analysis of what's going wrong. Some of the 'common sense' diagnoses of problems are:

- 'It's the system', or
- 'The lazy so and so won't work', or
- 'This organisation is so political'.

In order to obtain an accurate picture of what goes wrong in organisations and what steps can be taken to put it right, it can be useful to consider a systems' view of organisational life.

A systems' view is one which says that everything is made up of a number of elements connected in some way or another and that changes in any of these elements will effect the other elements which are connected to it.

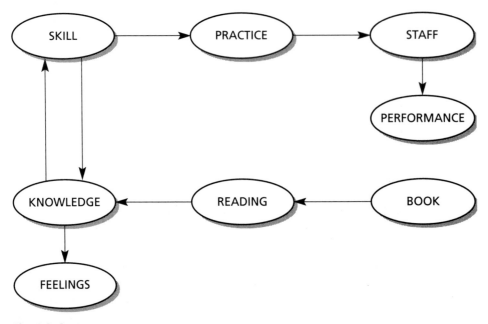

Fig. 1.2 Systems map

Systems' viewpoints are sometimes arranged in a hierarchy in order to make them more easily understandable. Thus, a motor engine would be a system for converting fuel into power. It would be a subsystem for a car, which in turn would be a subsystem for a city transport system, and so on. A motor engine would also be a supersystem for a carburettor, which in turn would be a supersystem for a float chamber or fuel jets.

This book uses a systems' view of people management in that it states that you need to develop a skills system – the ability to communicate, negotiate, etc. in order to manage your relationship with people effectively. It also treats recruitment and selection as a system which will affect staff performance and team-building as a system which will affect leadership.

A systems' view can offer you a way to integrate a number of perspectives and arrive at a better diagnosis, which will in turn give you a better basis for taking action. A systems' approach can help you take a more effective and balanced approach to managing people. Systems' views give a three (or multi-) dimensional picture and systems' approaches give a three (or multi-) dimensional toolbox to change the picture.

How to use this book

You can use this book in a number of ways:

- purely as an assessment guide. We all like to find things out about ourselves, and this book will offer you insights into the way in which you manage and may offer you food for thought in the way in which you work with people in future. You can use this insight as a basis for discussion with family or friends and it may help to widen your desire to learn and develop your management practice. This book cannot perform miracles. It is designed to help you consider how you might develop as a manager. If you do not want to develop as a manager, it will not do anything for you at all.

- by dipping in and out of the input sections to deal with particular problems that you may be facing. These sections will not offer you 'one right way' to develop teams which will operate a flexible manufacturing system effectively. They will help you look at some of the underpinning issues which can be adapted to offer solutions to a range of problems, one of which might be yours.

- by reading it as a 'novel'. The book is built around the story of Presteign Ltd and the development of Sally Ann Thorn's own management skills and practice. I hope that the story of Presteign Ltd and its people management problems will encourage the reader to consider his or her own work or business situation and perhaps to try out some of the solutions which Sally and her team found worked for them. All the situations in which Sally and her team find themselves are based on the actual experience of people running smaller business units, although they are also applicable to other situations.

Many managers are unhappy managers because they are unclear about their responsibilities or because they are unsure about the sort of skills that they should bring to the managerial role. Changes in the role of the manager mean that managers are asking questions of themselves such as: 'What is a "good" manager? Do managers still tell people what to do? Do we need more "soft" skills such as listening and facilitating?'

Managing is not a specialist activity. As the speed of change in the world increases, specialist skills become obsolete quickly. One of the major conflicts of the next ten years is likely to be the conflict between specialist and generalist. Such a conflict will impact upon job markets, education, training and the way in which organisations are run. Many of the accepted tasks of a manager are seen as planning, directing, controlling and organising. In the face of sophisticated employees we can see a need to develop new resources and skills. Managerial resources consists of qualities such as:

- *The ability to learn:* learning is the way in which you increase your resources of knowledge, skill, ability to cope, conceptual grasp etc. It involves you in the effective organisation and objective setting.

- *The ability to communicate:* whilst not strictly speaking a resource, communication is the way in which you can maximise your use of other resources outside of yourself.

- *The ability to manage effort:* the chapter on stress management will help you look at some of the ways in which you can manage your physical self and your surroundings in order to release more effort.

- *The ability to manage time:* the chapter on time management will offer you some pathways through which you can manage time more effectively and release more time for yourself and your organisation.

Once you have understood how much of these qualities you already use, you might wish to look at how you might use these resources to build relationships in a variety of situations, such as recruitment, staff development, appraisal, delegation, and team building. Issues like communication, effective information and processing underpin all of these situations.

Finally, you might wish to integrate all of these qualities to develop an integrated model of people management. The final section offers you a structured path through which you can use the resources and skills outlined in the other sections. A manager should be able to deploy these skills and resources to develop a vision of the ultimate destination design and build the vehicle, draw the road map and fuel the journey. This is leadership as a function of management.

2 LEARNING TO LEARN

'There are three ways of learning. The first is by experience and this is the hardest. The second is by imitating and this is the easiest. The third is by meditation and this is the noblest'.
CONFUCIUS (KUNG FU TZE)

Learning is the first of the tools in the manager's toolbox. It is the 'maintainance' tool which helps keep all the other tools sharp, bright and ready to use. Where a manager fails to learn, he or she will be unable to see, hear or feel properly in order to use his or her other tools.

Learning is an essential management skill. It involves acquiring, sorting, analysing and storing information. Information is what underpins all human actions. You can learn by obtainng new information; by combining existing information into new patterns; by finding new meaning in existing information.

If you don't learn, you are handicapping yourself. A person who fails to learn is like someone who has been blindfolded and had wax plugs put in their ears from the age of let's say, eleven. The blindfold isn't very good because it lets in some light, the earplugs also let in some noise, but the world is fuzzy and the noises are unclear. This person is given a complicated task involving delicate work such as repairing an expensive watch. The person can't see the watch very well and although they received clear instructions, only caught about half of them. Rediscovering how to learn means that this person can take off the blindfold and unplug their ears. Rediscovering how to learn puts you in charge of your own learning.

The objectives of this chapter are:

► *to help you look at how learning is directly related to efficiency and effectiveness in your work;*

► *to help you identify some of the ways in which you learn and some of the blocks which might stop you learning;*

► *to look at how you might develop effective learning strategies and employ these in your work and business.*

SALLY got into the office late on Thursday morning. Her desk was already covered with telephone message slips and 'post it' notes. Jenny, the secretary, told her that Dave had already rung three times and wanted her down at the Elm Road site before ten o'clock to talk about the Wilmsdorf contract. Sally's ex-boyfriend had called round late the night before and had started another row about why they'd broken up. As usual, he blamed the hours she put in at Presteign and the way that she kept talking about work. By the time Sally had heard him out, it was two o'clock in the morning and the last thing she wanted to hear was another set of problems.

'Bloody hell, Jenny, just calm down. Go and make me a cup of coffee and let me sort through this stuff.'

Jenny gave Sally a wounded look and went out to the enclosure, cluttered with grimy cups, that posed for a kitchen in the commercial section. 'Wow!' thought Sally, 'the commercial section!' When Sally, Mike, Dave and Alan had started the company from scratch six years ago, there had been no such thing as a commercial section. Everyone had done everyone else's job. Sally missed the day-to-day contact that they had had then.

As Jenny came in with a chipped mug full of coffee, Sally reflected on just what had happened to the company. Looking back, it was hard to tell just what had happened. The day-to-day running of the marketing operations meant that you were constantly making decisions and plans on the run. Meetings followed meetings and just recently it was getting harder to keep hold of exactly where the company was going. She rarely saw Alan, Dave or Mike any more except at meetings which always revolved around one sort of problem or another. Much of the fun was going out of the business, although they seemed to be making plenty of money.

The telephone sounded abnormally loud and Sally jumped, spilling coffee over the papers on her desk. She swore and picked up the handset; it was Dave.

'Sal, where the hell are you? You were due here fifteen minutes ago.'

'Sorry, Dave, bad night last night – can I cancel?'

'You know that this is a scheduling meeting, Sal, and you need to know what's going on just as badly as the rest of us. Your new orders are causing problems for Alan and you just don't want to talk it out. This will be the second meeting you've tried to miss. When are you going to learn?'

When are you going to learn? Sal thought back to lunch the day before yesterday with Josh Slocum. Josh had bumped into her out of the blue and they'd arranged lunch on spec. Much of the time they'd talked about school and college. Josh had been a star, staying on to take a Master's in Psychology and finally a Doctorate in something or other.

Sally had thought that he would have gone into teaching, but he was evidently working for some sort of high-powered management consultancy company with links into two of the new Universities.

After making the usual consultancy jokes about borrowing your watch to tell you the time and then stealing it, Sally asked Josh what sort of consulting he was doing.

'I'm helping people learn how to learn, Sal', Josh had said with an amused look on his face.

'How does it pay?' said Sal.

'Okay for me', replied Josh, 'Better for the people who do it.'

□   □   □

When are you going to learn? Let's take a look at what we mean by learning. For most of us, learning is about school, college or university. Education involves us sitting quietly in large rooms with someone – generally older than we are and differently dressed – telling us about alphabets or tax law or economic modelling. Sessions like this can go on for hours, or what seems like hours, at a time.

It is hardly surprising that most of us see learning as something to be endured – get the exam, find the job, get the pay rise. Learning is, however, more than this. Learning is fundamental to human performance. Some psychologists and behaviourists go so far as to say that our specialisation as a species is that of learning rather than using tools or speech.

Because humans are fairly essential elements of a business, learning is also fundamental to business performance. It involves change and as such means that if your business fails to learn to meet changes in the market place, it will fail to perform properly. Increasingly, we see terms such as 'the learning organisation' or 'the learning company' in common use.

Reg Revans[1] identified an equation:

$$L \geq C$$

In other words, learning must equal, or be greater than, changes in the environment in order for a company to continue to function.

Quite simply, this means that if you don't learn to cope with the changes in the world around you, you will not acquire or maintain the competitive edge which is necessary for business success. If you don't learn you don't develop, and if you don't develop your organisation in the face of change your organisation will die.

What's in it for me?

Sally hadn't understood why Josh had been so keen on learning. It seemed like a load of academic rubbish with no practical application. Josh had already

[1]Professor Reg Revans, *Action Learning*, Blond and Briggs, 1980.

said that strategy was a word that consultants put in front of things to let them charge an extra £1,000 a day. Wasn't learning the same sort of thing ?

Josh had smiled again. 'You're a hard sell, Sally, but just think for a minute. Learning involves us in acquiring new knowledge and developing new skills and attitudes which make us more effective in our chosen area of work. We may believe that we've reached the top in our business, but learning is about growth and continuous development. If you feel that you have nothing more to learn, you're closing yourself to new opportunities. All sorts of stuff like Total Quality Management are tied up in learning.

'As a manager you will learn all the time. Learning is unavoidable. The trick is to learn quickly and to learn the right things. You must be familiar with the feeling of disappointment which comes from realising that you've recognised an opportunity too late.'

'I'll say' said Sally,' We lost out on orders at the Hamburg trade fair three months ago, but that's just a missed opportunity. It could happen to anybody – bad luck, that's all.'

'And companies that didn't lose out? Were they just lucky – or had they learnt in time? Effective learning means that you can identify opportunities for improvement or development for yourself or your business.'

□   □   □

There is a lot of evidence to suggest that as managers we are unable to 'see' ourselves. If we can't 'see' how we operate, we're unable to change our own practice. So, if we think that the best way to get people to do things is to manipulate them, or to withhold information from them or to shout at them, we'll tend to look for things which support that view. We'll keep on using that management strategy, despite the fact that it's not working.

This means that we'll use more and more effort less and less effectively when by learning you can change and develop your strategy to use less effort for more effectiveness, more 'bang for your buck'.

Learning helps you to broaden your range of understanding and increase the number of tools in your toolkit. Let's go back to the idea of a continuum of behaviour. A continuum is simply the whole range of behaviour which a manager could have at his or her disposal. So a continuum for 'helping' could range from 'doing things for people' to 'doing things so people can help themselves'.

One of the behavioural continua we could look at is that of decision making. At one end of this continuum it is possible to involve people in decision making to such a degree that all decisions are arrived at by democratic consensus. At the other end of this continuum it is possible to make all decisions as a manager without involving others at all. In some cases the first of these actions is appropriate. In others the second is appropriate, and in yet others are additional points along the continuum.

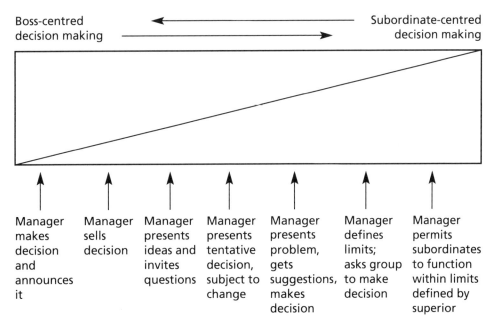

Boss-centred decision making ⟵ **Subordinate-centred decision making** ⟶

| Manager makes decision and announces it | Manager sells decision | Manager presents ideas and invites questions | Manager presents tentative decision, subject to change | Manager presents problem, gets suggestions, makes decision | Manager defines limits; asks group to make decision | Manager permits subordinates to function within limits defined by superior |

Fig. 2.1 Tannenbaum and Schmidt decision making continuum

We may, however, unknowingly become 'stuck' at one point or at one range in this behavioural continuum. Whatever it is that motivates us to act in a particular way will be dictated by the way in which we interpret the information we receive. The filter which interprets this information can be called our attitudes, values or personal theories about the world. All of these support ways of behaving with which we feel comfortable. These will have grown with us as we have grown and we rarely question the way in which we acquired them, or indeed, how effective they are.

Daniel Dennet[2] in his book *Consciousness Explained* tells a story about 'Shakey', one of the robots built at the Stanford Research Institute in California in the 1960s. Shakey the robot was built to tell the difference between boxes and other 3D shapes and to push the boxes off a table. Shakey was a pretty primitive robot as robots go, consisting of a box on wheels with a television eye. His 'brain' was a large mainframe computer in another room.

Shakey was programmed to identify the boxes by counting the number and type of vertices (where two or more lines join) and to categorise them. It did this by means of thousands of lines of binary programming consisting of zeros and ones which were able to differentiate between the different vertices. Dennett in his description of Shakey offers an imaginary situation where someone could ask Shakey how it knew which shapes to push off a table and which to leave on. In its imaginary reply Shakey could say

[2]Daniel Dennet, *Consciousness Explained*, Penguin, 1991.

1 'I photograph each shape and scan it against a 10,000 long digit shape in my memory, consisting of 0s and 1s. Then I . . .' (A very long answer if Shakey continues.) Or

2 'In my mind's eye, I look at the shapes. Identify the light and dark boundaries. Examine the vertices. If I've got a Y vertex bingo! It's a box.' Or

3 'I dunno. Some things just look boxy. It just comes to me. It's by intuition.'

Human beings have several levels of operation and response, just like Shakey. Learning will help you realise why a box is a box. Once you understand the 'why' of your own management practice you can modify it to meet new situations. Once you understand the 'why' of new situations you can take effective action to control and develop them.

How do we do it?

Although we may learn naturally, unexamined learning may lead us to learn the wrong things. The first step in learning is to consider our own personal learning skills, style and preferences. Whilst each of us learns in a unique way, there are a number of beliefs which all people share.

The first of these beliefs is that personal worth is related to and depends upon the success of our actions. Therefore 'I' must be competent. If 'I' believe 'I' am competent, I don't need to learn.

The second is that my sense of personal identity depends on being predictable to myself and also to others. Therefore 'I' must be consistent. This consistency supports my competence.

The third is that I believe that my survival as a person depends upon my ability to understand, explain and predict the world. Therefore 'I' must be in control. Learning involves relinquishing control because of needs for risk and discovery.

The final belief is that it is possible or desirable at least to go through life without feeling anxious, upset or guilty. Therefore 'I' must be comfortable. Learning isn't comfortable. As we'll see, learning is about change and change is uncomfortable.

LEARNING STYLES

Given that we all share these beliefs to some degree, learning is very much a matter of personal preferences and styles. Broadly these will be dictated by our upbringing. In the 1970's a psychologist called David Kolb identified four elements which made up learning[3]. These are:

[3]David Kolb, *Experiential Learning*, Prentice Hall, 1984.

SENSING/FEELING

Style four – 'The dynamic learner'

– integrates experience and application
– seeks hidden possibilities and excitement
– needs to know what can be done with things
– learns by trial and error
– perceives information concretely and processes it actively
– adaptable to and relishes change
– excels in situations calling for flexibility
– tends to take risks
– often reaches accurate conclusions in the absence of logical evidence
– functions by acting and testing experience
– *Strengths:* acting and carrying out plans
– *Goals:* making things happen, bringing action to concepts
– *Favourite Questions:* If? What can this become?

Style one – 'The innovative learner'

– integrates experience with 'self'
– seeks meaning, clarity and integrity
– needs to be personally involved
– absorbs reality
– perceives information concretely and processes it reflectively
– interested in people and culture
– divergent thinkers who believe in their own experience and excel in viewing concrete situations from many perspectives
– model themselves on those they respect
– learn by listening and sharing ideas
– function through social interaction
– *Strengths:* innovation and imagination (ideas people)
– *Goals:* self-involvement in important issues bringing unity to diversity
– *Favourite Questions:* Why? Why not?

DOING — WATCHING

Style three – 'The common sense learner'

– seeks usability, utility, results
– needs to know how things work
– learns by testing theories that seem sensible
– skill-oriented
– perceives information abstractly and processes it actively
– needs hands-on experiences
– enjoys problem solving
– restricts judgement to concrete things
– resents being given answers and has limited tolerance of 'fuzzy' ideas
– needs to know how things asked to do will help in real life
– functions through inference drawn from sensory experience
– *Strengths:* practical application of ideas
– *Goal:* bringing their view of the present into line with future security
– *Favourite Question:* How does it work?

Style two – 'The analytic learner'

– seeks facts
– needs to know what the experts think
– learns by thinking through ideas
– values sequential things, needs details
– perceives information abstractly and processes it reflectively
– less interested in people than ideas
– critiques information abstractly and processes it reflectively
– critiques information and collects data
– thorough and industrious, re-examining facts if situations are perplexing
– enjoys traditional classrooms
– functions by thinking things through and adapting to experts
– *Strengths:* creating concepts and models
– *Goals:* self-satisfaction, intellectual recognition
– *Favourite Question:* What?

THINKING

Fig. 2.2 Learning styles

Observing and reflecting = watching
Experiencing = feeling
Experimenting = doing
Conceptualising = thinking

If you are happier learning through watching and feeling you will tend to use an innovative learning style. Favourite questions will tend to be 'Why?' or 'Why not?' If you are happier thinking and doing you will tend to use a common sense learning style. Use Figure 2.2 to assess your own learning style. Are you happier learning by doing, watching, feeling or thinking?

Consider the two aspects of learning with which you are most happy to derive your learning style.

Right and left brain learning

Another important aspect of learning is our tendency to use one part of our brain more than another in our learning. The human brain consists of two halves: left and right. Each is connected, but where one half dominates our attitude to problem solving, learning or decision making we will display a clear preference for one type of learning.

Use the exercise below to determine your orientation to left or right brain learning. It should give you an idea of your learning preferences. Considering your own learning style and your own orientation will help you consider how to develop effective learning strategies which will help you improve your own performance.

ASSESSMENT EXERCISE

Respond to each of the statements in the first part of the exercise by completing the space which completes the statement so that it is true for you or more true for you more of the time than the alternative.

Section A

1. When planning my daily activities, I usually
   (a) make a list of things to do
   (b) picture the places I will go and the people I'll see

2. When I go to the cinema I usually sit in
   (a) the left side of the theatre
   (b) the right of the theatre

3. In order to prepare myself for a new difficult task I am likely to
   (a) compile extensive information about the task
   (b) visualise the problems and how I'll deal with them

4. My favourite problem solving approach is to
   (a) find the best way of solving the problem
   (b) think of a number of different ways of solving the problem

5. When I meet someone, I find it easier to
   (a) remember the person's name
   (b) remember the person's face

6. When I shop I
   (a) buy on impulse
   (b) only buy the best bargains after weighing up the costs and benefits

7. Generally, I absorb new ideas by
    (a) comparing and contrasting them with other ideas
    (b) applying them to 'real world' situations

8. When I need to motivate myself, I do so by
    (a) setting my own targets
    (b) competing against others

9. Daydreaming is
    (a) a viable tool for planning and problem solving
    (b) a waste of time

10. I am best at recalling
    (a) spatial arrangements – room layouts, where people sat
    (b) verbal or numerical data – names, ages, dates

11. When I am explaining something I prefer
    (a) to do it in writing
    (b) to do it by speaking

12. When someone gives me an assignment, I would rather have
    (a) specific instructions
    (b) flexible instructions

13. If describing a film that I have seen, I tend to describe
    (a) the scenes and action
    (b) the dialogue

14. If, I had a choice, I would rather work
    (a) by myself
    (b) on a team

15. When reading a paper, I read
    (a) to understand the main ideas
    (b) to understand details and facts

16. I tend to make decisions
    (a) after careful thought and analysis
    (b) by gut feeling or 'hunches'

17. I like to organise things
    (a) to show relationships
    (b) to show time or other sequence

18. I prefer solving problems
    (a) intuitively
    (b) logically and rationally

Section B

Place a tick against all the statements that are true about you.

19. I am outgoing and work well with others.

20. I am good at thinking up new ideas.

21. I can make sense of plans and diagrams.

22. I like to relax and do nothing.

23. I like to paint and sketch.

24. I postpone making telephone calls.

25. I like to sing in the bath.

26. I enjoy redecorating my home.

27. I have a place for everything and a system for doing things.

28. I can learn through reading books and instruction manuals.

29. I like to collect things.

30. I take notes at meetings and lectures.

31. I am results-oriented.

32. I enjoy planning projects in detail.

33. I like to read.

34. I enjoy crossword puzzles.

Scoring

Score your responses as follows. Circle your response.

	Left Brain	Right Brain
1.	a	b
2.	a	b
3.	a	b
4.	a	b
5.	a	b
6.	b	a
7.	b	a
8.	b	a
9.	b	a
10.	b	a
11.	b	a
12.	a	b

13.	b	a
14.	a	b
15.	b	a
16.	a	b
17.	b	a
18.	b	a

Statements 19-26 are right brain responses, add one point for each ticked.

Statements 27-34 are left brain responses, add one point for each ticked.

Add the two totals and this will give you your likely preference.

Where we show a preference for right brain thinking, we may demonstrate considerable creative, musical or artistic talents. Right brain thinkers tend to rely on feelings and intuition. They are good at recognising patterns with a minimum of information provided and may excel at solving complex problems requiring creativity and insight.

Left brain thinkers may demonstrate strong verbal, logical or analytical skills. Such a person tends to be meticulous and well organised and probably excels at planning, projecting costs and performing similar tasks requiring precise attention to detail.

Some people are able to use both the left and right side of their brains. Such a person may be flexible in his or her approach to learning and may be able to learn in a number of varying situations.

LEARNING AND CHANGE

Learning involves change and change can be painful. Elizabeth Kubler Ross,[4] a psychologist who carried out extensive work on the way in which people learn to cope with major changes in their lives including the death of someone close, found that people react to change in a similar way, although at different rates. This is embodied in the curve shown in Figure 2.3. It shows people's response to changes which they cannot control.

Stage 1 Shock in response to the event which signals change. – '*I don't believe it*'.

Stage 2 Denial of the reality of the change – '*It won't affect me*'.

Stage 3 Frustration and anger about the change. A tendency to blame, and a sense of injustice – '*Why me? What have I done to deserve it?*'

Stage 4 Depression and apathy – '*I'm fed up*'.

Stage 5 Experimenting with new behaviour. As a result of the pain suffered in Stage 4, a willingness to try something new – '*I'll give it a try*'.

[4]Elizabeth Kubler Ross, *Death – the Final Stage of Growth* Spectrum, 1975.

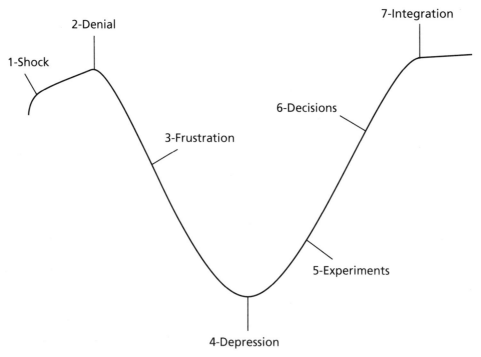

Fig. 2.3 Reactions to change.

Stage 6 Accepting the reality of the change – '*It's not as bad as I thought it would be*'.

Stage 7 Integrating the change into your life. Developing new attitudes and ways of behaving – '*I never thought it would work*'.

You may wish to identify the ways in which you have coped with change at work:

- over which you had no control;
- over which you had some control.

List some of the ways in which you deal with change effectively and try to decide if there are any stages at which you might get stuck. Consider also the ways in which partners, colleagues or employees might deal with change and what mechanisms you might use to help yourself and them. Does it, for instance, help to control the change or at least have a say in it? Does it help to know what the results of the change will be?

We can see that learning is not simply a process whereby information is poured into passive sponges which soak it up and regurgitate it at a later stage. Learning is an active process which is uniquely personal to you and which involves you in change. Learning can be blocked by your beliefs about yourself and can be hampered by a reluctance to change. Once you've decided your own learning preferences and attitudes towards change, you will be better placed to manage your own learning.

Developing effective learning strategies

The first step in managing your own learning is to set yourself clear objectives about learning. Unless you know what you want or need to learn, your learning is likely to be passive rather than active. What you need to learn will be dictated by your objectives. Clear personal objectives will help you to develop clear learning objectives.

Do not make the New Year's Resolution mistake. Most New Year's Resolutions fail because they are not specific or measurable. Humans get a sense of how well they are doing by having clear measurable targets. Without clear measurable targets they are unable to assess how well they are doing and are unable to improve their performance. For instance, a learning or training programme with the aim 'to improve safety on building sites' will be likely to fail. How can you measure increased safety on building sites? How can you link it to your training programme? A programme with the aim 'to increase the incidence of employees wearing safety helmets' will tend to be more successful. There is a clear objective if you want to change make sure that your objectives are SMART:

- **S**pecific
- **M**easurable
- **A**chievable
- **R**ealistic
- **T**imed

In setting your objectives you might want to consider the following exercise. Imagine, if you will, that you have been sufficiently fortunate to live until your one hundredth birthday. On your birthday a local radio talk show celebrity arrives at your house to interview you. She asks you the question: 'Looking back over your life which five things would you be most proud of ?' What would you like to be able to reply? Try to choose at least one thing from each area of your life – work, family, personal achievements etc.

This exercise may help you to consider your broad objectives. Once you've decided on your broad objectives, you can narrow these down to identify three things that you might need to do to bring one of these about. You might then wish to consider what you will have to learn to do this.

Learning involves managing information. This information may be found in books or in lectures or, perhaps more importantly in day-to-day interaction with new people and situations. Within the boundaries imposed by your own learning styles, preferences and attitudes, we can identify three elements of learning:

- the presentation of information;
- sorting and analysing information;
- recording information or remembering.

Let's look at each of these in turn.

PRESENTING INFORMATION

We've already seen that education/training and learning may not always be compatible. Carl Rogers said that the only learning which truly makes a difference is self-appropriated, self-discovered learning. If your experience of learning has been one in which teachers or trainers try to stuff you full of 'knowledge' in order to meet tests which have no relationship to anything that you experience in the important areas of your life, you are unlikely to see learning as a positive experience. You can manage the information available within the learning process by presenting this information to yourself in a different way. Let's look at some of the ways in which you can acquire new information.

- *Problem solving*. Every problem that you solve is likely to involve you in learning. Problem solving means bringing together new information or existing information into new patterns. Every problem genuinely solved or resolved is a learning.

- *Discovery*. Every time you find out something new you've been involved in learning. This new thing can be as fundamental as a discovery about the attitude or capacity of a friend or colleague, or as peripheral as a short cut to work or a new picnic site.

- *Example*. Psychologists call this behavioural modelling. We tend to 'learn' by copying other people who've developed what we see as successful strategies for dealing with their world. That's why small organisations take on the characteristics of larger organisations. Small organisations doing things for the first time will often turn to large organisations for solutions.

- *Instruction*. This is the type of learning to which we are often most resistant. It is in many ways the most unnatural form of learning because of its very nature. Learners in an instructional situation are rarely encouraged to learn or discuss what matters to them. They have solutions imposed upon them. In instructional situations collaboration is often frowned upon and the situation often demands clear answers to unclear questions. Instruction can involve a person or people that you don't know, telling you things that seem irrelevant.

- *Theories*. Theories are, as we've seen, 'maps' of how to get around the world. They are related to instructions but need not be. Essentially, theories are a distillation of other people's experience or distillation of your own experience. They are a method of patterning information.

- *Trial and error.* Guy Claxton in his book *Live and Learn*[5] calls this 'floundering'. Trial and error is perhaps the most painful method of learning but in some cases it leads to developing theories. In others, it can lead to a position where the individual concerned is determined henceforth to learn by example. Floundering is a primitive reaction to threat. When caught in a stressful situation people may flounder about, trying different methods of coping with the threat.

You can learn through using any or all of these strategies or approaches but each strategy will be dictated by personal preference, need and the type of learning that you require. Clearly, problem solving may be a better learning strategy than floundering or trial and error simply because it is less painful. If you use a problem solving approach to learning, you may benefit from using a structured approach such as that outlined below.

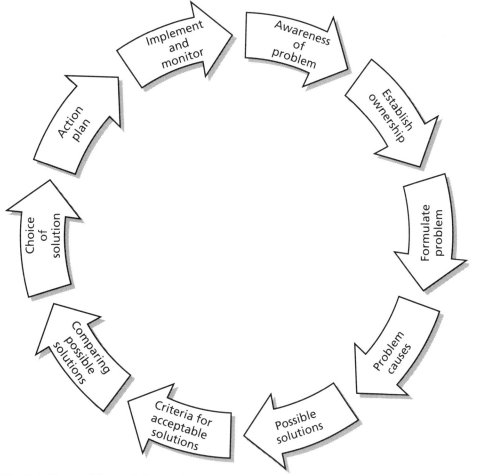

Fig. 2.4 The problem solving cycle

[5]Guy Claxton, *Live and Learn*, Harper and Row, 1984.

1. *Awareness of problem*

   List all relevant details of the problem. How it was identified, its characteristics and effects.

2. *Establish ownership*

   Is it your problem? If not, you don't need to solve it. If it's a shared problem work with, not for, the other person.

3. *Formulating a problem*

   Formulating problems in such a way as to aim at your intended goal. 'How can I get this job done?' rather than 'He won't do the job'. Try to ensure that formulation leaves the problem solution in your hands.

4. *Causes*

   Identify causes. Brainstorm if necessary, then restrict your list to probable causes. Check if your causes indicate a clear solution.

5. *Possible solutions*

   Brainstorm a list of possible solutions. Do not evaluate or judge. Do not limit yourself to feasibility.

6. *Determine criteria for acceptable solutions*

   Set out the requirements of a 'good' solution upon which you will make your final choice.

7. *Comparing solutions*

   Examine the routes and outcomes for your possible solutions. Look at their advantages and disadvantages. Don't dismiss options which seem unrealistic. They may have useful elements.

8. *Choice of solution*

   Choosing a solution means letting go of possibilities. More than one solution may be needed – beware of multiple problems. Look at the solution in various ways.

9. *Action plan*

   Your action plan will need to define a goal and break it into substages. Set dates, objectives and the resources (people, material) you will need.

10. *Implement and monitor*

    Put your plan into action and monitor it according to the acceptable criteria. Since problem situations change as we work on them you may find a series of 'action review' plan subcycles will be needed until the solution is attained.

SORTING AND ANALYSING INFORMATION

Learning using the problem-solving cycle gives you the opportunity to structure issues. Once issues are structured you can ***analyse*** them and act upon them. Without structure, issues are less controllable and learning is difficult to surface.

There are a number of other structuring techniques which can be used to analyse your own learning including the journalist's six questions:

What?
Who?
Why?
When?
Where?
How?

Asking these questions of problem or discovery situations can help your learning stay focused upon your objectives.

RECORDING INFORMATION OR REMEMBERING

The final element of learning, once you've acquired and analysed information is retention and retrieval. Retention and retrieval is generally seen as 'memory'. There are a number of ways in which you can manage your information retention and retrieval skills. The first of these is to organise information for retention. If information is organised in a way which helps it 'go in', it is much more likely to stay.

The first thing that you can do to organise for retention is to make use of a skill which we may possess from birth: that is, *clustering*. There is a considerable body of research which tends to show that people learn and remember through associative networks. Practically, this means that we will tend to make connections between knowledge that we already have and new learning. Effectively, we'll learn more readily when we can make a connection with what we enjoy learning.

One of the ways in which this connectionist model works is seen in a study carried out by the Russian psychiatrist, A. Luria. Luria worked extensively with a newspaper reporter whom he referred to as 'S'. S could effortlessly remember long lists of names and numbers. He did this by association. In order to remember a grocery list, for instance, he would visualise a familiar street and imagine walking down it and placing the objects in a specific place – eggs under a street light, bread in a doorway, etc. When S needed to recall the list he would imagine walking back down the street and recite the objects that he saw. Curiously, he only made a mistake when he 'put' an object in a place which was hard to see, such as a white egg in front of a white wall or licorice in the shadow of a building.

The second thing that you can do to aid retention and retrieval is to make information easier to use. This can involve using keywords. Keywords are the ones which are most loaded with meaning and which are likely to unlock your memory. Keywords can be used in two different ways to organise and store information for easy retrieval. The first of these is in *sprays*.

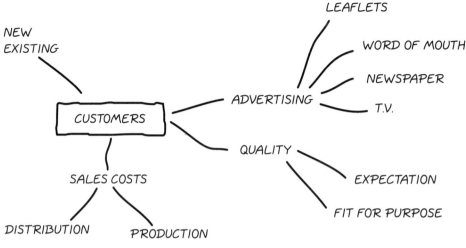

Fig. 2.5 'Sprays'

Sprays are a method of quickly jotting down ideas on a subject. They save time because you don't have to write words down in any particular order or produce sentences.

Another method of using key words is through **pattern notes**. You can use pattern notes as a basis for a presentation or in summarising what you've recently read. They are an absorbing and fruitful method of storing information for retrieval.

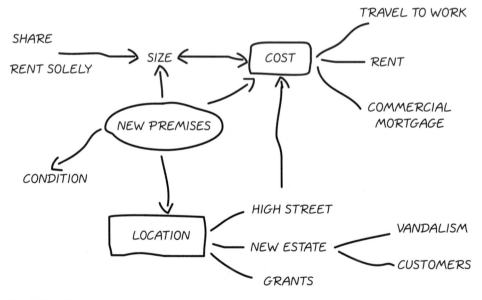

Fig. 2.6 Pattern maps

Feedback

Once you have developed your own information processing skills you might wish to examine the sort of information that you'll need to look out for. We've seen that you will learn much more readily if your learning is related to your objectives. This type of information, 'hot' information, can be called feedback. Let's look at what feedback can do. Feedback is the relevant information which will help you control your environment.

□   □   □

Sally remembered the time last summer when she'd had to prepare a presentation for a group of potential customers. Dave had set up the meeting and given her some background on the audience, but she'd had to learn a lot about their companies because the presentation had to be tailored. She supposed that the reward from potential orders was what had led her to work late at the library. But she didn't see that as anything but a 'one off.'

'I still don't see how learning is of use in everyday life.'

Josh looked at her in exasperation: 'There are some people who don't think water has any taste because they've drunk from the same source all their lives. Learning is a TFG for you, because you've done it all your life.'

'A TF what?' said Sally.

'A TFG – a 'taken for granted' – something you don't question. You need to question everything, particularly in a small business like yours, Sally – sales, stockholding, cost and debt control, everything. You've got to look for the causes rather than the symptoms if you're going to grow, or even hang on.'

'Okay', said Sally, 'But there is so much to learn. How do I know whether what I'm learning is the right thing.

Josh was really hitting his stride now. 'In lecturer mode' was what Sally and her friends had called it in college.

'It is the message which you receive when you try out a behaviour. For a small child exploring near a cooker, feedback is the feel of heat on its hand. When you climb a ladder you test for feedback by pressing against a rung before putting your whole weight on it. If the rung cracks, or gives out a noise which you don't recognise, you will climb down and check the ladder. In each case, learning has taken place. The child has learnt not to burn its hand and you have learnt not to injure yourself in a fall from a ladder.'

'You ignore feedback at your peril. Feedback is something that affects all areas of life: friendship – you've rung your old schoolfriend six or seven times, but she's never returned your call; business – stocks just don't seem to be moving at the moment or you don't open letters from your bank manager; health – you seem tired all the time, but unable to sleep, you've been smoking or drinking more recently. All of these areas mean that we are not only losing vital messages about what is happening to us, we are also losing the opportunity to change it. The bank manager's ignored letters can soon become a request to repay the overdraft facility.'

□   □   □

DEVELOPING YOUR OWN FEEDBACK SYSTEM

As human beings we are all recipients of feedback and givers of feedback. Receiving feedback and incorporating it into your future attitudes and behaviour is called learning. Giving feedback and making sure it is incorporated into other people's future attitudes and behaviour can be called teaching. It will help you to consider what sort of feedback will help you both learn and teach.

When you are learning, you may wish to learn in situations which appeal to your own learning style. You may also wish to consider the environment in which you learn and whether you learn most effectively in company or alone. Research shows that adults tend to learn more effectively in groups. Some of you will be working through this book on your own, and it may help to choose a mentor and to contract with that person to help you to carry through some of the exercises and learnings which are offered.

A mentor could be a friend or family member who will help you carry through the assignments set out in this workbook by offering feedback on progress and advice when you feel in need of it. Consider who would be likely to give you honest feedback. Honest feedback or criticism is a vital part of any system. No one actually enjoys criticism, because of the painful memories associated with it, but we should try to remember how essential it is. Climbing the ladder involves feedback about the strength of the rungs, the stability of the base, the movement at the top of the ladder. Running a business involves feedback about customer response, return on investment, staff performance, etc. As we will see in later sections, organisations and systems designed around effective feedback tend to succeed. Organisations and systems built around faith in product or other forms of ineffective feedback tend to fail. Choose a mentor who will both give you honest feedback and from whom you can accept that feedback.

In order to be effective feedback needs to be:

- specific
- immediate
- positive

This is just common sense. If you give people non-specific feedback, it will be disregarded. If Bill the caretaker has failed to lock up after the office has closed, or failed to remove the rubbish, he needs feedback about that failure. He doesn't need to be told that you're not happy with his work. Although this is common sense, many people duck the issue, causing major problems in the future. If you have agreed to do something and failed to deliver, you need feedback on what it is that you haven't done, not on your habit of biting your toenails in the bath.

Feedback also needs to be immediate. It needs to be linked strongly with the behaviour that you want to change either in time or in revisiting the incident. It is no use saying, either to yourself or others , 'Four months ago, you didn't take the rubbish out'. The behaviour has probably changed and the feedback will be seen as irrelevant and poorly motivated.

Feedback also needs to be positive. This is difficult, but as in the exercises above, you will find that you and others will learn more effectively if you are rewarded for changing behaviour rather than punished. If we are punished – even in minor ways – with the intention of changing us, we will tend to find other ways of avoiding the punishment rather than changing the behaviour. 'I'd be really grateful if you could take the rubbish out tonight, Bill' will work better in the long term than 'If you don't take the rubbish out I'll . . .'.

DEVELOPING CONFIDENCE AND MOTIVATION

Once we have decided that we want to learn, and how we can learn in a way which is both effective and with which we feel comfortable, the next stage is to develop motivation to learn effectively and the confidence to carry out effective learning.

Motivational strategies are about ensuring that we have the desire to put effective learning into action. Motivational strategies for ourselves are just as important as motivational strategies for our staff, and these fall broadly into two types.

Support strategies

Learning alone is often difficult. Motivation to learn alone can be low. Research shows that adults learn better when learning in the company of other adults or when supported in some way. Some psychologists use the concept of our self – who we are – as in 'internal community'. A group of different sub-personalities is directed by an over-manager. Each of these sub-personalities has different skills and abilities to bring to a problem. The idea of the internal community is one to which we will return when we look at putting a project into action.

This internal community is reflected by an external community of support which we use to assist us in our day-to-day tasks and problem solving. This community not only consists of people – family, friends, partners etc. but also of feelings about music, motor cars, politics and so forth.

When we are learning, it can help to identify what parts of this community or support system will assist us in learning. Obviously, we will need time to learn and understand, but it may be that you learn best in familiar surroundings, with music playing in the background, or in situations where you have to learn because failure to learn is a failure to succeed.

Reward strategies

The second strategy is to reward yourself for meeting the targets. You can reward yourself in many ways – with a trip out, a visit to friends, a meal or simply by congratulating yourself. Reward strategies can also involve simply learning new skills or strategies so that learning in itself becomes a reward.

If this chapter has helped to encourage your desire to learn, the next step is putting that desire into action. In trying out new ways of behaving, we all need help and support. We have looked at how you might develop support. We also need confidence where support is unavailable.

Developing confidence is something which can be done. Lack of confidence need not be an insuperable barrier to learning. Develop your own confidence by setting yourself targets and by taking on new experiences a few at a time. Don't set yourself up for failure by attempting too much. Set yourself achievable targets for learning. Increase these slowly. As you meet each target your confidence in learning will grow. Effectively, your theory about the world will have changed and become more robust.

Checklist for learning

1. I have identified my own learning styles and preferences.
2. I am aware of my own blocks to learning and can take steps to overcome them.
3. I can identify the ways in which I cope with change.
4. I can set specific learning related objectives.
5. I can use a variety of methods to develop learning opportunities.
6. I can use a variety of methods to retain and retrieve information.
7. I can identify a number of ways to motivate and support my learning.
8. I am in charge of my own learning.

Summary

- *Learning is a major management tool. It is how we solve problems and change the ways in which we work.*

■ *Unless we can learn, the way in which we change may not be the way we need to change.*

■ *People have different levels, ways, styles and skills in the way that they learn.*

■ *You can incorporate these into a personal learning plan which will help you sharpen your learning skills.*

■ *Some people are blocked from learning because of their attitude to change.*

■ *You can develop strategies to help overcome these blocks.*

■ *These should concentrate on feedback, which is the vital element of development, learning and business success.*

■ *You can develop a feedback system which will help you develop to achieve success. Receiving challenging feedback will help you to question your assumptions and work towards achieving effective learning.*

3 COMMUNICATION

'Officials are highly educated, but one-sided. In his own
department an official can grasp whole trains of thought from
a single word, but let him have something from another
department explained to him by the hour, he may nod
politely, but he won't understand a word of it.'

FRANZ KAFKA

In the last chapter we looked at learning as a way of acquiring and processing information. This chapter looks at one of the ways in which you can acquire and transmit information – communication.

Communication underpins everything a human being does. It enables a manager to set objectives, organise, motivate, appraise and develop. For a manager, communication can be seen as having two primary functions. The first of these is to gather information from the world in which you live. The second is to influence the behaviour of other people. Communication isn't just about giving messages, we expect to see some sign that the messages have been acted upon, such as a change in the way people behave.

Communication also helps in the construction of meaning through which you and others understand the world. It is the tool which managers can use to manage relationships. As we will see, good communication is a function of good relationships and vice versa. Without good relationships you are unlikely to have good communication and without effective communication you are unlikely to have good relationships. A tool doesn't, however, have a life of its own. It is irretrievably attached to the person who is using it. This means that the idea of who you are, your self-image, will impact heavily upon your ability to use the tool of communication.

Your self-image is made up of a number of things; your self-esteem, your role, the way other people see you, your emotions, etc. Each of these will affect the quality of your communication and the subsequent quality of the relationships you have with other people, such as customers, clients, friends, employees.

The objectives of this chapter are:

► *to demonstrate the issues which will impact upon the quality of communication and relationships;*

► *to offer a structured way of listening to other people;*

► *to offer a structured path for sending a message to other people.*

SALLY had had a long, hard day. The new software for the network was as temperamental a beast as she'd ever come across. There had been times when she'd wanted either to pick up the computer and throw it through the window, or run screaming from the room.

It didn't look as though it was going to get any better, either. She'd got a sticky problem that she knew she should have dealt with a long time ago. Judy Murray, one of the admin. staff, had got into an argument with Karen in packing because of some lost manifests. Karen swore blind that she'd sent them to Judy, who'd lost them. Judy swore blind that she'd never received them.

Sally wouldn't normally have interfered in an argument like that, but it had taken place in the front office when Dave had been talking to an important customer from Lowells. As she struck the retrieve key again, the screen of the Computer read 'Invalid path or driveway. Not reading drive C' for what seemed like the twenty-fifth time.

'Oh damn and blast it!' she shouted, 'Damn all computer programmers. Davy, get over here will you.'

Davy Allen, the kid who installed their software and handled debugging problems for them on a part-time basis, strolled over from the server unit where he was inputting code.

'What's up this time, Sal ?'

Davy was 28 and looked about 14. The girls in the office called him Davy Crockpot because he always had his head in a book or journal throughout the lunch breaks and seemed to do nothing but go on about serial networking and fuzzy logics.

'I've lost the whole package that I was working with', said Sally.

'I've told you before, Sally you're not talking to it properly. You need to spend as much time listening to the program as you do telling it what to do. It's just like communicating with humans really.'

'No, it isn't. I can at least tell humans to get lost. I can't tell this to get lost.'

'Yes you can, Sal, you can switch it off. It's just that you're letting other things affect your relationship with the computer.'

□   □   □

Communication as a two-way process

Communication is a two-way process. It is not merely about telling someone something or hearing what someone says. There are a number of factors which affect the quality of communication.

The first of these factors is the nature of the relationship in which the communication takes place. Remember that anyone or anything you have contact with is in some sort of relationship with you. Some relationships can be long-term, close ones, others can be brief and antagonistic. At work, even if you've only talked to someone once in five years, you still have a relationship with that person.

Good communication requires openness, self-disclosure and trust. Good relationships are both a result of and a support to good communication. A good relationship requires the people involved to:

- give and receive honest feedback;
- show that they value the other person;
- show respect for the needs of others;
- be willing to talk about themselves when this is appropriate;
- acknowledge other people's right to choose;
- realise that they will not be liked by everyone; and
- believe that most people will respond favourably if approached honestly.

Generally the qualities of an open, supportive relationships can be characterised by three fundamental components:

- *empathy,* being aware of the other person's viewpoint and understanding how they feel.
- *congruence,* being what you say you are. Behaving in the way that you say that you will. Giving the same message at verbal, and nonverbal levels. Honesty.
- *acceptance,* the ability to accept people for what they are. Separating a person's behaviour from what they 'are' and accepting them with all their faults and failings.

Apart from the quality of the relationship, other factors are likely to influence the communication process. Many of these are internal factors, such as your feelings about yourself or your emotional state at a particular moment in time.

Some of the factors which may affect the process of communication are:

- *Self-esteem* Your effectiveness in communicating will depend on how you feel about yourself. If you are confident with feelings of self-worth and adequacy, other people will tend to listen to what you say.
- *Clarity* This involves knowing what you want to say and how you want to say it. When messages are haphazard, unplanned or erratic they will be unclear.
- *Listening* This is much more than hearing. Few people are good listeners. About 75 per cent of oral communication is ignored, misunderstood or quickly forgotten. Effective listening is a positive process.
- *Willingness to learn* As you communicate you receive two sets of messages – those from others and those from yourself. Paying attention to these

messages and revising your communication strategies will enable you to communicate more effectively. Trying the same style of communication again and again will mean that you miss out on opportunities to communicate. Learning or experimenting with new styles may pay dividends.

- *Feelings* Human beings experience a constantly changing current of feelings and emotions. The culture in which we live means that many people have difficulty in handling the emotional aspect of communication. This can result in very real communication difficulties. One possible explanation of emotion is that it serves as a messenger in telling us whether or not we have reached our goals. We will feel anger, disappointment or anxiety if we fail to achieve the goals we have set ourselves and elation, happiness or contentment if we do achieve these goals. Because of the wide-ranging goals that we set ourselves, many of which are related, emotions can become confused. Emotions are best identified, observed, accepted and integrated into the way we set our goals. This helps with the last factor.

- *Self-disclosure* The ability to talk fully and truthfully about yourself is necessary to effective communications. The more two people know about each other, the more effective and efficient the communication will be. There are many blocks to self-disclosure – most people have fears. The effective communicator is one who can create a climate of trust where mutual self-disclosure can occur.

All of these factors will be affected by your upbringing and by the circumstances in which you find yourself. Differing situations will have different effects on your self-esteem and willingness to learn, so it is important to remain in possession of yourself.

□   □   □

Sally's office had turned into a battleground. Judy and Karen had stuck resolutely to their stories and the whole affair seemed to be turning into a schoolgirls' slanging match no matter how many times Sally intervened. After her conversation with Davy, and the experience with the computer that afternoon, Sally was keeping a close rein on her temper.

'You told me last week that you'd have those manifests ready on Thursday' said Karen triumphantly, as though her point was proved.

'I couldn't have them ready if you didn't send them, could I?' replied Judy.

'You could have rung up and checked – but you didn't. You must have had them. Admin. have never been any good. I didn't get my letters out last month until a good ten days after I'd given them in.'

Judy turned to Sally 'Have you seen those handwritten notes that we get from packing? 'They look like a monkey's written them or somebody from Tibet. You need the patience of a saint just to make sense of them.'

'Will you two just shut up and listen!' Sally said. 'Have you lost the ability to listen to me and to each other?' Sally wanted to add that they were acting like schoolkids, but thought better of it. 'These things tend to be misunderstandings, and if we can just listen to each other, I'm sure we can sort this out. If we don't listen, we'll be here all night and it still won't be sorted.'

□   □   □

What makes an effective listener

Whilst it may well be 'chicken and egg' regarding which comes first, we can say that effective communication involves two elements. One of these is sending a message and the other is identifying and understanding the other person's messages. This section deals with some strategies for the second of these. This skill is commonly called listening.

It seems ridiculous to say that most people are not good listeners. Unfortunately this is true. Early experiences in life teach us not to listen. Our role models – parents, teachers and other adults in our life – often teach us that children should be seen and not heard. Few adults actually listen to children, and it is perhaps not surprising that when we become adults we repeat these behaviours in our own lives.

ASSESSMENT EXERCISE

Answer yes or no to each of the following statements:

1. I've never had any formal training in listening.
2. I sometimes fail to attend when people are speaking.
3. I sometimes get distracted by other important issues.
4. I often already know what people are going to say before they say it.
5. I tend to interrupt because 'I've had this great idea', or for some other reason.
6. I miss some of what people are saying because I'm busy preparing my reply.
7. I generally listen to the words without focusing on the complete message.
8. I often hear what I expect to hear.

If you've said yes to more than three of the above questions you might want to consider your listening skills.

EFFECTIVE LISTENING TECHNIQUES

Listening consists of three important components.

Attending skills

This involves showing that you value the other person's message by:

- being open to what they say;
- leaning forward;
- maintaining appropriate eye contact;
- responding appropriately; and.
- avoiding distractions.

Following and supporting

The listener's most important task is to give the speaker 'permission' to talk by inviting them to talk, encouraging them to continue and responding with appropriate open questions. You can do this by

- Describing the person's body language. (*'You seem upset abut something.'*)
- Inviting them to talk. (*'It might be useful for you to have a word with me about . . .'*)

Encouraging people to talk involves the use of phrases such as 'Go on', 'I see'. Asking open questions demonstrates interest and encourages the speaker to talk further.

Reflective listening

There is a school of practice which believes that the listener should clear themselves for the speaker's message. This involves avoiding giving any information back to the speaker other than information which he or she has first given the listener, but which demonstrates that you understand what is being said:

- paraphrasing the speaker's words, (*'So it made you angry'*);
- testing for understanding (*'You seem to be saying that'*, *'Is that right?'*);
- summarising briefly (*'So you've been involved with the bookkeeping for over six months. You've had no support from me and you've felt angry at the lack of feedback'*).

You can use the formula 'You feel . . . because . . .' to help the speaker reflect on his or her own feelings and also to your feelings with facts. Reflective listening is a powerful communication tool which improves with practice.

Ground rules

Remember however that reflective listening will be ineffective unless you observe the rules.

- You should not fake understanding.
- You should not tell the speaker you know how they feel. It is a presumption, and often an offensive one, to believe that one person can know what it is like to wear another person's shoes.
- You should not answer the verbal element of the speaker's questions, but try to reflect the feeling contained in the question.
- You should try to improve your sensitivity and focus on feelings.
- You should develop empathy in your tone and manner, show that you mirror the speaker's feelings.
- Reflect in concrete terms rather than in vague terms 'So you feel unhappy because of the overtime you put in for the last three weeks' rather than 'You're miserable because there's too much work '.

TURNING BLOCKS TO ADVANTAGE

We have looked at some of the skills which might help you communicate effectively. This section looks at some of the things which block effective communication. Many of these blocks are associated with feelings which, as we saw earlier, are an important part of the communication. Look for the way in which feelings show that communication isn't working. This may be related to one of the following.

- *Presence* Are the people involved really 'there'? Does one or both of them want to be somewhere else? If so, this might indicate that they do not really want to communicate.
- *Attitudes* Do the people involved show respect and acceptance towards each other? Indifference or hostility may reflect a problem around feelings.
- *Objectives* Do people know what they really want from the communication? Feelings here may be an indicator of an unwillingness to be involved, a lack of trust or a need for more time. Ambiguity or mixed messages can mean that objectives are confused or deceptive and ruin communication.
- *Skills* People might simply not have the skills to communicate effectively. Lack of articulation or inappropriate language are often blocks to communication. Communication skills can be developed through learning and practice. You can, with access to a video camera, practise talking about yourself for three minutes. Ask yourself or a friend who will give you appropriate feedback whether the person talking draws and holds attention? What elements can you improve to make communication easier?

- *Beliefs* People continually make assumptions about each other on the basis of issues such as gender, race, occupation. These conscious and unconscious assumptions incorporate factors about what you expect people to know, what you have told them and what they have understood. Such assumptions also constitute beliefs about how people should behave. When these beliefs are not fulfilled, communication problems may arise.

- *Interest* Almost everyone knows people with whom they would not be completely honest or open. Such feelings may come from a lack of trust or feelings of vulnerability. You may be formal with these people or avoid them. This is one way in which people try to control others or try to protect themselves. Identifying the needs which are being fulfilled by behaving in this way can help improve communication.

Once you have identified these blocks, you may, if you wish, take steps to get around them or even to turn them to your own advantage. Use the following questions to assess whether communication is likely to be effective.

1. Is the relationship in which the communication is going to take place a supportive one?
2. If not, does it have areas of mutual agreement or interest?
3. If not, can areas of mutual agreement or interest be developed?
4. Do I feel confident in communicating my message?
5. If not, why not?
6. Can I increase my confidence either through changing the content of the message or the way in which it is delivered or the person who delivers it?
7. Do I have the skill to deliver this message?
8. If not, how will I develop these skills?

As we've noted above, the other essential component of communication is sending your own message. The processes through which we do this are something which we rarely consider. The most common strategy for dealing with a failure to have our own message accepted and understood is to 'turn up the volume', as if this would make the message more acceptable or understandable. The following section offers you a method which will help you in making sure that your message is received and understood.

Sending your message

Once you have considered the factors which are likely to affect communication, it may help you to consider the following eight stage model for sending your message. Like any effective process, it will involve you in preparation. Time spent in preparation is, as they say, seldom wasted. The process is something which good communicators do instinctively. Different transactions will call for a different emphasis, but all of these stages are necessary at some point for effective communication.

THE 8-STAGE MESSAGE

1. Prepare the message

The first part of the communication process is to prepare your message. Many people start a communication without knowing exactly what their message is or what they want it to achieve. Stop before you start your communications and ask yourself 'Why am I doing this?' If you have a clear objective, this will help you keep to the point. Always come to the point quickly, explanation can come later.

Use this checklist to prepare your message.

- Who is the message for?
- Is this the best place and time?
- What is the message?
- Are the main points clear?
- What outcome do I want?
- Is there any action required?
- And if so, is it specific and measurable?
- Does it contain all and only all the information my listener needs to know?

2. Prepare yourself

The second stage is to prepare yourself for the likely reception. Some communications are likely to result in rejection or ignorance. Prepare for rejection by valuing yourself. You can do this by choosing a place and a time for your message which brings out the best in you. Your message will be inescapably linked with you. Unless you value yourself and show it, it is unlikely that your listener will value your message.

3. Signalling for attention

People do not automatically respond to what you say. They may respond to what they think you've said. The more ready the recipient is to receive your message, the clearer its transmission is likely to be. It is helpful to expect a positive response when you attempt to gain your listener's attention. In face-to-face communication you can attract attention by:

- asking for it (*'Excuse me but could I have your attention for a moment'*);
- using humour;
- using eye contact;
- increasing vocal intensity; and
- body gesture and positioning.

Remember that important communications are best not left to chance encounters and that you should make sure you have the other person's attention before you begin your message.

4. Preparing the listener

It can be helpful here to consider how you would like to receive information. Where people feel threatened, they are unlikely to receive your message clearly. When emotional issues are being discussed, the temptation may be to speak as quickly as possible to deal with the painful issue quickly. This is not useful. After gaining the listener's attention, you should consider how you can help prepare them to receive your message. If your message contains new information, which the listener is not prepared to receive, you can

- say what it is that you want to say ('I'd just like to take a moment to tell you about . . .');
- tell them what benefits they might expect from listening ('I think it might be helpful for you to consider . . .');
- check that they are willing to communicate;
- warn them of the importance of your communication; and
- ask rhetorical questions to awaken interest ('You might ask yourself what does this have to do with . . .)'.

5. Sending the message

This is the actual 'moment of truth'. Remember that a message will communicate at a number of different levels. The content of the message needs to be the same over all these levels – emotional, content, etc. When sending your message, keep your objective clear. Use simple language, avoid unnecessary detail and emphasise the main points. Relate what you are saying to the emotions as well as the mind.

- Speak audibly.
- Vary your pitch, tone and volume.
- Respond to signs of confusion or disinterest.

- Pause for questions and clarification.
- Summarise to help understanding.
- Talk 'to' people not 'at' them.
- Switch approaches if yours is not working.

6. Receiving and understanding

Listening is the primary skill needed here. This is an active process which we looked at in the last section. Beware of preoccupation with your message, switching off because you disagree, getting hooked on detail. Checking for understanding here can include statements such as, 'Have I been clear about this?' Using statements such as 'Do you understand?' places the onus on the listener and may be less useful.

7. Closing

The penultimate stage is to close the communication. A conversation which has served its purpose should be closed effectively. You can close a conversation by signalling that you are preparing for closure. This can be done by:

- asking for action ('So we can now . . .') or reaction ('How do you feel about this?');
- suggesting ways forward;
- summarising what has been discussed;
- arranging another meeting;
- indicating that you have finished; and
- thanking the other person for their time.

8. Following up

In many cases, conversations may need to be followed up. For instance, a telephone or face-to-face conversation can be summarised in a memo or a letter for the benefit of people who may be affected by the conversation or simply for your own records.

□   □   □

'Seems like an awful lot of trouble to go to just to do something that I've done all my life', Sally said.

'Well, Sal, just think about how much time, money and effort it's cost you in your life sorting out simple mistakes that were caused by someone not listening. The flight recorder on the plane that crashed into the mountain in the States last year showed that the co-pilot had told the pilot that he was too low but the pilot didn't listen. When the Challenger shuttle spacecraft was destroyed, the disaster occurred because no one would listen to the engineers at Morton Thiokol where they made the O-rings. How much trouble do you want to go to?'

□   □   □

Overall, communication is a contract which will impact on, and be affected by, the nature of the relationship in which it takes place. It may be helpful to think about the contract as imposing a number of obligations upon the speaker – to speak clearly, to come quickly to the point, to prepare the listener etc. Similar obligations are imposed upon the listener – maintaining eye contact, responding appropriately, checking and paraphrasing, etc. Where the contractors within the relationship fail to carry out these obligations, the purpose of the contract will be frustrated or, even worse, one of the contractors may resent the 'breach of contract' and take action against the other person. This may lead to conflict.

Body language

There are a number of powerful methods of communication other than spoken language. Body language can reinforce your verbal message or discount it. It is often the basis upon which people decide whether or not you are worth listening to. Consider the following issues.

SPEAKING BODY LANGUAGE

You may be able to bring to mind occasions when important messages have been undermined by the speaker's body language. Use the following tips to avoid this type of pitfall:

- Face the other person, but do not stand in direct opposition.
- Maintain a natural, receptive posture.
- Lean slightly towards the person.
- Place yourself close enough so that you are both comfortable.
- Match the body language of the speaker without imitating obviously or mimicking.
- Avoid extremes of dress or behaviour unless you are in the business of drawing attention to yourself.

Remember that much of our behaviour has a basis in our biology. Much of body language is about communicating non-threatening behaviour to others of the same species who once would have seen our very presence as a challenge.

The reason that we tend to interview people face-to-face is that the situation is perceived as potentially threatening. Human vision receives most strongly those things which are directly in front of it. Our peripheral vision is very weak and consequently we like to have potential threats where we can see them. Unfortunately, direct eye contact can also communicate a number of other attitudes and behaviour, so care should be taken.

READING BODY LANGUAGE

Everyone has a great deal of experience in reading and interpreting body language. You can train yourself to become more sensitive to body language by:

- treating each element of body language as reflecting a statement made by the person who says it: this can be simple as in the way a person dresses, or more complex as in lack of eye contact;
- looking for signal clusters: one element of body language in isolation may not be a useful message indicator, but a cluster of non-verbal statements may give meaning to an underlying message.

Formal interviews

One of the most common communicative situations which you might face as a manager is the formal interview. The formal interview is used in a number of areas, such as recruitment and selection, appraisal and discipline, and many people find it difficult.

The first question that you need to ask yourself before you commence a formal interview process is whether it needs to be a formal interview. Many people use formal interviews because they've always been involved in them. As an information-gathering process, the formal interview has some disadvantages in that it can restrict the type and amount of information available. Formal interviews tend to place relationships on a formal basis with the consequence that the exchange of information is limited to work roles. A recruitment interview may, for instance, need to obtain a more rounded or complex picture of candidates. Formal processes are designed to exclude emotion from communicative processes. They are seen at their most formal in legal proceedings where the individuals involved have roles assigned by dress and communication is preceded by honorifics.

The advantage of formal interviews is that they offer a structured framework to which can help avoid the likelihood of acquiring subjective or inaccurate information. Information is exchanged in a 'safe' manner, uncontaminated by emotion or irrelevant facts.

Essentially interviews are an information-gathering process and as such we need to consider three issues. The first of these is the structure of the interview. The second issue which you may need to consider is the type of information-gathering mechanisms which you intend to use. These can be looked at as questions which help or hinder the information-gathering process.

THE INTERVIEW STRUCTURE

Most researchers into the interview process offer an interview structure in three stages: opening, body and closure.

Opening

The purpose of the opening of an interview is to set the scene, welcome people and put them at ease. This is an essential part of both building a relationship and of preparing people for the exchange of information for which the interview is designed. It is possible to consider three elements within the scene-setting exercise itself.

1. *Perceptual Scene-Setting* This involves the interviewer managing the setting in which the interview takes place. The surroundings would be organised to provide an atmosphere of privacy and incoming calls would be blocked. The interview could take place in armchairs, around a coffee table rather than across a desk. In managing perceptions, you can create an impression which will last.

2. *Social Scene-Setting* This is another essential element in building a relationship with the respondent in an interview. The way in which a person is met, greeted and the concern shown for their comfort (offers of coffee, etc.) will contribute to the good impression which the respondent will acquire.

3. *Factual Scene-Setting* The final scene-setting element of the opening stage is that of giving the respondent information which helps them to understand the purpose and likely content of the interview. This type of scene-setting is designed to orient the respondent. As we will see in the section on appraisal, it is possible to take a number of approaches to the appraisal interview. For example, where an employee believes that an appraisal interview is going to be about performance and accountability and the manager intends that it is about development, the mismatch in perceptions is likely to result in an ineffective interview.

Body

The body of an interview is designed to gather and give information for a number of purposes using the sort of questions outlined below and the listening skills we've already looked at.

Closure

The final stage of the interview is that of closure. It is important that in closing the interview that you do not leave the respondent with a feeling that they have not had the opportunity to respond fully to questions. Premature closure of an interview will leave respondents with that kind of feeling.

This means that the interviewer should prepare the respondent for closure. This can be done non-verbally or by simply saying, 'We'll need to draw things to a close shortly'. Once the interview has begun to close, it is the responsibility of the interviewer to tie things up by summarising what has been agreed or discussed, or by asking if the respondent has any questions. This can be termed 'factual closure' The other element of closure also corresponds to the opening. This is 'social closure' and may include an expression of appreciation or thanks. Ending the interview on a positive note will prepare the way for further contacts and preserve the relationship which has begun.

QUESTIONS TO GATHER INFORMATION

Once you have decided how you intend to structure the interview, the next issue to consider is the type of questions which you might use to gather information. Broadly, we can identify questions by their characteristics in helping or hindering the information-gathering process. Further specific examples of these questions are given in the chapter on appraisal.

Helping questions

These first types of question will help to build a potentially fruitful relationship.

1. *Questions conveying trust.* Questions that elicit the listener's aid or suggestions can indicate that the speaker has faith in the listener. For example, a manager may ask, 'How do you think I should deal with this problem?' When a manager and an employee show an open trusting relationship, the employee may also ask this type of question.

2. *Clarifying questions.* Clarifying questions are the type asked for the purposes of obtaining useful information. This kind of question is frequently asked in connection with paraphrasing, mirroring, or reflecting what the other person has said: 'you're worried about your lack of knowledge of the new system. Is that so?'

3. *Empathetic questions.* Empathetic questions are those that deal with the other person's feelings; they are asked for the purpose of expressing concern rather than finding solutions to problems. For example, you might ask, 'How did you feel when Sandy sent the wrong order to the customer?' Such questions indicate concern about the effect of an event on the other person.

4. *Open questions.* The most useful questions are those which have no implicit answers, instead they stimulate reflection and thought on the part of the other person. Open questions invite the other person to be creative in exploring the various possible dimensions of an issue.

Probing questions

Probing questions are designed to encourage the respondent to expand upon initial responses. Interviewers will often fail to use probing questions and may be left with a wealth of 'shallow' information which is not an awful lot of use. Probes could be used to respond to the statement 'I felt dissatisfied about . . .' and examples could include, 'In what way were you dissatisfied?' or 'can you tell me more about your dissatisfaction?'

Hindering questions

Types of questions which may tend to hinder the process of communicating include the following:

1. *Critical questions* Questions used to criticise, reprimand, or express doubt about the other person's abilities create a gap between the speaker and the respondent; in addition, a sarcastic tone may be received as criticism, even if the actual words do not seem critical.

2. *Testing questions* Questions asked to determine whether someone is right or wrong. This type of question can imply a superior attitude on the part of the speaker, and may make the respondent feel as if he or she is on the witness stand undergoing cross-examination.

3. *Leading questions* The speaker may unwittingly ask a question that evokes the answer that he or she wants, which may or may not be the real answer. A leading question almost seduces the respondent into giving the desired answer, which stops further exploration of the issue and may provide information that is misleading or incorrect.

4. *Closed questions* questions which invite 'yes' or 'no' answers. 'Did you leave your last job because of the effect of the recession on the industry?' is a closed question. Closed questions in sensitive areas such as performance or reasons for leaving a job are also likely to leave the respondent feeling as if they have not been given the opportunity to explain their side of the story and may lead to resentment.

In addition to the types of questions asked, it is possible to consider another element of the communicative process in interviews and that is the framework or structure.

OBJECTIVES

The final issue in 'formal' interviews is the nature of the information which you want to gather. In recruitment interviews this may be information about a person's work experience, potential commitment to the organisation, potential, performance ability or ability to work as a team member. In appraisal interviews this may be information with regard to current performance, relationships at work, agreement with regard to objectives. In disciplinary interviews it may be information with regard to the reasons behind actions or attitudes. As we will see later in the book, the need for clear objectives in information gathering is essential in any interview or meeting. Without clear objectives an interview or meeting may be a frustrating experience.

Once you feel happy with your communication skills you may wish to consider communication in relationships where power is involved. Such relationships are generally the most important ones in our lives and involve us in communicating through negotiation, persuasion and dealing with conflict.

Checklist for communication

1. I can understand and manage my relationship through communication.

2. I can manage myself when I communicate.

3. I can listen effectively across a range of communication channels.

4. I can send messages effectively across a range of communication channels including body language.

5. I can structure formal and informal interviews.

6. I can use a wide range of questions when gathering information.

7. I can control the communication process.

Summary

- *Communication is affected by a number of issues. The first are those which impact upon the idea of who you are and include factors such as self-esteem.*

- *The second set of issues which affect the communication process are linked to the nature of the relationship in which the communication takes place.*

- *Good relationships will help good communication and vice versa.*

- *Good communication is a two-way process which involves both listening and speaking.*

- *Listening consists of attending, following and reflecting the content of the message that the speaker gives.*

- *Sending the message involves eight stages including preparation, signalling for attention, preparing the listener, sending the message, checking for understanding and closure.*

- *Blocks to effective communication can be identified and turned to advantage.*

- *Communication is not only about verbal messages. It is about a whole range of messages including body language or non-verbal behaviour.*

- *Communication process can also be formal and it may help to consider both structure and process in formal communication.*

4 NEGOTIATION AND WORKING WITH CONFLICT

'Let us begin anew – remembering on both sides that civility is not a sign of weakness and sincerity is always subject to proof. Let us never negotiate out of fear. But let us never fear to negotiate.'

JOHN F. KENNEDY

Once you have developed confidence in communication and in the relationship in which the communication takes place, you may wish to consider two further issues in the communication process. The first of these is the question of power in relationships and this involves you in negotiation.

All human interactions are characterised by some sort of negotiation between or among people trying to give and take from one another. This process of exchange is continual and often goes unnoticed. (We will see in Chapter 13 on team building how important role negotiation is within groups.) Take time for a moment to consider why you occupy the position that you now do. How much negotiation did it take – at home, at school, at work, elsewhere – to enable your occupation of this position?

The second issue which you may need to consider is where relationships break down, either because one party holds all the power or for some other reason. When a relationship breaks down, communication either comes to an end because one or both parties withdraw, or else communications take an extreme form which is unacceptable to one of the parties.

The objectives of this chapter are:

► *to help you recognise the need for negotiation;*

► *to introduce the idea of power in negotiation;*

► *to help you identify different negotiation strategies;*

► *to help you identify your preferred style of negotiation;*

► *to help you consider conflict and to recognise its impact;*

► *to introduce strategies for managing conflict.*

What is negotiation about?

Because negotiation is a function of communication, it is also a function of the relationship in which the negotiation takes place. We have seen the way in which the nature of a relationship impacts heavily upon the quality of communication within it. The nature of the relationship also impacts upon the likelihood of satisfactory outcomes within the negotiating process.

We looked earlier at some of the things in a relationship which can help you communicate more effectively. We need to consider the question of relationships from another viewpoint – that of power – and how this viewpoint is likely to affect negotiating tactics.

Once we have identified someone or something, we are in a relationship with it. We need to incorporate him, her or it into the way in which we see the world. To some degree, as these relationships become more complex, we can identify them through a growing degree of dependence. Dependence is the degree to which we need someone or something. Likewise, power rests on the degree to which you are dependent. It is not only about liking people or wanting to be with them. It is also about not liking people, but needing them to fulfil one or more of our objectives. You may, for instance, be dependent on a close friend for warmth, company and support. You may also be dependent upon a bank manager for financial support or a customer or client in order that your work continues. Dependence is sometimes hard to admit because it defines vulnerability. The more dependent we are, the more we see ourselves as being vulnerable. Of course, other people are also dependent upon us, but some people find it very hard to confront their own vulnerability. You can dismiss the whole question of vulnerability by refusing to accept that you are dependent.

Consider for a moment the following exercise. You can use it to assess how you feel about dependence on others.

EXERCISE

If you feel that the following statements are true of you or reflect your belief

> *all the time*, score five points
> *much of the time*, score four points
> *some of the time*, score three points
> *rarely*, score two points
> *never*, score one point

1. I feel strongly that there can only be one boss in an organisation.
2. A person's worth is seen in the things that he or she does.
3. I tend to be jealous of my own projects and plans.

4. I like to win by whatever means.

5. I am self-sufficient.

The total possible score is 25 points. The higher your score, the more independent of other people you feel that you are. Where your score is high, you may wish to consider how you exercise power and how you react to power being exercised over you. How would you redefine power?

TYPES OF POWER

French and Raven,[1] two sociologists, identified eight types of power in research that they carried out in the 1950s.

1. Positional power

This type of power is one that comes from one person's position in relation to another. For instance, a manager may have power because of the position which he or she occupies, whereas a supervisor may have less power because of the way in which people perceive their relative positions. Bear in mind that this type of power is given to the person in question by the people who are subject to it. This type of power is characterised by a need for the relationship to continue.

2. Information power

As individuals, the more information that we have, the more we feel able to control what is going on about us. This form of control involves one person having more information than another and using this information to control the other person's uncertainty. People can become dependent upon others because of their need to control their own uncertainty.

3. Control of rewards

This is about having the power to reward for desired performance or behaviour. This type of power creates dependency upon the person giving the reward.

4. Coercive power

This is about having the power to punish for failure to behave in a desired fashion. This type of power is also likely to create dependency. People can depend on not being punished as well as depend on being rewarded.

1. J.R.P. French and B.H. Raven, 'The Bases of Social Power' in *Studies in Social Power*, D. Cartwright (Ed.) Institute for Social Power, 1959.

5. Alliances and networks

This is an extended form of information power together with positional power.

6. Access to and control of agendas

If a person or an organisation can control the agenda in a negotiating situation, they can effectively set the ground rules. This means that they can legislate for the introduction of items which are favourable to themselves and for items which are unfavourable to be blocked. If the agenda is controlled, one of the parties to a relationship can be dependent upon the other to explain the rules for communication and subsequently negotiation.

7. Control of meaning and symbols

This type of power is one whereby one party will dominate the other by means of their use of language or the setting in which the relationship takes place. The legal system is a system which uses control of meaning to a great extent with its own language and many arcane symbols to support its power. Bank managers and solicitors use this type of power to some extent also. Consider the setting of your bank manager's office and the content of your discussions.

8. Personal power

This type of power may also be called 'referent' power. It is the type of power which springs from wanting to be like someone, because you feel that they have some desirable quality or qualities.

USING POWER

All negotiation is about power. Because there are always power imbalances in a relationship, negotiation goes on all the time. No matter what your overall approach to negotiation, you may need to consider the nature of power. Remember that the power in the relationship will influence the negotiation process and that negotiation is not limited to a formal 'across the table' session.

It is, of course, very rare that you will find that there is only one type of power in a relationship. In the bank manager example, he or she is likely to have six or seven of the types of power which we've discussed. Once you've identified the types of power which are involved in the relationship, you can cast your strategy in a way which will help you work successfully in that relationship.

Let's carry the bank manager analogy a bit further. He or she is likely to have several types of power over you. He (if it is a he) has positional power, information power, at least about the bank's lending policies and possibly about similar organisations to yours. He will have reward power and conceivably coercive power, although this is likely to be illusory. He will have access to alliances and networks, and control of agendas through demands for a business plan. He will certainly have control of meaning and symbols in the form of his office setting and the way in which he dresses.

Much of this power is dependency inducing. You will be dependent upon a bank manager for his knowledge of the bank's lending policies, his ability to reward or coerce if you have already been rewarded. Where he controls the agenda, you will be dependent upon him to explain the rules.

Negotiation is about developing strategies that will decrease or increase the dependency of one of the parties in a negotiation. The bank manager will use strategies which will attempt to increase the customer's dependency, whether or not he or she is a borrower. The customer should use strategies which reduce his or her dependence on the bank. These can correspond to the power strategies which the bank manager may wittingly or unwittingly use.

- The first type of strategy is knowing the area in which you are going to negotiate. If you are asking for money, the more you know both about the current state of the lending market and the particular scheme for which you are seeking money, the less dependent you will be upon the bank manager.

- The second is to maintain flexibility in your commitment to one bank. Banks will, within certain limits, protect themselves by exchanging information about classes of customer. This does not mean that you should not approach as many sources of finance as possible. If a bank manager is aware that you are not dependent on him, your negotiating position will be much stronger.

- The third is to develop your own networks and alliances. When a bank manager knows that you know other people in the area which you propose to work, your potential dependency upon him as the only source of finance or information is reduced.

- The fourth is to manipulate rewards so that the manager will feel good about helping you. You may have rewards in your power that you do not use or realise that you have. People can feel rewarded when they are involved in an obviously successful project for which they can expect to receive praise. The bank manager is not immune to rewards.

- The fifth is to manipulate meaning and symbol yourself. Your first meeting with a bank manager is likely to be on his territory. Respond by inviting him to a second meeting on yours. Set a stage for his visit.

- The sixth is to use your own personal power. If you appear confident and relaxed, whilst committed to your project, you may be able to induce a manager to help you because of this.

The prime rule of successful negotiation is to manage the context of the relationship in which the negotiation takes place from the very beginning.

TACTICS IN NEGOTIATION

Let's look for a moment at the sort of things, apart from power, which are likely to effect the negotiation process.

- The first of these is, again, the nature of the relationship between the parties. If you value the relationship you will generally use collaborative strategies. We will see in the next section how collaboration seems to demonstrate concern for the other party.

- The second of these is your own, or the other negotiating party's level of skill in communicating. Much of this may be seen as communication confidence and you can build this by means of the sort of strategies which we talked about in Chapter 2 on learning to learn.

- The third is the amount of time available to the parties. Studies have shown that parties who face tight deadlines when negotiating will tend to use competitive strategies, although these are likely to be the most time-intensive where parties are more or less equal in power.

- Fourthly, clarity of objectives impacts upon the negotiation process. If you have clear goals you will be more likely to enjoy a focused discussion in which the objectives can be used to define progress and as a measure of success.

- Fifthly, you may need to take into account the way in which openness affects the negotiation process. As we have seen, openness is a major factor in contributing to communication effectiveness. It is also a major factor in contributing to negotiation success. You might think that a knowledge of the other party's positional strength would mean that party is at a disadvantage. Research seems to prove the opposite to be true. Knowledge of the other party's relative weakness seems to lead the negotiating party into responding collaboratively. Such information needs to be honest and relevant.

Much of the above section has dealt with relational issues within the negotiation process. Managing the relationship is only part of the job. The other element is about your tactics: within the relationship that you set up, you will have some choice regarding the tactics which you use in the negotiation process. There are two broad ways of negotiating, part of which is dictated by the nature of the relationship and part of which will be dictated by personal preference.

EXERCISE

Consider the statements below and the extent to which you generally engage in the behaviours which they describe when negotiating.

If you 'never' engage in the behaviour, answer 1.
If you seldom engage in the behaviour, answer 2.

If you *sometimes* engage in the behaviour answer, 3.
If you *often* engage in the behaviour, answer 4.
If you *always* engage in the behaviour, answer 5.

1. When I negotiate I try to win.
2. When I negotiate I try to win, but if I can't, I make sure the other person can't win either.
3. I tend to blame other people for the problem.
4. I would conceal my true intentions.
5. I would discredit the other person's position.
6. I'd try to work towards a situation acceptable to both parties.
7. I'd reveal my true intentions at the beginning of a negotiation.
8. I'd give the first concession.
9. I'd try to stay flexible about the means to a settlement.
10. I'd never personally attack the other negotiator.

Statements 1–5 are characteristics of a competitive negotiator. The highest score is 25, the lowest is 5. The higher your score to these statements the more you will prefer a competitive style of negotiation.

Statements 6–10 are characteristics of collaborative negotiation. The highest possible score is 25, the lowest 5. The higher your score on these statements, the more likely you are to engage in collaborative negotiation.

Competitive negotiation incorporates an approach in which the objective is not only to win, but to make the other party lose. Collaborative negotiation is the type of approach in which the objective is to arrive at a solution in which both parties are satisfied with the result.

Negotiating roles

Before we look at these approaches in more detail, let's look at some of the roles which you might take on in a negotiation.

It is possible to identify five roles in the process of negotiation and the particular strengths of each of them.

1. *The factual negotiator*

    (a) knowing all the facts related to the negotiation;
    (b) asking factual questions;
    (c) covering all the bases to make sure that no facts are left out;
    (d) providing information.

Factual negotiators tend to leave aside emotional issues such as 'face', which is a person's desire for a positive identity. (People like to feel and look good and will react hostilely to attacks which make them feel or look bad.) They can get most involved in details about the negotiation.

2. *The relational negotiator*

  (a) establishing relationships with the other party;
  (b) being sensitive to the other party's emotional issues;
  (c) building trust;
  (d) perceiving the position of the other party.

Relational negotiation can lose sight of the reasons for negotiation and the objectives in their anxiety to build relationships. They can also give away information without realising it. Their sensitivity can make them become emotional and lose perspective.

3. *The intuitive negotiator*

  (a) coming up with unexpected solutions or ways of approach;
  (b) sorting the wheat from the chaff – the key issues from the irrelevant detail;
  (c) visualising the implications of a proposal;
  (d) accurately guessing the progress of negotiation;
  (e) seeing the 'big picture'.

The intuitive negotiator can be dangerous because of their wildness. They may also have very little discipline.

4. *The logical negotiator*

  (a) set the rules of the negotiation;
  (b) develop an agenda;
  (c) argue a logical rather than emotional way;
  (d) adapt their position to meet changing situations.

The logical negotiator can sometimes see the process of negotiation as being more important than the content.

Finally, all these approaches or roles need to be co-ordinated by the lead negotiator, who is responsible for all of the above roles and who makes the final decision about strategy, etc.

Consider the four roles above and decide which you feel most comfortable with:

1. factual

2. relational

3. intuitive

4. logical

It is likely that there will be some of all of these in your own make-up as a negotiator. If the intuitive negotiator is strongest, you will need to develop discipline. If your logical negotiator is most prominent, you may need to develop relationship building skills. Consider how you might do this. Now let's look at the two broad approaches to negotiation which we mentioned earlier.

Competitive negotiation

You can assess the characteristics of a potential negotiating situation by looking at these factors.

1. Do both parties need the relationship to continue?

2. Are both parties skilled in negotiation and communication?

3. Is there sufficient time for the negotiation to take place?

4. Are there clear objectives?

5. Is there effective information exchange between the parties involved?

If you answer 'no' to more than two of these questions, the negotiation is likely to be a competitive one. Where these factors seem to indicate that the negotiation is likely to be a competitive one, you will need to consider some of the informal ground rules for competitive negotiation. Competitive negotiation may be uncomfortable and ultimately self-defeating, but it happens, and in order to succeed you will need to consider a number of factors.

OPENING BID

In a competitive negotiation you may need to give some consideration to the way in which the negotiation begins. As we've seen, the secret of successful negotiations is to manage the context of the relationship in which the negotiation takes place. This will help balance the power between the parties and maintain communication. Where it is not possible to manage the context of the relationship, you will need to use strategies which increase the dependency of the other party by limiting information, controlling agendas and so on.

The first rule of competitive negotiation is that you should try to avoid making the opening bid. The opening bid gives a great deal of information to the other party and making it will decrease the opposing party's dependency on you.

The corollary to this rule is that if you are forced to make the opening bid, it should be just under the point at which your opponent will be insulted. This both gives as little information as possible to the opposing party, and avoids the possibility of their withdrawal. If your opening offer does insult your opponent, it is possible that he or she may withdraw and both parties will suffer loss.

The way that you pitch your opening offer will depend on a combination of the information that you have about your opponent's position, your own perceived strength, and the amount of time available. One of the skills of competitive or value-claiming negotiation is estimating the opponent's real needs as opposed to his or her expressed desires. This involves the use of listening skills and the interpretation of body language.

CONCESSIONS

In similar fashion to the opening bid strategy, the competitive negotiator will need to consider the effect of concessions. Concessions in a competitive situation are seen as a sign of weakness or dependency. The second rule of competitive negotiation is that you should keep concessions to a minimum. The size of the first concession will also give away information about your best alternative to a negotiated agreement (BATNA). The BATNA of a party involved in negotiation is a vital piece of information which will tell the other party exactly how far they can go before the negotiation breaks down. In competitive negotiation, your BATNA should always be hidden.

CONFLICT

Within a negotiating situation, there are certain rules which relate to conflict. If the parties ignore these rules, the negotiation is likely to break down into futile argument with little result for either party.

The first rule with regard to arguments is to make sure that your position is strong and clear. It is important to be well prepared and to keep your arguments well supported and to the point. The more relevant information that you have, the more effective your argument is likely to be. Irrelevant arguments are not likely to lend you credibility and a fuzzy position will indicate weakness.

The second rule with regard to conflict is to make sure that your arguments are capable of persuading your opponent. In order to do this, you will need as much information as possible about your opponent.

The final rule for competitive negotiation is that you should avoid attacking or threatening your opponent, except as a last resort. Threats to use power may work in the short term, but you send potentially dangerous messages when you threaten. The first is that your negotiating position is one which does not have an adequate alternative. Unless you have an alternative to a negotiated settlement, your position will be perceived as weak by an experienced negotiator. Threats communicate your desperation and can bring the negotiation to an end.

We've looked at broad tactics. The specific types of behaviour which you can use in a competitive negotiation may include:

- being sarcastic in an attempt to produce emotional reactions and provoke the other party to reveal information;

- misunderstanding the other party deliberately through a mistaken summary or question;

- exaggerating by amplifying what the other person has said; using words like 'always', 'never', 'impossible', 'extremely', 'nobody', which can pre-empt another person's extreme position;

- making an unexpected move by introducing a surprise topic which has nothing to do with the subject, which can cause the other negotiator to lose track of the argument;

- overloading the other person with questions or too much information, in order to put them in a position where they are forced to ask you for help;

- using silence right after a question or a statement made by the other party – if you do not talk there is a good chance he or she may start again and disclose further information.

You can see that communication is used even in competitive situations. Competitive strategies require that you find out as much as possible about the opponent in order to prepare your message. This then leads to knowing what your message is, and preparing yourself for delivery. Negotiation is often an extremely intense form of communication because of the way in which it is affected by power issues. Let's look briefly at the other type of strategy available to the negotiator.

Collaborative negotiation

Competitive negotiation is about one party achieving power over another party, whereas collaborative negotiation is about both parties balancing the power between them. They look for solutions which will create value for all the parties involved in the negotiating process – to create a so called 'win-win' situation.

Amongst the best known proponents of win-win negotiation strategies are two Harvard professors, Roger Fisher and William Ury,[1] who produce a model of 'principled bargaining' built around four strategies.

1. *Separate the people from the problem* – involves communicative strategies which accept the people as human beings and focus on the problem as a separate issue.

2. *Focus on interests, not positions* – involves avoiding the opposing party's positional stance, but looking for the underlying interests; a communication strategy which looks at the underlying message.

[1]Roger Fisher and William Ury, *Getting to Yes*, Hutchinson, 1990.

3. *Invest options for mutual gain* – creating new opportunities based on the free exchange of information about individual need.

4. *Insist on objective criteria* – creating or using external standards which are untouched by the bargaining process.

Collaborative negotiation can be much less intense because of the parties' attitude to power within the negotiation. Where parties set out to balance power in a relationship, this gives clear messages about the quality of the relationship and the degree to which the parties wish it to continue.

Collaborative negotiating is characterised by the following type of behaviours.

OPENING

The opening of a collaborative negotiation will involve you in gathering as much information as possible, but also in disclosing information to develop solutions which are acceptable to both parties. This will involve behaviours such as considering a high number of alternatives for each issue, using open questions to gather information and actively helping the other party to expand his or her ideas about potential solutions.

CONCESSIONS

Collaborative negotiation is aimed at levelling power imbalance within the relationship. As such, focus is maintained on long-term rather than short-term implications. Sarcastic or irritating remarks should be avoided. These include

- positive value judgements about yourself, e.g. 'my generous offer';
- counterproposals which may cloud the issue;
- argument dilution – five reasons for doing something are less persuasive than just one good one.

CONFLICT

Similar rules about conflict pertain to both competitive and collaborative negotiation. In collaborative negotiation you may need to structure the issues and address them separately. We will look at questions of structure in the section on negotiation.

Specific behaviours in collaborative negotiation would include effective communication behaviour such as actively listening, paraphrasing, sermonising and disclosing. A useful communication tactic is to label behaviour by giving advanced warnings. 'I would like to ask you a question . . .' or 'I feel that I need to tell you that . . .'. Behavioural labelling slows down the negotiation process and gives both parties time to gather their thoughts and prepare responses.

Negotiation is very much about power in communication. We have seen how power effects the type and quality of communication when both parties are interested in achieving some area of agreement. Let's now turn to those areas where we need to communicate with someone and that person refuses to communicate with us, or where situations are so intense that communication is obscured. In these types of situation we will need to use other skills.

Using communication in difficult situations

We have seen that well managed relationships are a major factor in successful communication and that successful communication leads to better managed relationships, but what do we do when the person will not listen or engage in communication with us? What do we do when we see either the person or the situation as difficult? What do we do when the relationship breaks down and we find ourselves in conflict?

A major block to effective communication is the perceived difficulty in a situation or of a person. We react to difficult situations and people in different ways – avoidance, embarrassment, fear, anger.

We can use effective communication as a way of managing difficult people and situations. Communication can involve influence and persuasion, assertion and negotiation. Use the following exercise to help you identify your usual method of dealing with difficult people or situations.

ASSESSMENT EXERCISE

When you encounter a difficult situation or person do you feel:

- invaded, attacked or at fault?
- rejected, ignored or helpless?
- engaged in dialogue?

As you meet various people throughout the day, try to determine whether they reflect a dominant pattern in your relationship with them? Are you happy with your findings? How could you improve things? Did you notice any pattern in your responses to difficult people? Could you change this response? What else could you do if you encountered this type of situation again?

Try to remember difficult people whom you've handled well. What helped you in these situations and what can you do to repeat this?

If you are faced with a difficult person or situation, it is probably one in which there is a high level of perceived threat or where communication is confused. You may wish to take stock of your communication skills: Is your message clear? Are you listening to the other person? Is your message acceptable to them?

Unfortunately, communication may not be enough and what were previously 'difficult' situations can often lead to conflict. Conflict is a situation where relationships have broken down. The determinants of our behaviour in conflict will often lead us to fight or flight when faced with difficult people or situations likely to lead to conflict. These primitive behaviours, i.e. attacking or running away, can be managed by taking a number of factors into consideration. The first of these is self-image or self-regard and regard for others.

Many of us are concerned about conflict and rarely deal with it comfortably. We see it as destructive and something to be avoided where possible. Kilman and Thomas,[2] working in 1975, identified a range of attitudes to conflict and potential conflict which depended on our regard for ourselves and our regard for others.

This model shows that if you have a low concern for your own and another party's needs or interests, you will tend to use an avoiding style in conflict. The people involved feel little motivation to confront or work to resolve the conflict, because they have only low needs to satisfy.

People who are not concerned about their own needs, but are very concerned with the other person's, will tend to show an accommodating style of conflict management. They will give in and sacrifice their own low needs. On the other hand, individuals who have a high concern for their own needs and a low concern for the other person's needs will demonstrate a competitive style.

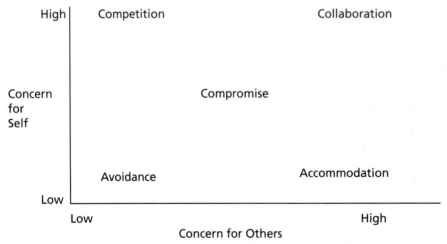

Fig 4.1 Kilman and Thomas conflict management style

[2]Kilman R.H. and Thomas K.W., 'Interpersonal Conflict Handling Behaviour as reflectors of Jungian Personality dimensions', *Psychological Reports*, **37**, 971–80

People with high concern for their own needs and high concerns for the needs of others will tend to display a compromising style which splits the difference to gain a solution to the conflict. This style is often seen as the 'best' style to adopt, but it is the collaborative style which requires the most communicative skill. A collaborative approach will work to generate new solutions acceptable to both parties.

Kilmann and Thomas's work is important but there are factors which impact on this theory. The first is that no one will use just one style in a conflict situation. The second is that the nature of the relationship will affect the process. As you move towards a collaborative style, you give messages which show a desire to improve the relationship. The last is that the parties' background and culture will affect their attitude to conflict. Some Far Eastern cultures are expected to avoid conflict at all costs. Consider all of these factors when you assess either your own conflict style or that of others.

FUNCTIONS OF CONFLICT

Before we go on to look at some of the ways in which you can deal with conflict, let's try and analyse what it is that conflict does. It can be a constructive force. As a central part of everyone's life, it helps people bring to the surface issues which they would not normally talk about. It can help bring people closer together. We've seen already however, that many people find conflict difficult to handle and destructive. Conflict does not need to be destructive. The following section offers a way of identifying the two types of conflict: constructive and destructive conflict.

Constructive conflicts

1. tend to be centred on interests rather than needs;
2. tend to be open and dealt with openly;
3. are capable of helping a relationship develop;
4. focus on flexible methods for solving disputes; and
5. help both parties reach their objectives.

Destructive conflicts

1. tend to be centred on people's needs rather than interests or issues of fact;
2. focus on personalities, not action or behaviours: 'You are an awkward so-and-so' rather than 'You've been awkward recently, what's been wrong?'
3. involve face-saving and preservation of power;

4. attack relationships;

5. concentrate on 'quick fix', short term solutions; and

6. tend to repeat themselves.

SELF ASSESSMENT EXERCISE

Consider the following conversation. Try to identify the sort of communication which is likely to lead to constructive conflict and the sort likely to lead to destructive conflicts.

1. DAVE 'I think that we need to close down the packing department and start again from scratch.'

2. SALLY 'I don't agree. I think that if we recruit the new staff and sort out the management we'll be okay.'

3. DAVE 'Yes, but look what it will cost in time and effort. Steve was useless and we can't be sure we'll get anything better.'

4. SALLY 'I know Steve was bad, but he wasn't that bad. We've all made mistakes.'

5. DAVE 'But Steve was your mistake, not mine.'

6. SALLY 'What about Alan Sugarman – he was your mistake. You always go on about other people.'

7. DAVE 'No, I don't. And I never made as bad a mistake as you did. The whole Norham Road site's gone down the drain since you took it over.'

Clearly, this conversation is moving from constructive conflict in statements 1, 2, 3 and 4 to destructive conflict in 5, 6 and 7. There are a number of strategies which Sally or Dave can take to resolve the conflict, but it is likely that neither will be able to tell how or where the conflict came about.

MAPPING CONFLICT

Once you've identified the nature of the conflict, you might wish to consider how conflict came about. Conflict doesn't just happen it develops through clearly identifiable stages. These stages are, however, often not identified by the parties involved in the conflict. These stages can be labelled as follows:

1. *No Conflict* The first stage is, of course, no conflict at all. This stage means that there are either no differences between the parties or else one or more of the parties are afraid for one reason or another to express a difference. This is a stage where parties may be avoiding conflict.

2. *Unexpressed Conflict* This stage occurs when one party feels that there is something wrong, but will not or cannot express it. Many of us may have been in situations where we feel that there is something wrong with a relationship, but the other party refuses to identify the problem. The classic case is of the husband–wife relationship where the husband or wife asks what is wrong, only to be answered nothing. Such unexpressed conflicts can turn into open conflict very quickly.

3. *Problem Identification* This stage will involve one or both parties identifying the issues which are generally interest issues which can be addressed easily at this stage. If issues are relational or emotional, however, it may be that the next stage of conflict is reached.

4. *Dispute* The fourth stage is one where conflict has started to get out of hand. Parties will bring in issues which are not related to the problem, just as Karen and Judy did at the beginning of the chapter on communication. A party's needs have not been met so he or she will escalate the conflict, although there is a stage in which parties may try to involve others in the conflict, to try to obtain help.

5. *Help* The fifth stage may involve other people either in an official or unofficial capacity. Individuals will appeal to a third party to attempt to resolve the conflict. Such a strategy can be dangerous for the third party, but generally their aim should be to get the parties talking again before the situation degenerates further into the penultimate stage.

6. *Flight or Fight* The sixth stage is one in which people tend to become very emotional and may allow the conflict to degenerate into physical or verbal agression – hitting the other party or name calling. The conflict is such that the parties involved no longer feel safe and will be forced to leave the relationship or attempt to destroy the other party or the relationship itself.

7. *The Conflict Cycle* The final stage can demonstrate that conflict repeats itself. Once we get into stage 6 it is very difficult to emerge. People need to feel safe when they communicate and effective communication helps them feel safe. As soon as safety is challenged, conflict can be perpetuated because we can't take the risk of talking to the other party. People in this position will often legitimise their position by talking about 'principles' or 'rights' as though the conflict is outside of themselves. Such conflicts may be impossible to handle.

Once you understand the nature of conflict and the way it has come about, the next stage is to manage it. The first stage in managing conflict is to structure and analyse the underlying issues.

STRUCTURING THE ISSUES

When conflict takes place, individuals tend to bring unnecessary baggage. Few, if any of us, stop to analyse the issues when our boyfriend has been caught seeing someone else or the sales manager orders some printing without clearing it through the boss. Conflict here moves quickly through its stages, with no attempt to examine the issues. Nonetheless, if we want to manage conflict we have to consider the issues. This can be done by means of: DRIVE.

D Data or factual issues relate to the facts about the problem. We may be in conflict because the April invoices have gone missing, which threatens our potential safety.

R Relational issues reflect the nature of the relationship. The nature of conflict about the invoices will depend on the nature of the relationship. In a weak relationship, conflict is likely to be of a longer duration.

I Interest issues impact upon what needs the parties are trying to serve and what they are trying to achieve to meet those needs.

V Value issues involve individual sets of values which dictate attitudes. Issues here are about assumptions of what is 'right' or 'wrong'.

E Emotional issues are tied to the way in which a person's individual goals and needs are met. This set of issues includes concepts such as pride, dignity and fairness.

MANAGING CONFLICT

Once you've analysed and structured the issues in conflict, you can look at some of the tools you can use to manage them. Remember, though, that it helps to be as creative as possible in searching for solutions to overcome conflict. The narrower your search for information and solutions, the less successful your conflict management strategy is likely to be.

There are a number of broad strategies which may help you to manage conflict. The first of these is in the field of *enquiry*. Once you have structured the issues, you may need to find out why the issues have led to conflict. Enquiry can involve:

- *checking* by using your own words to paraphrase what the other person has said and to ask if they feel that you have understood. This is an adaptation of the reflective listening techniques we saw in Chapter 3.
- *interpreting* by offering your own understanding of the situation. 'I think that you are angry because . . . but you aren't saying so. Is that true?'

- *feedback* and negative feedback to give your own feelings about the person's behaviour before asking for their opinion. 'You've heard how I feel, is there anything you want to say?' Feedback can include disclosure 'I don't like to tell you this, but I am . . .'

The second broad strategy is *control.* Control involves you in stepping back from the issues that are generating the conflict and your feelings about it.

Control techniques can include relaxation exercises such as those outlined in the chapter on managing stress. Other methods include 'RDA statements'.

Resent
Demand
Appreciate

Thus you might say to your partner:

'I resent the fact that you didn't wash the pots last night.'
'I demand that you do your share of the housework.'
'I appreciate the fact that you cleaned the bathroom last week.'

This helps to develop the elements of a contract for future behaviour. 'RDA' statements should concentrate on past behaviour. That is what the difficult person does or says, and not what you consider that person to be.

A variant of RDA statements is the 4R series. Using this model you:

Receive the other person's comments without interrupting. This shows that you are listening and value the other person's statement.

Repeat the other person's comments as objectively as possible. This can help the other person open up about the problem.

Request the other person's proposed way of dealing with the problem. People who are unable to deal with conflict are often unable to offer solutions, instead releasing tension and wanting to talk about the problem.

Review the possible options. The final strategy is assertiveness. Assertiveness training became very popular in the late 1980s. Although there is little clinical evidence which suggests that it works. Nonetheless assertion can be a useful way of communicating in the context of a good relationship. Assertiveness is about honestly disclosing your feelings in away which is acceptable to the other person in the relationship.

Assertion techniques include 'broken record'. This involves you in repeating your statement using the same tone of voice and volume. 'I appreciate you are busy but . . .' and briefly stating what you need or want, your belief or opinion. Assertiveness is really only honesty or congruence in communicaiton.

Whatever method you use dealing with conflict or potential conflict involves you attempting to restore effective communication as soon as possible. Because conflict can involve emotional, value, interest and relational issues our reaction is often dictated by our primitive behaviour patterns. Our initial reaction is to run away or turn and fight. In order to deal with these reactions we need to step outside the issues and to manage ourselves. without managing our 'self' we are immediately discarding half of the resources within the relationship which we need to manage.

Checklist for conflict management

1. I understand how my own self-concept will impact upon my work with conflict.

2. I can identify the type of conflict I may be involved in.

3. I can identify the stages of conflict.

4. I can structure the issues in conflict.

5. I can employ a range of communication methods to manage conflict.

6. I can control conflict.

Summary

- *Negotiation goes on constantly.*

- *Negotiation is about power in relationships.*

- *It is possible to identify eight different types of power in relationships, all of which are functions of dependency.*

- *Strategies in negotiation can broadly be grouped into two types, collaborative and competitive.*

- *Collaborative negotiation involves a flexible attitude to process and a search for common goals.*

- *Competitive negotiation involves an inflexible attitude and a desire to beat the opposition.*

- *Each of these strategies will dictate different tactics.*

- *Within these tactics it is possible to identify a number of roles.*

- *Negotiation can break down into conflict.*

- *In dealing with conflict 'self' is very important.*

- *It is possible to identify two types of conflict, constructive and destructive.*

- *Managing conflict involves recognition of conflict and structuring the issues to resume communication.*

- *There are a number of techniques which you can use to do this including DRIVE, RDA statements and 4R responses.*

5 PRESENTATION

'**The most precious things in speech are pauses.'**
Attributed to RALPH RICHARDSON

As a manager, you don't just have a relationship with individuals, you will also have a relationship with groups. A manager may also need to build a relationship with a group and may not have the opportunity to do this incrementally by building individual relationships and aggregating them.

Where you need to build a relationship with a group quickly, one of the best ways of doing this is by means of a presentation. For the purposes of this chapter 'presentation' is about communicating and building a relationship with groups of people.

The objectives of this chapter are:

▶ *to consider a structure for carrying out one way presentations;*

▶ *to help you look at methods of delivering a one way presentation;*

▶ *to introduce the idea of a two way presentation;*

▶ *to consider some ways in which you can manage yourself when presenting.*

'THE problem,' Sally said, 'is that I'm always nervous. I just know that I'm going to make a fool of myself and so I come on as being really aggressive. By the time that I'm into what I've got to say, my audience are either so annoyed with me that they're not listening or are looking at me like rabbits at a snake.'

Josh started laughing. 'Well, Sally', he said, 'it's one way of getting people's attention, but you might not get your message across in a way which builds a successful relationship'. 'Broadly, we can split presentations into one-way and two-way communication strategies. Using a one-way strategy, we can do a number of things to help our nervousness.'

□   □   □

Preliminaries

WHY ARE PRESENTATIONS DIFFICULT?

When you communicate with an individual you receive constant feedback and can tailor your communication to respond to that feedback. When you present to groups there is either no feedback at all (the audience can throw rotten tomatoes, but by then its often too late) or there is too much feedback from too many sources and we can't respond to the different messages. This is one of the reasons why people often find it hard to make presentations.

All too often, a presentation can turn into an example of one-way communication to which the audience may have to listen, but which they will not hear. So, how do we work with a group that consists of individuals from whom we don't receive much feedback or from which we get too much?

The first thing is to decide which of the elements of the 8-stage message in Chapter 3, are useful in communicating with groups. The first of these is preparation.

PREPARING YOUR PRESENTATION

Communication in groups should always have an objective and because a group consists of many individuals this objective should be clear and specific. The objectives should also be realistic and preferably measurable so that you can achieve them and measure this achievement.

The first rule is to decide what you want to say. You should ensure that you have identified your audience and what your audience expects and needs. If you are in doubt, try to interview one of your audience before the presentation.

The second rule is to decide to whom you want to say it. Time spent in planning is never wasted. Knowing your audience is crucial; are they expecting information, to be entertained, a sales pitch? What do they already know? What do they need to know? Remember that you are in charge of the presentation and that you can obtain information by asking and by actively searching for it.

The third rule is to organise your presentation in a way which suits your material and your audience. Generally speaking, you must shape your material in a way which will make it easy for your audience to assimilate. This usually requires an introduction, followed by the main body of the material you wish to present, ending with a summary of the main points or conclusion.

There are a number of ways of organising your information for maximum effect.

Topical

This requires that you divide the speech into various topics and arrange them in the most effective order, dealing with each issue separately and linking them at the beginning and/or end. This format is useful for transferring information.

Historic or time sequence

This requires that the information is related in the time sequence it occurred. This type of organisation can be used for speeches which aim to teach or instruct.

Spatial

This type of presentation could be structured in relation to varied geographical locations, such as a presentation in a building or on a site.

Logical

This format is useful when presenting a reasoned argument or proof. Each point supports the proof or provides a basis for subsequent points. Deduction (given A and B, then C must follow), proposition and other features of logical argument feature.

Residual reasoning

Structuring a presentation whereby each apparent solution to a problem is shown to be ineffective or unsuitable. This process is carried out until you are left with one worthwhile solution – the one which you are promoting. This uses the problem-solving cycle to provide a sequence for information.

Emotional

This form of speech is also known as oratory. Rather than appealing to the audience's intellect, this type of presentation appeals to their emotions. Points should be arranged from the strongest to the weakest and be persuasive with the aim of motivating or inciting action in the audience.

The first minutes of a presentation are extremely important. You never get a second chance to make a good first impression. Whilst it may not be necessary to start every speech or presentation with a joke, it can be helpful to find some way to build an immediate rapport with your audience. This will help you gain acceptance from your audience and prepare the way for your message.

You can check that your audience understand you. It may help to start with an area that you know they understand before you take them into new territory. Above all, try to prepare your audience. Once you have prepared your audience you can also motivate their desire to know what you want to tell them. If your audience feels safe, you can help them want to know by showing them the consequences of failing to listen to your message.

Keep relating to the audience by trying to think of their questions. Use the phrase 'This is all very well, but it doesn't answer the question . . .'. Do not assemble facts without narrative. Make your presentation tell a story, but don't try to pack in too much. Once you have considered the layout and plan for your presentation, consider how you will wish to deliver it.

□ □ □

'Okay' Sally said 'I've got a good idea why I'm nervous and how to prepare. That hasn't stopped the butterflies mating in my stomach and perspiration dripping down the back of my blouse.'

'I thought that ladies glowed, Sal' said Josh, grinning.

'Maybe I'm not a lady, Josh, but I'd watch it if I were you, or else you'll find out the hard way.'

'Sorry, Sal, no offence. Anyway delivery is going to depend on your audience, and your preferred style. You can either deliver a one-way presentation or make it more participative and turn it into a two-way presentation.'

'What's the difference?'

'Well, look at it this way . . .'

□ □ □

Delivering your presentation

ONE-WAY PRESENTATIONS

Delivery of your presentation is contingent upon a number of factors. The first of these is process. In order to explore process issues in your presentation, it is helpful to forget about content and look at what your audience is getting in terms of the means of presentation.

Means of presentation can include

Talk	Overhead projectors
Working demonstrations	Slides
Blackboard	Model demonstrations
Flip chart	Tape recordings
Film	Video

Any means that you choose should be integrated into a smooth whole. Don't be afraid to drop sections and don't crowd the presentation.

Research shows that the attention of an audience varies over a 40-minute period. It starts high, drops slowly after the first ten minutes and then more rapidly, reaching its lowest point after 30 minutes. It then rises sharply and is high for the last five minutes. Try to present your most important points for the audience at the beginning and the end of the presentations.

Vary your means of presentation to maintain audience attention after the first five minutes. This can mean breaking up longer presentations with visuals and with breaks. Do not be afraid to give your audience a break, but try to break at a high point.

As you deliver your presentation, initial instinct is to minimise the perceived threat from the audience. The sort of behaviours which you might see as minimising threat are in actual fact likelier to raise potential audience hostility, causing more of the behaviours which hinder presentation in the first place.

Behaviours which contribute to this cycle include dashing through the presentation in order to minimise the pain, avoiding eye contact with the audience and mumbling or talking to the visual aid, careless ad libs or non-stop jokes in an attempt to ingratiate yourself with your audience. All of these behaviours are based on primitive behavioural patterns which are designed to show that we aren't important enough to hurt or that we're really one of the audience.

Using words

You should avoid reading a prepared paper. A natural style of speech is one which you control. Set your own pace and signpost your presentation so that your audience know where you are going. Try to remember to place your facts in a way which will help your audience want to know them. Set your facts in a narrative ('The major issue was the loss of orders through misplaced invoices – this product . . .') or as the answer to a problem ('We didn't know what to do until we . . .'). Listening to stories is something that humans like to do. When delivering the message, you should try to make it as easy for your audience to listen as possible. You may, for example, use examples to make your presentation real. Develop examples from your own experience or that of a customer in order to relate to your audience's experience.

Analogy and metaphor help people to understand by making the subject matter simple and embedding it in their existing experience, too. ('This product is like a guard dog – it will protect your premises, keep you company on cold winter nights – and what's more it never needs feeding.')

Using visual aids

You can break up your presentations in a number of ways, but visual aids are often the most powerful. Visual aids themselves can be used in a number of ways:

- to explain your presentation – a picture is worth a thousand words;
- to corroborate your presentation;
- to give impact to your presentation.

Choose your visual aids carefully to suit the needs of your audience. As a means of presentation, they should be integrated into your presentation. Visual aids are only a tool which can help you create an impact with your presentation. If you cannot manage them you should not use them.

A good visual

is

BIG and BOLD

Clear and Concise

Stimulates Interest

Attracts attention

Gets the message across

Blocks to presentation

Presentations as part of the communication process are designed to do one of three things. The first of these is to increase the audience's knowledge or understanding of the presenter's position or message. The second is to achieve changes in the way they feel about the presenter's position or message. The third is to achieve changes in the way the audience behave or act (you might want them to buy something that they haven't bought before). A presentation is one of the many ways in which we seek to change things. Effectively a presentation is an educative method, a way of helping people to learn, even if it's only about the benefits of your product or service. As we saw in Chapter 2, learning and change are two ways of saying the same thing. Much work has been done on the effectiveness of achieving change through one-way presentation or lecture.

In education 'chalk and talk' is probably one of the most common methods of delivering a message to a group. It has, however, been criticised as one of the most ineffective ways in which a message can be delivered. John Holt, an American educator and author, has said that the 'biggest enemy to learning is the talking teacher'. Criticisms of the lecture include charges that:

- It is dull, boring and therefore a waste of time.
- It makes the audience passive.
- It causes a loss of motivation, curiosity and creativity.
- Since it is a one way communication device, the presenter finds it difficult to tell whether the message is getting through.
- It ignores the varying listening and understanding rates of participants.
- It ignores the varying learning skills and styles of participants.
- Delivery may be poor and fail to connect with the participant's learning needs.
- Retention of the information is low – much is lost in the first 24 hours and much of the rest is lost thereafter.
- It endorses the concept of the authority figure and the speaker may talk down to the audience. Patronising attitudes are not likely to endear the speaker to the listener particularly when the speaker is asking the listener to do something.

Summary of one way presentations

Overall, we may say that one-way presentations are useful in transmitting information to an audience which has to listen or has expressed a desire to listen. One-way presentations are less useful where we actually need to persuade a reluctant audience. So far, we have looked at what it is that a presenter can do to work with a passive audience. This can be summarised as follows:

Preparing your position

- Know your subject and prepare well.
- Know your audience.
- Don't read from a manuscript, use general notes only.
- Avoid heavy statistics.
- Include practical 'how to' materials.
- Study yourself in action on videotape.

Delivering your presentation

- State your objectives early on in the talk, remember that learners are eager to find the answer to the question 'What's in it for me?'.
- Watch your delivery technique – vary pace, use voice variations, movement and poses.
- Watch your beginnings – get their interest at the outset.
- Watch your endings – give them a message they will remember.
- Maintain eye contact.
- Demonstrate energy and enthusiasm.
- Demonstrate confidence, sincerity and conviction.
- Personalise your talk, talk about yourself, your experience, your own mistakes.
- Use 'you' a lot to build audience rapport.
- Use everyday language and a conversational tone.
- Assess and reassess your audience in the course of your talk and make adjustment as necessary.
- Use humour, anecdotes, examples, analyses.
- Breathe properly.
- Dress properly.
- Finish on time.
- Introduce surprise.

Supporting your presentation

- Use good visual aids.
- Use handouts.

TWO-WAY PRESENTATIONS

As we've seen, one-way presentations may be useful when working with an audience which expects you to give them information. When working with an audience that is hostile or expects to be persuaded, an accomplished and skilled communicator can use one-way presentations to achieve his or her aims, but you may find it easier to build a relationship with the audience which involves them from the start.

We have already seen that the anxiety created by making a presentation rests in part on the lack of feedback from your audience. It is also caused by the isolation which you establish as soon as you stand up in front of an audience. This isolation reinforces the 'us and them' feeling in both your audience and yourself and can be a barrier to building a relationship.

Depending on the nature of the audience group – age, expectations, position etc. – you can use a number of methods to involve your audience from the beginning and to break down the barriers which block your relationship with your audience.

Consider the following methods.

Case analysis

Give participants a short case, incident or problem study before you are due to give the presentation. Use the discussion generated by this study as an introduction to the formal lecture.

Problem census

Before you begin your talk, ask the audience for areas of special interest, concerns or problems which they hope will be covered in the session. Post them on flipchart and check off those that you intend to deal with.

Involvement incident

Ask everyone to jot down on a sheet of paper a real life incident, problem or event that relates to your topic. Encourage some people to share their incident or problem with the total group.

Interest development

Start the lecture off with a short, simple involving exercise, puzzle or game. It should be pertinent to the topic and make its point in relatively short order.

Structural note taking

Ask the group members to set out on notepaper the following columns as a lecture monitor chart:

I agree/accept	I reject/disagree	I have this question

Ask them to use the chart as a guide to note-taking and tell them that at a point approximately half-way through the talk you will ask them to discuss their notes with a neighbour or in a small group.

Two things

Give participants a two stage assignment. For example, in a talk on leadership ask them to list on the left-hand side of a sheet of paper three to six individuals whom they might consider to be significant leaders, then later in the talk ask them to write on the right-hand side two to four qualities which justify the 'leader' label.

As well as attempting to involve participants at the outset of the lecture, you may wish to consider the following techniques for involving one or two individuals in the group, during the lecture.

Appoint various individuals to execute specialist roles:

1. *Stretch monitor* this participant stands up and calls 'stretch' whenever he/she feels it's necessary. (Remember that 'the mind can only absorb as much as the seat can endure'.)

2. *Handout distributor*(s)

3. *A timer* (if needed)

4. *Jargon stopper* this assignment entails standing up and raising a hand when an unexplained word or concept is used by the lecturer or a participant.

In larger groups it may be helpful to appoint four or five participants as 'card carrying members' to display large posters carrying keypoints. These participants can be asked to stand up and display their posters at the beginning of the lecture, to punctuate the lecture, or at the end. A talk on persuasive communication, for instance, may include posters with

Message is in the receiver	Watch your wording
Make EGO appeals	Anticipate resistance

TURNING ALL PRESENTATIONS INTO TWO-WAY PRESENTATIONS

The final issue within the presentation is the question and answer period at the end. A question and answer section has the following purposes:

- to check understanding and retention;
- to correct misunderstandings;
- to learn of knowledge gaps;
- to learn of resistances to the points made in the presentation;
- to check whether the presentation met needs;
- to provide a chance to discuss and apply the new learning;
- to summarise or re-emphasise.

Each of these objectives is designed to meet a genuine presentation goal. Questions are, however, often difficult to elicit. People are conditioned from a very early age to avoid asking questions – they can be dangerous, embarrassing or show your ignorance. People may also dislike being questioned for fear of displaying ignorance, being 'bested' by the questioner or because of time pressure.

The questions and answer section can, however, be the most important part of the whole presentation. Remember to leave sufficient time for this. If your group does not ask questions you can 'model' by asking yourself a question. ('So, what does it mean to be a manager in today's recessionary climate?')

Do not be afraid that you cannot answer a question. No one can know everything about a subject. If you honestly don't know the answer, open the question up to the whole group ('We honestly don't know the answer to that one yet, Fred, perhaps the people here might have some idea of how they see it going?') or offer to answer later.

Try to encourage questioners by showing your appreciation ('That's a very good question') and avoid arguments with questioners.

Finally it may help you to consider the following exercise and checklist when you are about to make a presentation. The following section on 'Personal Performance' is designed to help you relax and set internal objectives for the presentation. The checklist is to help you focus on what you need to do.

PERSONAL PERFORMANCE

Remember that the behaviour of the presenter is important. You will effect the information which you give rather than the other way around. Do not overlook the need to project qualities such as openness, receptivity, confidence and interest. All of these will help build an effective relationship between speaker and audience.

If you are to give a presentation – at a sales meeting, in a speech, or in an interview – picture a range of possible scenarios. Begin with an ideal outcome. Imagine that you're performing in top shape with things happening exactly as you want them to. Then picture a mediocre outcome, with you stumbling over yourself. In the process of rehearsing these scenarios, you prepare yourself for mishaps and problems. Then, once you have worked through the possibilities, focus on the ideal images. Allow yourself to perform marvellously.

Checklist for presentation

1. I know what I'm talking about.

2. I know what message I'm trying to put across.

3. I have considered the needs of the audience when preparing my message.

4. I have organised my presentation according to a defined plan.

5. I am using visual or other aids to 'visualise' my presentation and hold the audience's attention.

6. I have a clear idea of what I want to achieve.

7. I intend to involve the audience by means of questions and demonstrations.

8. I intend to check the audience's understanding.

9. I have rehearsed my presentation until I'm happy with it.

10. I can use anecdotes or humour effectively to hold audience attention.

11. I am in control of this presentation.

☐   ☐   ☐

Sally took a deep breath, stood up by the flipchart pad, and turned to her audience. Smiling, she said 'Good morning, and welcome to Presteign's presentation on our position with regard to our tender for your new product design. This morning we're going to have a presentation with a difference . . .'

☐   ☐   ☐

Summary

■ *Presentation is about communicating with groups.*

■ *Many of the difficulties faced by presenters involve lack of feedback or inaccurate feedback from the group.*

■ *Presentations can be split into one-way and two-way presentations.*

■ *In all presentations preparation is vital.*

■ *In two-way presentations there are a number of techniques which you can use to release and channel feedback.*

■ *Ultimately, all presentations can be two-way presentations by using a question and answer period effectively.*

6 STRESS MANAGEMENT

'One has two duties – to be worried and not to be worried.'

E. M. FORSTER

So far in this book we've considered the management of relationships and the tools which you can use to manage relationships with others. As we've seen, the idea of 'self' is a vital part of the management of relationships since your 'self' contributes towards the creation of the relationship.

In managing the self, there are a number of resources available to you. The most crucial of these resources are effort and time. This chapter helps you to consider how you might best manage your own effort and the next chapter will look at the management of time.

The objectives of this chapter are:

► *to define 'stress';*

► *to examine some of the theories which attempt to explain 'stress';*

► *to look at some self-management techniques with regard to stress.*

THE common-sense definition of stress is simply having too much to do with too little time to do it. Stress is, however, much more than this. Stress is the result of the human inability to adapt to changing circumstances in their lives. Stress is not necessarily a bad thing. The physical and mental responses to perceived threats or opportunities equip us to cope adequately.

These physical and mental responses to threat typically follow a reaction involving three stages. The first of these stages is shock where performance will be reduced. The second stage is where performance increases dramatically and can remain at levels well above normal functioning. The final stage is where the stressor – the thing causing stress – remains in place for a long time and ultimately the individual becomes exhausted.

There are a number of steps in developing a stress management strategy:

- identifying your personal stress management style;
- identifying the stressors which are causing your own stress;
- developing short-term strategies for managing stress;
- developing medium term management technique for managing stress;
- removing the causes of stress in the stressors.

Stress management strategies

Each of us will manage stress in different ways. In addition, different people are able to handle different levels of stress. Some of us find one type of situation stressful where others see it as a welcome challenge.

These individual differences can be split into two types. The first of these is linked with personality 'traits' or characteristics. The literature on stress seems to identify a number of characteristics which enable people to deal more effectively with stress. These include a high level of commitment to the work, a high level of sense of control and preparedness to see stressors as a welcome challenge. Additionally, a sense of 'mastery' as confidence or the ability to meet challenges will buffer the negative effects of stress.

Research into individual differences and stress have also identified some negative personality aspects which tend to increase the level of stress and to cause physical or physiological breakdown. These have been broadly labelled as Type A personality behaviours. Type A personality behaviour is characterised by a sustained drive towards poorly defined goals, competitiveness and a need for achievement or aggression, preoccupation with deadlines, chronic haste and impatience. Studies have shown that this type of behaviour in its extreme forms can be linked with heart disease, although these studies are by no means conclusive.

The second type of difference is in the individual's perception of the stress factors. This will to some degree be affected by an individual's personality but there are other factors which will affect perception such as reactivity – the degree to which individuals react to situations – and this may be genetically determined. Social class, education and age will also affect perception, as will the way in which social support mechanisms contribute to individual views of the world.

Consider the following exercise to assess your own disposition towards stress.

EXERCISE

Your stress reaction strategies:

1. You are confronted by an angry customer at work. He or she seems angry and upset. Your inclination would be to:
    A. Agree that they are correct, offer apologies and offer to put it right despite your already full workload.
    B. Respond by fighting back, taking exception to the customer's stance and raising your voice.
    C. Try to gather accurate information, agreeing with the facts that you know to be true. Agree to investigate.
    D. Blame the problem on factors beyond your control.

2. You have bought a new electrical appliance, say, a toaster or a kettle. When you get it home you realise it has a fault and needs to be returned. The last time you returned something to the shop, which is only a small one, the manager had been upset and reluctant to exchange the product. You then:
    A. Avoid going back to the shop or try to go back when the manager isn't present to avoid confrontation.
    B. Enter the shop prepared for a fight. Take the initiative and demand an exchange or your money back.
    C. Explain the situation, demonstrate your understanding of the shop's position, but politely ask for an exchange.
    D. You place the blame on the manufacturer.

3. One of your staff has been asking you about pay rises for some weeks now. Her performance is not really up to scratch. She comes into your office and asks aggressively what you're going to do about pay. You then:
    A. Agree that she should be paid at least 7 per cent, although the budget will have to be squeezed.
    B. React just as aggressively and tell her that if she's not careful, she won't get a pay rise.
    C. Sit down with her and try to find out why she feels that she should be

paid more and agree to look at the problem.

D. Tell her that the budget just won't stand it and that it's not your fault.

4. You are snowed under with work, your colleagues ask you to take on another job because they need to go to a trade show. You then:
  A. Agree to take on the job.
  B. Storm out of the room, saying that you couldn't possibly take the job on.
  C. Ask them why it's necessary for them both to attend the trade show, what the benefits are and whether someone else could do the job.
  D. Remind them of the fact that they didn't do the job that you'd asked them to do last month.

Interpretation

Mostly A s. If you've scored mostly A s you tend to use denial strategies. You will tend to take on more pressure than you can comfortably handle. Develop assertiveness skills as outlined in the chapter on negotiation. Develop your physical capacity for dealing with stress.

Mostly B s. Your stress reaction strategy is to fight harder. You may need to consider developing relaxation skills as outlined on page 90 of this chapter and communication skills as set out in Chapter 4 on negotiation.

Mostly C s. You are an enquirer. Your stress management skills are probably fairly well established You may wish to consider some of the short term stress management strategies.

Mostly D s. You deal with stress by distracting and drawing attention to other issues. You may wish to consider some of the objective setting exercises in the chapter on time management.

Ineffective stress management strategies fall into three groups. The first type is *withdrawal*; this involves retreating from the stressful or potentially stressful situation. Absenteeism is a sign of withdrawal. A similar reaction to withdrawal is *denial*; this involves avoiding the subject of stress by denying that you are stressed.

The second type of strategies are *protective*. Protective strategies include seeing the problem as someone else's. This is exacerbated when you are stressed as one of the symptoms of stress is to blame others for your problems.

The third type of strategies are *compensatory*. These can include using props such as alcohol, tobacco or other substances. Other compensatory strategies involve being obsessional about minor details at work.

The final type are ***distracting*** strategies. Distracting strategies can include being overemotional. If you use distraction to cope with stress you will be prone to outbursts of anger, anxiety or other emotions.

Causes of stress

We can group the causes of stress at work into four broad categories.

- The first of these is the actual physical environment; that is, the location in which the work is carried out, the physical components of the work, surroundings, etc.

- The second is the individual's role requirement in the workplace, which includes factors such as the expectations held about a person's title and content, the relationships between people at work, variety and character of work, etc.

- The third is the individual's developmental needs, which would include business or career development.

- The fourth is the conflict between roles at work and roles in other areas of life, which would include work – family conflict, work – friendship conflict, work – self-concept conflict.

□   □   □

'This all seems fairly irrelevant to me, Josh,' said Sal, 'I don't see how it's going to help me sort out the fact that I'm tired all the time and some days, it feels like I'm going nuts.'

'Sal, unless you know where it's coming from, you're not likely to know how to deal with stress.'

□   □   □

Consider the following exercise, which is designed to help you identify the causes of stress in your life within the four categories outlined above. Answer 'yes' or 'no' where each of the following statements is generally true for you.

EXERCISE

1. *Physical environment*
   (a) I work in overcrowded conditions
   (b) I work in an open-plan office
   (c) My work station or office is generally untidy and crowded
   (d) My workplace could be physically dangerous

2. *Role requirements*
   (a) People look to me to solve problems and maintain good working relations
   (b) I don't really enjoy good relationships with my staff
   (c) I am often involved in handling customer complaints
   (d) I sometimes feel that people expect too much of me

3. *Developmental needs*
   (a) I don't have a clear idea of where it is that I am going
   (b) I can't really identify opportunities to expand my role at work
   (c) I spend much of my time reacting to situations rather than working on what needs to be done
   (d) I haven't much choice in what I do

4. *Work role and life role conflict*
   (a) I am unhappy when I find myself making trade-offs between friends and family and work
   (b) I find that I have little to talk about other than work with friends
   (c) I find that my impatience with issues at work often spills over into my life at home
   (d) I rarely have time for exercise, entertaining or being entertained (cinema, theatre, concerts, etc.)

You score two points for every 'yes' answer and no points for a 'no' answer. The higher your score in each of the four areas, the more likely these are to be a source of work stress.

Managing Stress

Once you have identified the causes of stress in your working life and your own personal management strategies, you can take steps to improve these strategies.

Many of the types of strategy which we saw earlier in the chapter are dysfunctional. They can involve you in a descending spiral of compensation, distraction, denial or withdrawal. Functional strategies are much more positive and useful. These can be broken down into three types:

- managing stress in the short term
- managing stress in the long term
- removing the causes of stress

Each of these strategies will be helpful in certain circumstances. In this sense stress is a little like crime. Managing stress in the short term can be likened to catching the criminal as he or she commits the crime. Managing stress in the long term can be seen as crime prevention and removing the causes of stress can be seen as eliminating crime altogether. Let's look at catching the criminal first.

SHORT-TERM STRATEGIES

Stress causes tension. This reduces the blood supply to the muscles which causes a build-up of waste products in the system and feelings of tiredness together with various aches and pains. Tension means that your body is fighting against itself and your circulatory system needs to work harder to get the blood around your body, which can result in high blood pressure.

If you are under constant stress – 'Eustress' – you can find that your body adjusts to the presence of stress and you find it difficult to notice its effects.

Your sense of what it feels like to relax becomes distorted. You may not feel as though you have slept properly and you may become irritable and restless.

The first thing that you need to do is to learn to pause. The intransitive verb 'to relax' means to wait, stop or linger upon. Relaxation is not just about staying in bed on a Sunday morning or drinking a gin and tonic at the end of the day or going on two weeks' holiday, although these active symbols of relaxation can be important; it is also about learning to pause frequently throughout the day.

When you're under pressure, you can get into the habit of over–reacting to stimuli, unable to slow down or to take a break. This is the road to what Linda Cherniss, a researcher into stress-related problems, and her colleagues called 'burnout'. These are the mental symptoms of stress.

Evaluate yourself on the 'burnout' scale opposite.

If you learn to pause, you can manage the likelihood of becoming burnt out. Pausing can clear your mind, reduce some of your tensions and help you make the most of your own energy and time. Pauses can be shallow, medium or deep.

Shallow pause

The shallow pause can be done anytime or anywhere.

1. Breathe in slowly and deeply to a count of five, expanding your abdomen as you do so.
2. Put both feet on the floor and rest your hands in your lap.
3. Breathe out slowly to a count of five, maintaining the spinal stretch which happened when you breathed in. Let your breath become natural.

Medium pause

Before you begin, try to ensure that you will not be interrupted for at least five minutes. Sit with your feet flat on the floor and your knees comfortably apart. Place your hands in your lap. Keep the base of your spine in contact with the back of the chair and your spine upright. Close your eyes.

THE ROAD TO BURNOUT

Stage 1 Energy, enthusiasm	Stage 2 Bouts of irritation sense of anxiety, feelings of guilt.	Stage 3 General discontent Increasing anger, guilt, lowered self esteem.	Stage 4 Withdrawal illness sense of failure.
Symptoms	Symptoms	Symptoms	Symptoms
Too busy for holidays	Complaints about other work	Lack of enjoyment	Absenteeism
Reluctant to take days off	Long hours	Constant tiredness	Avoiding colleagues, customers, suppliers
Take work home	Poor time management	Lack of commitment to work/home	Reluctant to communicate
Inadequate work/family/ friends balance	Too many commitments		Physical ailments
Frustration with results			Alcohol or drug abuse
Unable to refuse more work			

- Take a slow, deep breath in, expanding your abdomen, then slowly breathe out.
- Taking your next breath, focus on your head and the muscle group behind your ears. Relax. Then relax the top of your head, forehead, eyelids and face.
- Exhale. Take your next breath and work downwards, relaxing the muscle groups in your throat, neck and shoulders. Exhale.
- Take another breath and relax your left arm, down to your hand, palm and fingers, then back up to your left shoulder. Exhale.
- Repeat for our right arm.
- Now relax your back, abdomen, pelvis, buttocks, legs and feet.
- Take one more slow breath in and out. Stretch your hands and feet and open your eyes.

Deep pause

There are a number of methods of deep relaxation, which include the following.

3 Minute breathing exercise

● Pick a chair which allows you to rest your arms on its side and supports your back, but allows your feet to rest firmly on the floor.

● Sit back and take a few moments to do nothing at all. Focus your gaze on a spot in the middle distance.

● Feel the strain and tension start to melt away.

● Place your hands on your stomach with fingertips touching. Fill your lungs with air which will push out your diaphragm and push your fingertips apart. When they are wide apart, breathe in and let them meet again. Keep your shoulders relaxed and still.

● Now start, breathe in and let out your stomach to a slow count of three, then breathe out to a count of three. Keep a slow, gentle rhythm. Feel your stomach muscles assist your breathing. Repeat seven times.

● Take your hands away, but keep the rhythm going. Rest your hands along the arms of the chair.

● Imagine that you have 'switched off' your stress response and feel the complete air exchange which this has allowed, exchanging fresh, oxygenated blood for carbon dioxide carrying blood at the cellular level. All the chemicals which cause tiredness are breathed away.

● Keep this gentle, quiet breathing going for a full three minutes or longer.

This can be combined with visualisation exercises.

Pleasant memories

Take some time to recall pleasant memories, relax your body as fully as possible and let your memories float freely through your mind. Touch lightly on heartfelt memories – summer holidays, your old room, close friends, early childhood experiences, walking to school in the sun, snow or rain, waking up refreshed and looking forward to the rest of the day.

Visualisation exercise

Visualise a blackboard. In the upper left-hand corner, watch the letters of your name appear slowly, one at a time. Pause for a moment and look at the word. Then in the upper right-hand corner of the blackboard watch the letters of the word 'relax' appear, one at a time. Pause for a moment and look at the words. Then on the line down watch the words appear again, just as slowly.

JOHN RELAX
JOHN RELAX
JOHN RELAX

Medium-term strategies

Once you've mastered methods which will help you 'catch the criminal', the next set of strategies involves setting up your own crime prevention programme. We've seen how important relationships are in managing people. Relationships are also important in offering support. Everything which offers support can be called a support network.

Everyone, whether they acknowledge it or not, has a support network. Support can be physical, emotional, intellectual, recognitive (shows you've been recognised for who you are) through to financial or spiritual. It can range from a simple 'hello' right through to a shoulder to cry on or the loan of a house for six months. It can be a pet or a favourite car. Whatever gives support should be recognised and acknowledged.

As we've seen throughout this book, the quality of relationships with people is one of the most important factors in managing people. You may wish to map your support network and you can do this by constructing a sociogram. Take a large piece of paper and draw yourself in the centre. Then map out all the other people, groups, objects, animals, activities etc that you see as supportive.

You may wish to put those which are important to you closer and the less important ones further away. Put in arrows to show the direction of support – is it mutual or one-way?

Your map may include a number of people such as friends, family, colleagues, employees, relatives, teachers etc.

In our society we tend to have an ambivalent attitude to support. Working in a small organisation can lead to a sense of isolation. This isolation reinforces one's sense of individuality and ultimately this can lead to the feeling that one is surrounded by 'enemies' or 'incompetents'. Additionally, needing support can be seen as weakness.

It can help to think about your attitude towards support. Consider the following exercise.

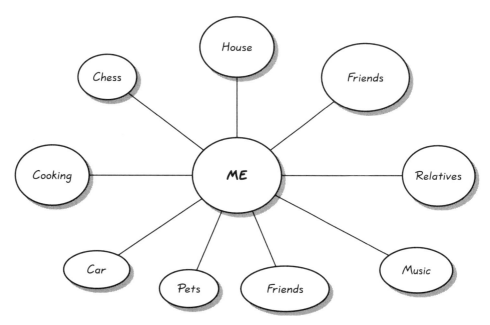

Fig. 6.1 My support network

ASSESSMENT EXERCISE

Consider the following statement and place a circle around the letter that you feel corresponds most closely with that statement. If you agree, circle the letter 'A'. If you neither agree, nor disagree, circle the letter 'B'. If you disagree circle the letter 'C'.

1. You need to compete to survive.	A	B	C
2. You can't afford to rely on people.	A	B	C
3. I sometimes feel limited by the concerns of friends and family.	A	B	C
4. I don't talk about work much outside of work.	A	B	C
5. I always seen to be the one who sorts out problems at home or work.	A	B	C
6. This whole exercise is namby-pamby.	A	B	C

Interpreting your score

For each A score 3, for each B score 2, for each C score 1.

Score: 15–18 You may wish to consider your attitude towards support systems. Consider the support system exercise which we looked at earlier and repeat it for negative support systems. Consider who takes support from you, saps your energy and undermines you.

Score: 10–15 You seem to have a fairly neutral attitude towards the idea of support systems. You may not feel strongly that you need a support network and accept the network that you have without carrying out maintenance activities. Consider the exercise earlier to examine what it is that you want and need from a support network.

Score: 6–10 This score may indicate that you have a positive attitude towards support and may have an adequate support network in place. You may also wish to consider the exercise earlier to determine your support needs.

Support is about sharing, and a supportive relationship is one which encourages sharing of problems and successes. It is unrealistic, however, to expect that one person can offer all the support which you need. Different people will offer different types of support and support can be grouped under three main headings.

1. *Nurturing support* helps you prepare to achieve things. It can involve people believing in you, offering advice about the best way to proceed or just listening to your concerns about a situation.

2. *Energising support* is more confrontative. It tends to challenge your beliefs and preconceived ideas. This type of support will involve people asking you difficult questions, pointing out potential problems or unrealistic plans. It can also involve them in suggesting new potential courses of action.

3. *Relaxing support* offers you a change in focus and a shift away from problems and concerns. People offering relaxing support will suggest that you go out to take your mind off current problems or will mediate on or restate the problem so it doesn't seem as bad as it first did.

Now that you've mapped your relationships and you're aware of the type of support which you can expect, you could take the opportunity to decide both how these relationships are supportive and how you can both limit non-supportive relationships and encourage new ones.

ASSESSMENT EXERCISE

Draw four columns on a piece of paper and make a list of the relationships you've identified. Consider whether each of these is supportive or non-supportive, and write this in column two.

Then consider the type of support that you get from each of these relationships before deciding whether there are any gaps in the type of support that you need. Write this in the third column.

Finally, in the fourth column, identify the type of actions which you intend to take to maintain present relationships, limit or end relationships which are non-supportive or develop new supportive relationships.

These three types of action are considered in more detail below.

1. Maintaining supportive relationships

As you will see in the chapter on team building, relationships between people need maintenance. Maintenance activities can be as simple as just staying in touch with the occasional telephone call or letter, asking how people are, or remembering birthdays and special occasions. All of these activities will show that you value the relationship and are willing to invest time and effort in it.

2. Ending or limiting support relationships

When you evaluate a relationship, you may find that it is draining or unsupportive and you have to take on the task of changing or ending it. You can do this by telling the person or people how you feel, identifying what you have appreciated or enjoyed and acknowledging that it is over.

In some cases there is too great a price to pay in ending a relationship, for instance, in a financial or work relationship. In cases like this you need to take steps to limit your relationship with that person to the basic components – the financial or work elements – and find other sources to acquire the support you need.

3. Developing new supportive relationships

We often embark upon relationships without considering the costs and benefits which they are likely to bring. We become 'friends' because we 'like' someone. We enter into intimate relationships because of physical attraction. These instant relationships may be moderated by experience, but this can be a painful process as we unpack the emotional and other resources which have gone into making the relationship what it is.

When developing new relationships it can help to have clear objectives about what you are looking for and what you do not need. You then need to consider who might best meet your needs and not give you what you don't need.

The next step is to make the potential contract clear. You need to state what you can bring to the relationship and what you are looking for. You don't need to do this all at one time, but the framework must be clear. All too often we can enter into a relationship without offering a clear framework, because of fear that somehow we are unacceptable to the other person. This is likely to lead to problems in that either we are forced to act as if we were someone other than ourselves, or the other person is forced to make a radical adjustment in their perception of us, placing the relationship under strain.

Making the contract clear involves showing your own support needs, finding out the other person's support needs, the extent of commitment and what other exchanges, financial, intimate or otherwise, will take place. This is not to say that the relationship will not change over time and under day-to-day pressure, requiring constant readjustment and maintenance, but that exchanges should always be openly acknowledged.

As well as managing your relationships to support you in your management strategies, you can also manage yourself. The other medium-term management strategy is to embark on a health maintainence programme.

HEALTH MAINTAINENCE

An American survey in the 1970s identified seven personal health practices which were highly correlated with physical health:

1. sleeping seven to eight hours daily;

2. eating breakfast every day;

3. rarely eating between meals;

4. being at or near correct height–weight ratios;

5. never smoking cigarettes;

6. moderate or no use of alcohol;

7. regular physical activity.

As well as managing stress through developing support networks and using relaxation exercises, stress can be managed through a physical maintenance programme.

The physical symptoms of beneficial stress mean that:

• The heart beats faster to pump more blood into the muscles and other tissues.

- Blood pressure rises to speed circulation.
- More of the substances which create blood clotting are released in the case of accident or wounding.
- Breathing rate increases and becomes shallow.
- Oxygen and nutrients reach the muscles more quickly. Wastes are evacuated more quickly.
- Steroids are released to power the system.
- Glycogen is released for energy.
- Pupils dilate to let in more light. Senses are heightened.

Stress prepares your body for action. Problems arise, however, when the body is unable to take action – fight or flight – and when these levels of arousal are maintained at too high a level for too long. Physical maintenance can help address these problems. A maintenance programme will involve two components.

1. *Diet:* coping with the pace of life today means that we tend to increase our use of stimulants and sugars. Ninety years ago we ate less than four pounds of sugar per annum. Our per capita consumption is now over four pounds a week. As well as sugars, which are designed to give us quick, easy access to energy, we also use a great deal of caffeine which stimulates our physical responses. Cutting down on sugars and caffeine will enable you to develop more sustained responses to physical symptoms of stress. It is difficult however, to replace sugars and caffeine at one stroke. Try to develop an incremental strategy which replaces one cup of coffee with a glass of water, or one chocolate bar with a piece of fruit.

2. The second component of a physical maintenance programme is ***physical exercise***. Exercise will also help you to develop a sustainable response to stress. As part of a planned programme of exercise, your cardiovascular and muscular systems will be strengthened enabling you to cope with physical stress. This programme needs to fit into your own needs.

Long-term strategies

The final type of strategy involves eliminating 'crime' altogether – removing the 'stressors', the causes of stress. Let's return for a moment to the second exercise you completed in this chapter which looked at the causes of stress. These fell into four areas:

- physical environment
- role requirements

- developmental needs
- role conflicts

Eliminating stressors in the physical environment should be fairly easy. If your workplace is noisy, poorly lit, overcrowded or dangerous, you can take steps to remedy this by moving or sound-proofing, better lighting, putting safety factors in place. Remember that stress is cumulative and stress in one area will impact upon stress in another area.

Eliminating stressors with regard to people's expectations of your role will be more difficult. Remember to manage your relationships honestly and use some of the communication strategies outlined in Chapter 3. This will cut down on role stressors.

Developmental stressors are also difficult to manage because, as children, we may have been told that we are going to get it all and we never do: life is full of contradictions and trade-offs. Developmental stressors can be managed by maintaining a balance between the demands of your work life and your social, personal or family life. Try to keep an open attitude towards learning.

Role conflict stressors are linked to those experienced through frustrations about personal or work and career development. Whilst individuals can hold a number of roles (e.g. wife, mother, manager, friend), these roles can sometimes conflict at work. Again, honesty in relationships combined with a strategy which uses pauses to demarcate clearly the lines between roles, will contribute to the removal of this type of stressor.

Checklist for stress management

1. I understand my existing strategy for dealing with stress.

2. I understand what causes stress in my work.

3. I can use short term strategies to manage stress including relaxation and visualisation.

4. I can use medium term strategies to manage stress including building support and health maintainence.

5. I can remove stressors.

6. I can actively manage my stress levels.

Summary

- *Stress management is about managing yourself and your effort in order to be a more effective manager.*

- *Stress is an extreme form of a normal human syndrome.*

- *For short periods stress is good for you.*

- *Over longer periods it can become harmful.*

- *The first stage in managing stress is to identify it.*

- *The second stage is to manage it in the short term through relaxation, exercise and emotional management.*

- *The medium-term management of stress will involve you in the development of support networks – relationships which will help dilute the effects of stress.*

- *The long-term management of stress involves removing stressors through combinations of the above two strategies.*

7 TIME MANAGEMENT

The way that each person experiences time is related to his awareness, his motivation, his knowledge, and his interests: it is an aspect of his uniqueness. Getting acquainted with how each person uses time is an important factor in every relationship – no two people use it in exactly the same way.

VIRGINIA SATIR

Time is perhaps the most important resource available to you as a manager. It is certainly the only irreplaceable resource. All other resources – money, effort, information – are replaceable. Time isn't. The way in which you use time is individual to you and will, in the same way as learning or stress management, depend on your personality, preferences and skills.

The objectives of this chapter are:

➤ *to recognise your own time management skills and style;*

➤ *to develop a structured approach to managing time;*

➤ *to identify some time management tools.*

Perhaps the most salient way of looking at time stems from the Greek philosopher who identified time as a river into which no one can step twice. The second step will be into a different river. Time is the coin that you use to buy the benefits of experience. Spending it wisely will benefit you as both a manager and a person.

□　　□　　□

Neil and Karen had been looking at one of the training leaflets that periodically came through to Norham Road. Sally walked over to them and said:

'Better time management, huh? I wouldn't have have thought that either of you have enough time to go on a time management course.'

'No, Sal, you're right. It seems like a lot of money to be told how to use a filofax', Karen responded.

'Anyway,' said Neil, 'we're going to be working until eight again tonight, Sal, the second shift were held up because Bill was late in machine set-up again. That will put us back by six hours on the schedule. I honestly don't know what he's playing at. Bill needs a time management course, if anybody does.'

'Why was Bill late?', asked Sally.

'I don't know, something to do with admin not giving him the message.'

'It always comes down to admin,' said Sally, angrily.

'You can't blame them Sal' said Karen, 'they're under deadline pressure to get the new brochures sent out – Dave's orders.'

'Maybe we do need to think about time then,' said Sally 'we never seem to have enough.'

'The last company I worked for had a consultancy firm in to train us in time management, Sally,' said Neil. 'It cost them a fortune and things weren't noticeably better'.

□　　□　　□

In the preceding chapter we looked at managing stress in order to develop effort and energy. We saw that this was an important management tool. Managing pressure needs to be placed in the context of managing your own time.

Time personality

As we saw at the beginning of the chapter, the way in which you use time is unique and individual to you.

It is possible to identify time use in four broad areas:

1. *immediate time pressure reaction*, which at one extreme involves harassed lack of control and at the other involves adoptive flexibility and relaxed time mastery;

2. *long-term personal direction*, which involves continuity and steady purpose as opposed to discontinuity and lack of direction;

3. *time use* – efficient scheduling versus procrastination;

4. *consistency of approach*, involving dependability at one end of the scale and inconsistency and changeability at the other end of the scale.

Within these four areas there seems to be some relationship between personality and time. As we've seen, your personality, style and skills affect the way in which you manage learning and stress. So will your personality affect the way in which you manage time.

Consider the following questionnaire to assess your own time personality.

ASSESSMENT EXERCISE

Choose the statements which most accurately reflect your approach.

1. **A.** My colleagues often say I'm like a cat on hot bricks.
    B. I see myself as quite a happy-go-lucky person.
    C. I believe strongly in a place for everything and everything in its place.
    D. I tend to buy things on impulse.

2. **A.** I'm good at seeing patterns and possibilities.
    B. I feel very strongly that I am an important person.
    C. I tend to take the initiative with new projects.
    D. I lack patience.

3. **A.** I tend to think about myself quite a bit.
    B. I tend to be calm in time of crisis.
    C. I have systems for most things in my life.
    D. I tend to follow my hunches.

4. **A.** I am sensitive to other people's feelings.
    B. I like to do a job well.
    C. I pay attention to details.
    D. I tend to let people know how I'm feeling.

5. **A.** I work best under pressure.
    B. I feel comfortable with new tasks.
    C. I spend a lot of time planning.
    D. I rarely plan in areas of my life.

Interpretation

Mostly A s **A** statements tend to show high levels of emotionality, nervous tension, imagination, introspection and sensitivity. **A** s tend to be flexible, and responsive to short-term time challenges.

Mostly B s **B** statements show high levels of elation, self-esteem and a strong sense of identity. **B** s tend to be able to plan in the longer term.

Mostly C s **C** statements tend to demonstrate a need for precision and orderliness with levels of confidence and initiative. **C** s tend to schedule efficiently.

Mostly D s **D** statements tend to demonstrate high levels of ability in using emotion, together with impulsiveness. **D** s tend to show a lack of consistency.

Use the grid below to map out your areas of time management strengths and opportunity for development. Identify your A, B, C and D scores as points on the grid and connect the points. The more of each quadrant that is filled, the less you will need to develop that particular area of time use.

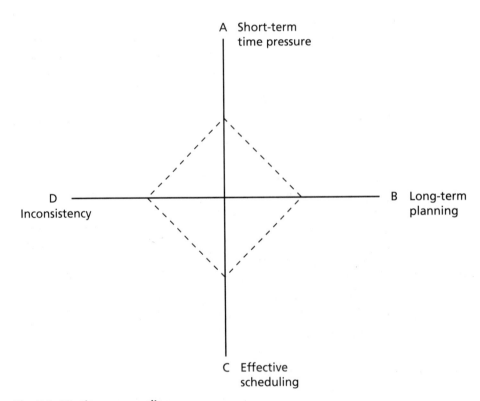

Fig. 7.1 My time personality

Structuring your use of time

Generally, time management involves eight steps, some of which will be necessary for everyone who attempts to manage their time. Others may only be necessary for people who suffer from immediate time pressure need or long-term personal direction.

The eight key elements of time management are:

1. Finding out where your time goes

Because of the problems that we've already looked at in learning about ourselves, you can often end the day wondering where your time has gone. You know that you've completed a number of jobs. You may even have crossed them off a 'to do' list, but where has the time gone? And what about the tasks you haven't completed or that have just occurred to you? Finding out where your time goes may involve you in writing a time diary or developing a sampling plan for your time.

2. Learning why your time goes where it does

As we've seen, some of the underlying reasons for time use will be because of your perception of time. Your perception of time will be created to some degree by the society in which you live and work. Studies have shown that Brazilians did not consider themselves 'late' until they were approximately 34 minutes beyond the time of their appointment. Americans considered themselves late when missing their appointments by 19 minutes. Learning why your time goes where it does will involve you in some self-examination and in developing an attitude which values time.

3. Minimising your time commitments

As well as valuing time, the most productive resource you need to learn to value is yourself. Often managers may take on more work than they can comfortably handle out of a mistaken belief that they are pleasing someone or meeting their own need for approval. In addition, organisations can ask managers for such a total commitment that every waking hour should be spent at one's desk. This idea is regarded with some suspicion in Europe where managers who consistently work late are seen as deficient in workload and time management.

4. Prioritising

The ability to prioritise is the key element of any time management strategy. People already prioritise to such a degree that it is difficult to believe that they cannot prioritise effectively in all areas of their life. Later in the chapter, we'll look at using priority grids or the 80:20 rule of ABC analysis to help prioritise difficult decisions and also the benefits of changing desires as well as actions.

5. Cutting down on time-wasting activities

This involves actually taking action to manage the time wasters in your life once you've actually identified them.

6. Avoiding the diversion trap

Everyone needs to spend some time on activities which are not immediately related to productivity. Avoiding the diversion trap is about managing yourself to ensure that the activities that are personally useful to you are protected.

7. Locating information quickly

Up to 20 per cent of your time is spent in searching for or handling information. The information explosion needs new ways of storing and handling information.

8. Organising for personal time control

As we've seen, time use is an intensely personal thing. This means that time management needs to fit in with your own personal needs. That is why plans, 'to do' lists, diaries, etc. need to fit in with your existing skills and style. Your time management will not improve simply because you develop a 'to do' list.

FINDING OUT WHY YOUR TIME GOES WHERE IT DOES

Time impacts upon you in a number of different areas. We've already looked at the elements of immediate time pressure, long-term time pressure, time use and consistency. Within each of these areas there are personal styles and orientations. Everyone feels the impact of time in three areas.

Physical impact

The physical arena consists of the way in which events at work affect your time use. How does work come into your life? Is it controllable with orders or presentations made by appointment, or is it reactive as customers or clients turn up off the street unannounced. If your work comes in uncontrolled 'bursts', what steps can you take to manage the workflow? Could you, for instance, put in place a filtering system so that initial enquiries were met by staff employed for that purpose and passed on for your attention only if they meet particular criteria?

Other issues in the physical arena might consist of the way your work is physically handed out. If you have to communicate between administrative staff and customers, you may wish to consider the layout of your workplace to cut down on time spent communicating or processing work.

As well as workflow and the physical coordination of work, other physical constraints include the actual time that your workday begins and ends. If you work from 8.30 am to 6.00 pm, you may wish to consider why you follow this pattern. Is it the most effective one to follow? Do not take work patterns for granted. If most of your productive work is carried out in the morning, perhaps you should consider how you can adopt a flexible pattern to fit in with your needs.

A significant change in the way in which people work can be seen in the adoption of an 'annual hours' system, where employees are contracted to perform a number of hours over a year. This gives employers increased flexibility in organising work with employees contracted to work a number of hours which can vary from week to week.

Finally, a question which you might wish to ask yourself is how you actually coordinate your time? Do you have specific times for specific activities? Do you have clear goals for your time? This question impacts upon the second area of time use – the psychological impact of time

Psychological impact

One of the major issues in time management is the psychological impact of time. Instruction manuals, time management courses, time management systems all tend to have one thing in common: they concentrate on 'doing'. Systems and courses all tell us that we can change what we do.

Changing behaviour in response to a new time management course or system is difficult. Changes in behaviour are rooted, as we will see later on in the book, in a system of needs and values. We have already considered some of the reasons why you might have difficulty in managing time in that time is personal to you.

Another problem which you might have in managing time is in your ability to say 'no' to new tasks. Consider the following questions when you analyse where your time goes.

- How worried are you about deadlines?
- Are your time estimates generally correct?
- How realistic is your sense of time?

If your answers are 'very', 'no' and 'not very' to these questions, it may be that you take on too much because of a deep-rooted need for approval. Throughout the first part of this book, you have been asked to consider your own motivation

– to learn to handle stress, to negotiate. Your motivation is the underlying purpose to your behaviour. Without understanding your own purposes, you will find it difficult to modify the way in which you use time.

All behaviours serve some purpose. If a behaviour doesn't serve some purpose, you won't do it. If you're doing it, it serves a purpose at some level.

Although you may feel that your time management, stress management or learning habits are causing you distress, they will be serving some objectives. This means that you have developed/learned trained incapacities. Trained incapacities is a term used by Folger and Poole to refer to the sorts of behaviours which we learn and which are useful to us in one situation, but which we carry through into other situations where they are not useful.

An example of a trained incapacity could be seen in Sally, who feels that her stress management strategies require her to carry out physical exercise at the local fitness centre. Travelling to the fitness centre, buying the shoes and clothes for training are causing her problems. She is losing out in other areas of her life.

A method to identify and deal with trained incapacities suggest that you

- determine what goal your behaviour is actually serving;
- decide what value or values underpin the goal;
- decide whether those values are still important to you; and
- establish another set of goals which are consistent with the values, but also consistent with the overall patterns of behaviour in your life at present.

Continuing Sally's story, we can look at what this would mean for her behaviour. Sally can identify that she wants to train four times a week in order to keep fit. She can still keep fit by cycling to work twice a week and going to the local gym once a week. Sally has changed her goals which underpin her objectives. She'll still reach her objectives, but by a slightly different route.

Biological impact

The final area in which time impacts upon your life is the biological arena. As we saw in the chapter on managing stress, we are so 'comfortable' in our bodies, that we rarely question what we need to do to maintain and support them. Time's biological impact can be measured by asking the following questions: 'At what time of day am I most productive?'

Many people find that they are best at a particular time of day. If you are most active and productive first thing in the morning, coordinate your work so that your most difficult or complex tasks are tackled in the mornings. Conversely, identify the time of day at which you are least effective and timetable simple routine tasks for this period.

Finally, you can ask yourself how other people's biological clocks affect you. We will look in more detail at using other people's time in the chapter on delegation but you might wish to assess how other people's most/least productive times might impact upon your work scheduling.

Once you've identified where your time goes and why it goes where it does, you can take steps to begin to actively manage your time. This will involve you in cutting down on diversions and time-wasting activities and minimising your time commitment.

Minimising your time commitments

Once you've looked backwards to analyse your use of time, the next step is to look forward to plan and forecast your use of time. Forecasting in your use of time is a major problem which you may face. The setting of unrealistic deadlines and completion dates will impact upon many areas of your work. As well as the domino effect of unrealistic deadlines, these will have an effect upon your own self-confidence and self-image. In the chapter on learning to learn we saw the positive effects of reward schedules on performance. Punishment schedules can have a negative effect and continual failure to meet deadlines will act as a self-inflicted punishment.

You can make use of a number of strategies when setting deadlines and completion dates which will help you minimise your time commitments. The first of these steps is not to say 'yes' too quickly. We saw earlier that need for approval will dictate your response to demand upon your time. You should remember that whilst accepting impossible deadlines may make you popular in the short term, continual failure to meet them will make you fairly unpopular.

The second strategy is to check your resources beforehand. We've already seen that effort and time are a manager's primary resources. He or she can also make use of other resources through communication and learning. Consider which of your resources is likely to be brought to bear upon the problem. If time is short you can increase effort. If effort and time are short you can use communication and learn to mobilise other resources.

Remember that if you continually use one resource management strategy you may exhaust it. Before you agree to take on a new task consider what you will need and what resources you have available to meet the deadline.

The third strategy is to avoid overcommitment. Time resources are similar to effort resources and even financial resources. We tend to spend them and immediately forget that we've done so. Research seems to indicate that whilst people suffering from depression think of the past, to an extreme degree normal people think generally of the present and the future. This means that normal people will see what's gone is gone.

This means that you can easily take on small tasks which by themselves may not make much of a demand upon time but which when they come together are unmanageable. Try to consider the time diary which we saw earlier in the chapter and limit your commitments through saying no.

Cutting down on time wasters

As we've already seen, procrastination or time wasting activities will often satisfy a need which you've consciously forgotten but which your unconscious behaviour pattern 'remembers' .

You may also procrastinate because of the perceived risk in failing at the task or even perhaps completing it: task failure may lead to censure from colleagues or customers: task success may lead into areas of new work which you do not feel ready to undertake. We've looked at the former already in identifying the goals which the original behaviours are attempting to fulfil and replacing the behavioural pattern with one which fulfils the old goals and the new needs on discarding the old goals.

When risk is the problem in changing behaviour, you may wish to consider using *affirmation*. Affirmation is a fairly simple self-programming exercise which is used by high-performing sports teams. It has also been used by the creators of self-improvement programmes such as Dale Carnegie and Dr Coué, whose maxim or affirmation, 'Every day in every way I am getting better and better', became the butt of jokes. This does not mean that because affirmations are simple, they should be discredited; they are a powerful way of changing behaviour.

An affirmation is a written statement about oneself which is intended to formalise a personal goal. An affirmation needs to be positive, personal and in the present tense such as

'I contact at least ten new clients each week.'

'I complete my to do list every day.'

'I make and use a priorities grid'.

If you decide to use affirmation as a way of dealing with behavioural change, be sure to

● Write each affirmation in bold, block capitals on an index card or sheet of paper.

● Read the affirmation aloud to yourself at least three times a day for at least twenty one days.

Although you may feel that affirmations are simplistic mumbo-jumbo, there is evidence in the field of social psychology to suggest that as well as being conditioned or socialised by external pressures (family, friends, school), we can condition or socialise ourselves. Affirmations strengthen and develop new potential behavioural pathways.

A similar method to affirmation is that of *visualisation*. Visualisation involves using some of the relaxation exercises which we saw in Chapter 6 on stress management. Once you have completed these relaxation exercise, you can take some time to remember a time in your life when you were under a great deal of time pressure. Try to remember the reasons why you were under pressure. Identify the main cause of the pressure.

Once you've identified the reasons for your time pressure in the past let that time go and try to think of your present situation. What time pressures affect you now. What is their source? How have they occurred?

The next stage in visualisation is to imagine a time in the future when you are dealing successfully with time pressures. At this future date you have mastered time pressure; you are cool, flexible and adaptable. Concentrate on this vision and make it as real as you can. Build the vision around a particular issue or example and share your vision with the other people who impact upon your time.

Visualisation is a method which you can use in developing your ability to see different ways of behaving. All too often we believe that the way in which we believe is the only possible way and block off visions of a possible future. Visualisation needs to be used regularly and can be used in conjunction with affirmation to change behaviour.

Information management

The next major step in managing your time is to manage your information storage, management and retrieval.

Richard Saul Wurman identifies what he calls 'information anxiety'. He categorises this as human inability to cope with the exponential growth of data caused by speeded up information processing and identifies 'five rings' of information:

1. *Internal* information consists of the messages which enable our bodies to run, synapses to fire, digestive systems to work.

2. *Conversational* information comes to us in the formal and informal exchanges we have with other people.

3. *Reference* information is the information which 'runs the systems of our world'.

4. *News* information encompasses current events which may influence our vision of the world.

5. *Cultural* information encompasses history, philosophy, the arts and every other source of information which determines our attitudes and beliefs as well as the nature of society as a whole.

We can use categories such as these to identify the types of information which will impact upon our own time management. It is possible to classify all information into three types:

A current operating information;

B problem-solving information;

C resource information.

We can identify current operating information as being that which you need on a day-to-day basis in order to operate within your organisation. This is top priority information and needs to be classified as 'A', problem-solving.

'B' information is that which you might need in a hurry and which will be important when you do need it, but which does not directly impact upon your day-to-day work. This is only top priority information part of the time and can be graded as such 'B'.

Resource information is something which you need irregularly. Resource information actively contributes to your productivity infrequently and is thus graded 'C'.

You can categorise information in this way by using this ABC rule to prioritise your information needs.

PRIORITISATION

We have seen that prioritisation is an essential step in managing yourself and your time. Everyone prioritises all the time. It is a human trait. Without the ability to prioritise the human race would not have developed, because all possible events would have the same valency or value. Choice, which is fundamental to development, would not occur.

As individuals, we often fail to prioritise in a structured way. We tend to prioritise on the basis of criteria which are based deep in our psychology; if an opportunity seems to be likely to satisfy our immediate needs, we will disregard the possible future costs of putting that opportunity first.

Objective setting

Before you begin to prioritise, however you will need to develop clear objectives. We've already seen how these objectives need to fulfil your needs. Unless there is a clear link between your objectives and your needs, you are unlikely to 'own' your objectives and thus plan effectively to meet them.

Whilst it may sound stupid to say that managers do not have clear objectives, it is often true. Managers as individuals may not have clear goals or may have adopted goals which 'seem' good ones, but which do not satisfy their own needs. We saw at the beginning of the chapter how some people are 'good' at working through immediate time pressure whilst others are 'good' at maintaining purpose over a longer period. Espousing and maintaining clear goals and purposes is a skill or preference in the same way.

ASSESSMENT EXERCISE

Objectives can be formulated by generating a set of questions about what you want from your life in five years' time and then answering the questions. The questions (and answers) should be as specific as possible. Although you will want to generate your own questions, here are some examples.

1. Five years from now what do I want my personal life to be like?
   (a) What sort of skills and training do I want?
   (b) What sort of friends do I want?
   (c) What do I want to look like?
   (d) How do I want to manage my relationship?
   (e) Where do I want to live?

2. Five years from now what do I want my working life to be like?
   (a) What do I want my job to be in?
   (b) What do I want my annual income to be?
   (c) What sort of associations and networks do I want to belong to?
   (d) What awards do I want to win?
   (e) What sort of balance do I want between work and social/family life?

3. Five years from now, what do I want my family/social life to be like?
   (a) What responsibilities do I want to take on for family by . . .?
   (b) What sort of holidays do I want to take?
   (c) What sort of relationship do I want to be in?
   (d) If I have children, what do I want for them in terms of
       ● education?
       ● family life?
       ● friends?

You may find it difficult to decide on and be specific about five-year goals. If so, try the exercise for six-month or one-year goals. Your goal statements should be written down to include four key elements:

● result desired;

● minimum acceptable standard;

● target date;

● maximum cost in time and money.

An example of a key one-year target for working life might be

I shall increase the average order my customers place (result) by at least eight per cent (standard) no later than September 30 (target date), by increasing my customer call time three hours a week with no more than £500 spent on monthly promotion costs (cost).

Consider how your six month or one year goals can contribute to a five-year plan.

Once you've decided your goals you can then prioritise in a structured manner.

Using grids

If we identify an activity or a behaviour which contributes to the achievement of your goals as productive and one which does not as unproductive, we can derive the matrix shown in Fig.7.2.

Let's label the quadrants as follows:

First quadrant = A
Third quadrant = B
Second quadrant = C
Fourth quadrant = D

You can use these labels to classify your time and the activities upon which you spend your time. Use the grid to match your best or class A time with class A or most productive activities.

Once you've identified your major productive activities and planned to develop the most productive time to them you can then decide how to organise for time management.

	Productive uses	Non-productive uses
Major uses	First Quadrant	Third Quadrant
Minor uses	Second Quadrant	Fourth Quadrant

Fig. 7.2 Time use matrix

ORGANISING FOR TIME MANAGEMENT

An effective organisation system for time management isn't just an organiser or a card file. Overall it's a series of arrangements involving people, paper, physical objects, space and priorities which support your goals and objectives.

The arrangements are the result of behaviours – things that you do and say – which you engage in each and every day. If your relationship with your staff or colleagues is costing you time, it means that the way which you behave is inconsistent with your goals. If you find that systems or paperwork are stealing your time, this means that the way in which you behave is inconsistent with your goals.

Only you can organise a system for time management which brings your goals and your behaviour into line. You may wish to consider some of the tools available to you for time management.

These can include information systems management tools, such as personal computers or manual filing systems which use A, B, C, D categorisation and prioritisation. Other information systems management tools are simple card indexes or Rolodex. Don't underestimate a time management tool just because of its simplicity or lack of cost. Sometimes cheap and simple tools are best. They can also include scheduling and prioritising tools such as diaries and personal or electronic organisers. Again, use the tools which you feel happy with. Your management of time is your own business. If you are happy and effective using a simple diary, that's fine.

The final group of tools that you can use are patterning tools. Patterning tools are what you can use to break action down into a regular set of steps or responses in order to cut down on your information search time. Patterning tools include procedures: if A happens, then you pull switch B and raise pressure on the 'go' light valve. If B happens, you ask the customer for her name and address and fill in form Y. They also include checklists and patterning tools which are often used in situations which are potentially dangerous in order to ensure that a minimum standard of behaviour is used. Checklists are used, for instance, in preflight checks on board aircraft and in high risk chemical production. This is not to say that you cannot use checklists in day-to-day situations to cut down on time lost through searching for information in regularly occurring situations.

Checklist for time management

1. I have a good idea of my strengths and weaknesses in managing time.

2. I can map where my time goes.

3. I know why my time goes where it does.

4. I can prioritise tasks effectively.

5. I can prioritise information quickly.

6. I understand the purposes which my time wasting behaviour serves.

7. I can use affirmation or visualisation to change these diversionary and procrastinating behaviours.

8. I can use a variety of tools to manage my time.

9. I control my time.

Summary

- *Each of us has his or her own time management style.*

- *Some common factors can be identified in four broad areas:*
  - *immediate time pressure;*
  - *long-term goals;*
  - *ability to schedule;*
  - *consistency.*

- *Within these areas you can take a number of steps to manage your time.*

- *Taking these steps will involve you in analysing your time loss before you can change.*

- *Changing your existing time management strategy will involve you in looking at needs and values as well as behaviours.*

- *Without actively managing your needs and values, your behaviour is unlikely to change.*

8 RECRUITMENT AND SELECTION

'You never saw such a commotion, in all your life, as when my
Uncle Podger undertook to do a job.'

J.K. JEROME

This chapter is designed to offer you a framework through which you can
address questions around the recruitment and selection process. Some of the
skills discussed are core skills, that is, they will cross into a number of different
areas of managing people. Interviewing for recruitment and interviewing for
appraisal, for instance, use virtually the same skills. Advertising for recruitment
and advertising for sales are not significantly different.

The objectives of this chapter are:

► *to help you identify your own recruitment and selection orientation and
its strengths and weaknesses;*

► *to offer you a framework through which you can develop an effective
recruitment and selection process for your own organisation.*

Basic principles

THE recruitment and selection process is sort of a cross between fishing and fish farming. First of all, you need to decide what particular fish it is that you want to catch. This is the process of job definition and analysis. Then you need to develop an adequate stock of the right sort of fish. This is the process of recruitment. This will involve you in the decision about what sort of lures you will need and how you will spread your groundbait. Once you have caught your fish, you will need to check that it is the right sort, before you net and finally land your catch. This is the process of selection and since we are involved in running a business unit and not leisure activities, the better the selection methods, the more likely you are to land the right sort of fish.

□   □   □

Sally Ann wasn't really sure where she had gone wrong. She'd interviewed Steve personally. He'd come across as bright, hard-working and dependable. His application form had shown that he had more qualifications than half of the people working with the company. His references had been excellent.

The truth was, though, that he couldn't do the job. He didn't fit in with the rest of the team in the packing section and he couldn't keep to agreed targets; in addition to which he'd been off sick for so many days that Sally didn't know where she was or what they were paying him for. Sally had tried all sorts of remedies. She'd had him in for talks in the office which had gone on for what seemed like hours. Steve had been charming, nice, admitted that there was a problem, but done nothing about it. When she'd called him in the second time, it had been exactly the same, as if they'd never had the first conversation. It was like trying to pin down smoke.

Finally, she'd got frustrated and shouted at him, talking about performance review, and he'd left. He'd not been in the office for four days now, without a phone call or message, and Sally hoped that he'd left.

The problem now was finding a replacement.The packing team were already shorthanded and it was coming up to the busiest time of year. What bothered Sally was making the same mistake again. She did not want to go through the dreadful trail of advertising, interviewing and appointing. The last time it had taken three days out of a very busy schedule and, if truth be told, she didn't much like it anyway.

As Jenny came in with the second post, Sally looked up and said 'Hi Jen, I don't suppose you know anybody who'd want to run the packing department, do you? Pay's about £15,000.'

'I suppose it depends on what you're looking for, Sal.'

'Oh, I don't know – graduate, early twenties, bit of work experience – has to look like Kevin Costner.'

Jenny smiled: 'Is that why you chose Steve in the first place ?'

'No, it flipping well isn't. I chose Steve because I thought he could do the job.'

'Sorry, sorry . . . I didn't mean anything. It's just that you don't seem all that clear about what you wanted.'

Sally had to admit that this was true. She had a fuzzy picture in her mind about the sort of person she wanted for the job, but it was fuzzy in the extreme. What she supposed she'd had in mind was somebody that she could get along with, someone like she'd been when she first started the business. She'd worked in packing for long enough, together with half a dozen other jobs, why couldn't she find someone with that commitment to the business? Recruiting was about finding someone you can work with, someone who you could get along with, wasn't it?

'Anyway', continued Jenny, 'I got the impression when you interviewed me that you weren't sure what you wanted. It was all very friendly, and I was pleased to get the job, you know that, but we're growing now and I think that maybe you need to think about what we're doing. Steve wasn't the only no-hoper we've had in the last year. What about Eddie's friend Alan – and Sue Sugarman? I think we're wasting our money advertising.'

Sally thought about what Josh had said when she'd last talked to him. 'You have all the answers – you're just not looking in the right place for them. Remember to set up your framework and always question all your assumptions.'

'Right' thought Sally, 'what's the framework and what are my assumptions here?'

□   □   □

When we consider recruitment and selection, it can help to set out a framework and look at what both these elements are designed to do. Sally thought that the purpose of recruitment was to find someone she could get along with, probably someone like herself. This is simply wrong.

The purpose of recruitment is to attract a sufficiently large number of well-qualified candidates to fill the requirements of a job. The purpose of selection is to define accurately what those requirements are and to use effective processes to ensure that the candidate fits the job requirements.

ASSESSMENT EXERCISE

Use the following exercise to assess your own preferences in the process of recruitment and selection. This may seem like labouring the obvious, but as Sally found out, the obvious can easily get lost.

Consider the following statements. Each describes a behaviour or an emotion which an interviewer can demonstrate or feel.

Score yourself on the following rating:

Score 5 if the statement is always or almost always true of you.
Score 4 if the statement is always true of you.
Score 3 if the statement is often true of you.
Score 2 if the statement is rarely true of you.
Score 1 if the statement is never true of you.

1. I would attempt to put pressure on the candidate if the job involves working under pressure.

2. I have never received formal interview training.

3. I would skip over potentially embarrassing situations in an interview.

4. I would tend to make my decisions on 'gut feelings'.

5. I feel embarrassed when interviewing for a job and find it hard to tell people that they haven't been successful.

6. I'd try to paint as 'rosy' a picture as possible for the candidate at interview.

7. I wouldn't notify unsuccessful candidates or else I'd write to them.

8. I'd find it difficult to give unsuccessful candidates feedback about the reasons for my decision not to appoint.

9. I rarely have clear objectives when I interview.

10. I don't generally have much of an idea about what I'm going to say in an interview, or how I'm going to follow up.

Each question scores a maximum of 5 points. Questions 1, 3, 5, 6, 7 and 8 deal with questions of the interviewer/candidate relationship. A score of 20 or over indicates that you may need to consider the nature of your relationship with the people you interview. Is it an honest one? Can it be managed more effectively. Questions 2, 4, 9 and 10 deal with the structure and objectives of the interview. Scores lower than 12 indicate that you may wish to think about how you set objectives for an interview and how you design its structure.

DIFFERENT APPROACHES TO THE TASK

Recruitment and selection are perhaps the two most important steps that the manager can take. Generally in business we can see a range of attitudes to recruitment which range from the casual ('We've known Bill for years, he can do the job') to the intense which can involve the use of expensive selection techniques such as biodata or assessment centres. Many feel that recruitment is something which can be addressed casually. This tends to be true particularly when unemployment is high, because of the relative ease with which people can be removed and replaced.

There are generally three common mistakes which lead to a recruitment failure:

- A general lack of clear objectives about what it is that the job requires. This situation worsens when more than one person is involved in the recruitment and selection process, as three or four people will often each have a different idea of what it is that they are looking for to fill the post.
- Failure to understand just what it is that the selection process is designed to do.
- Failure to use an appropriate range of selection methods for the type of job which is involved.

The rest of the chapter offers you a path which will help you decide just what it is that the post requires, and the best ways in which to fill it.

Recruitment and selection can be seen as a two-stage process. Recruitment is the process whereby the optimum number of suitably qualified candidates are attracted to apply for the post. Selection can be seen as a process whereby this potentially large group of individuals needs to be filtered through a variety of criteria in order to determine their suitability for the needs of the job and the needs of the business. This may not be the case where an organisation needs a particular highly skilled individual, when the process may place much more emphasis on recruitment rather than selection.

Recruitment and selection should be considered as two separate processes, otherwise one or both may fail. If you filter wrongly at recruitment, you may end up with a pool of poor candidates. If you attract at selection, you may end up with a poor fit between the job and the job-holder.

The criteria which are set for the selection process can vary widely, particularly when the job is a new one, and few people within the organisation have any idea of what the new post will involve, or the type of person who would be likely to fill it satisfactorily. When the duties involved in a new post are poorly defined, individuals involved in the selection process often fall back on personal rather than job criteria. It is at this point that the selection process, can become blurred because the objectives are no longer about the candidate's ability to meet the requirements of the job, but about whether or not the person will fit into the rest of the team, the person's appearance, race or sex, the person's academic record.

This is not to say that such qualities are not important, but that they may not be the most salient feature in the selection process. Reliance on this type of criteria can lead to the appointment of a person who is popular with the rest of the employees but cannot do the job, a person who is smart but rude, a person who is academically accomplished but lacks any commitment to the work.

The first rule of effective selection is that you should know what you want. If more than one person is involved in the selection process that this information should be shared with everyone involved. Where possible have a written statement of what it is that you are looking for which includes the knowledge, skills and attitudes required to do the job.

DETERMINING NEED

□　　□　　□

'Okay', Sally thought, 'I know what recruitment and selection are *for*, I've set my framework. How the hell do I find out what my assumptions are?'

Sally called through to Jenny. 'See if you can get hold of Dr. Joshua Slocum at the Centre for the Study of Management Learning, the number's in the card file.'

As Sally put the phone down, it rang almost immediately. It was Dave ringing about the new Health and Safety regulations. He said that he'd thought he had all the regulations covered, but a friend of his had told him that some new ones had been introduced in the previous month. He wanted to know how he was going to find out what the new regs were without ringing the Inspectorate themselves.

'I suppose it's just a case of going to the right place for the information, Dave,' Sally said. 'Try the business library.'

Dave rang off and Jenny called through to say that Dr. Slocum was not in the country at present and was not expected back for some weeks. Sally supposed that it was difficult to go to the right place if your information source wasn't in the country. Then she remembered something else that Josh had said: never think that information can only be sourced in one way. Information lies all around you.

□　　□　　□

Developing the framework

Let us look now at some of the ways in which Sally can develop a set of criteria which will help us select an appropriate candidate for the job. In order to decide on criteria, Sally will need information about the following factors:

- What does the job involve? What sort of tasks? What sort of skills will be needed to carry out those tasks? Manual skills, clerical skills, selling skills, leadership skills? What sort of knowledge? Knowledge of a particular milling machine or software package? Knowledge of a foreign language? What sort of attitudes? Does the job holder need to be friendly, flexible, caring?

● What context is the job performed in? Is it in constant contact with customers or other staff? What types of knowledge, skills and attitudes will the job-holder need to fulfil the tasks within the job What levels of reponsibility are there? Who would the job-holder report to and what type of supervison will they require? How would working conditions impact upon the type of person who would fit the job requirements?

Once Sally has developed her list of factors, she can ask herself where she would be likely to find such information. In a smaller organisation of, let's say three or four people, most of the people working there are likely to know quite a lot about the requirements of the job, because they are already doing all or part of it. The growth of a company to beyond six or seven people means that it is not all that easy any more. Sally may think that she knows what a job entails, but often a manager only knows what managing the job entails, and this is quite a different set of information.

Let's look at the likeliest sources of effective job information. Often we can assume that the boss is the most likely person to know what the job requires. As we will see, however, *doing* is a different skill to *managing*.

You may find that as you develop your management skills you become more distant from the job and need to look elsewhere for your information.

COLLECTING JOB INFORMATION

There are a number of sources of information and methods which Sally can use to collect it in developing a clear picture of the job requirements. Some of these are complex and may not seem worth the effort. Listed below are some of the sources of information from which she might gain a clearer picture.

● *The person who has held the job in the past.* This person will have a great deal of information about the job, although it well may be biased. In the case of a new job, this source is unavailable and you will need to consider the next most accurate source

● *The group or team in which the job is to be performed.* It is likely that in a smaller business unit, working under pressure, the people in post will to some extent be doing the job already if there is a need for it in the first place. This group can often include the boss or the person who is going to supervise the new job.

● *The boss or the person who is directly responsible for supervising the new job.* This may be the most *inaccurate* source of job-related information in that the boss or supervisor may offer criteria which are related to their own personal preferences and not to the needs of the job. This is, however, the most common source of job-related information.

Another useful source of information is **expert information**. This can be from external sources or experts. Your local library may have a copy of the American Dictionary of Occupational Title (DOT). This lists thousands of job titles with brief descriptions and a skeleton job description for each. Experts who work in other organisations can be consulted informally.

Where possible you should always use more than one information source when deciding what it is that the job requires. Do not make assumptions that you alone know what a job entails. You may be wrong.

Once you have decided on the sources of information that you intend to use, you may wish to consider how you intend to collect it. When collecting information we need to use 'good enough' methods which will give the best possible picture of the needs of the post. We can use three main rule of thumb methods.

1. *Observation*. This applies where there is already a person in post to observe.

2. *Individual interview*. Again this is of more use where there is already a postholder to interview.

3. *Group interview*. This means involving the group or team who, as we've already seen, may be already doing the job between them and asking them just what it is likely to involve and what type of person would be needed to fill it.

□   □   □

The wind was freezing and black clouds promised snow later on that morning. Sally wished she'd stayed in the office. It wasn't much warmer, but at least you could warm your hands around a cup of coffee. The packing shed was right at the end of the yard and Sally was shivering uncontrollably when she reached it.

Neil and Karen looked up in surprise when she burst through the door. The office was warmed by an old-fashioned stove and the windows were shuttered by steam and brown paper patches.

'Oh good, the kettle's on – milk and one sugar please,' Sally said looking at the kettle standing unplugged by the sink unit.

'Hello, Sal, we don't see you in here often,' said Neil.

'That's because I can never get a cup of coffee.'

'Sorry, Miss Thorn, I'll get you one right away,' said Karen.

'I just thought I'd see how things were going,' said Sally. 'Without Steve, that is. You've not heard anything, have you?'

'Not a thing,' said Neil, 'not that it makes much difference.'

'What was the problem with Steve anyway?'

Neil started on a diatribe in which he indicated that Steve had been about as much use as a chocolate fireguard. As he went on, Karen chipped in from time to time.

'Okay, okay,' said Sally, 'well, what sort of a person do you think that we need?'

After an hour of talking to the supervisors, Sally went out and looked at the packing work for half a day, and was amazed at how much it had changed. She also spoke to some of the packers.

Sally used individual and group interviews as well as observation. She stuck to her objectives in finding out what sort of skills and abilities the job needed. She could use the information she gathered to add to her own knowledge. After a day she'd got a pretty good idea of what the packing department did on a minute-by-minute basis; a day well spent considering that the post was likely to cost them £100,000 in the first five years, and was responsible for the company's initial image to the customer.

□   □   □

Once you've arrived at an accurate picture of what the job requires, you will need to communicate that information to the potential candidates and to your fellow interviewers if you are not inteviewing alone. Lack of confidence in communicating accurate job information can lead to poor outcomes for recruitment and selection. All too often job information is cooked up in the head of a manager and turned into a list of duties couched in vague terms called the job description. The job description often offers a list of duties and responsibilities, as in the example below.

Post Title: Packing Manager

Main Duties:

1. To supervise the staff within the packing plant.

2. To act as site manager in the absence of the directors.

3. To order packing materials and ensure that materials are packed within agreed quality standards.

4. To liaise with staff at the loading bay and the production departments to ensure the free flow of packed products.

5. To manage disciplinary issues within the packing plant.

6. To ensure compliance with health and safety standards.

7. Any other duties which may be deemed compatible with the post.

Responsible to: The Sales Director
Responsible for: 23 packing staff

The problems with even such an abbreviated job description is that it tells people what they are expected to *do* rather than what they need to *achieve*. The job description is a static rather than a dynamic document and is not likely to set accurate accountabilities for performance. The job description which may be augmented by a person specification is less than useful in that it fails to accurately describe the performance levels that you expect from the job holder.

Later in this book we will look at issues about the job contract. The job contract rests on the exchange of information between the employer and the employee. This exchange of information will determine the nature of their future relationship. If the potential employee is given information which suggests that the employer only wants to fill a post and that little thought has been given to the requirements of the job, then this will set the tone for their relationship. If, on the other hand, the prospective employee is given information which sets out performance measures and targets, this will assist in developing the relationship. More information on the job contract is given in Chapter 10.

RECRUITMENT METHODS

Once you have defined the requirements of the job and communicated this to the people who need to know, you can consider how you are going to recruit. Recruitment is the process of generating a pool of rainbow trout from which you can pick out the best rainbow trout. It is also about avoiding a pool of trout, chubb, piranhas and goldfish, simply in order to avoid the effort involved in throwing the wrong fish back. Often even professionals working in the field of recruitment and selection can lose sight of their objectives. In some cases individuals involved in the field can start to recruit before they actually know what the job requires, assuming (wrongly) that their recruitment methods will throw up any number of appropriate candidates.

Even if this is so, the effort expended in sorting through the unsuitable candidates will cost more than necessary and tax the stamina of the selectors. After you have interviewed the seventh or eighth unsuitable candidate you may be too tired to notice the ninth suitable one. Effective recruitment involves knowing what it is that you want. Fishing expeditions will largely be doomed to failure.

Effective recruitment is also largely a matter of common sense in using appropriate methods for the job vacancy that you wish to fill. Recruitment, like sales, is about communication – getting the right message to the right audience at the right time. Let's take a moment to look at the sort of channels which you, the recruiter, can use:

- word-of-mouth advertising;
- newspaper advertising;

- government recruitment agencies (job centres, etc.);
- careers service;
- training schemes;
- professional recruitment agencies;
- speculative applications.

Only you can decide what particular channel is an appropriate one for the job that you wish to advertise. All have their advantages and disadvantages. Some people, for instance, would never entertain speculative applications because many of them come from unemployed individuals; the same applies to Job Centres. You should, however, in the interests of common sense as well as fair practice, try to reach as many of the type of candidate that you want as possible. Don't disqualify before the selection process – or, indeed, at any stage – on the basis of your own prejudices.

□ □ □

Back in the office, Sally thought about some of the choices she'd made in the past. She'd often found the Job Centre unresponsive and had relied mostly on newspaper ads.

'Jenny, why did you apply for this job?'

'Because I needed one,' said Jenny glibly.

'All right, all right, but what appealed to you about ours?'

'It's not so much what was in it as what wasn't in it,' Jenny said. 'It didn't have a box number when four of the other posts did. The ad told me about you, well, about the company, and told me what the salary would be. It gave the impression of a small company, but a friendly one.'

□ □ □

Recruitment advertising

Recruitment advertising of any sort is about creating and managing the right impression with your potential candidate pool. At a minimum, this means disclosing the right information to this pool. Potential candidates will need to know:

- location
- salary package
- company description
- job title and content
- candidate requirements
- accurate and sympathetic reply instructions.

If you fail to meet these criteria, you may, at a stroke, alienate suitable candidates, attract unsuitable ones and leave the world in general with a sense of your incompetence. A recent job ad in a national daily advised candidates to re-apply for a post because the original applications had been stolen. Whilst this may have been honest, one has to question the wisdom of creating this type of impression.

SELECTION AS A TWO-WAY PROCESS

As we saw in the section on preparing job information, the selection process does not merely involve information gathering, it also involves information giving. This reflects the way in which good communication involves disclosure. Unfortunately, our early experiences may lead us to consider the selection process as something other than a process of information exchange. Some people may see it as an examination or a test. We will look at the value of setting up barriers which need to be overcome to join an organisation or group in Chapter 13 on teambuilding, but this should not obscure the process of information exchange. The issue which you will need to consider is the way in which you give and gather information as part of this process.

□   □   □

Sally had just put her coat on, and had almost reached the door when the telephone rang.

'Hello, Sally Ann, this is Josh, finally returning your call.'

'Hi Josh, where have you been?'

'You'd just be jealous if I told you. What's happening on the recruitment front?'

'Well I've sorted out the job information. What I'm not too sure about now is just what I do with it?'

'What do you want to do with it, Sally?' Josh asked.

'I've just said I don't know.'

'You're being lazy, Sal, I've told you that you've already got the answers. You're just not looking in the right place The information you've got is the material that you'll use to filter out your applicant pool. There are lots of methods that you can use to select, but all of them need to refer to your original job requirements.'

'What methods?'

'Am I paying for this call or what . . . oh, all right, Sal.'

□   □   □

CHOOSING YOUR SELECTION METHOD

It is a sad but indisputable fact that in any population of people who apply for a job, there will be a number who will not give accurate information about themselves. This may be because they do not know themselves or the information that you need. It may be because they want the job and don't think about their potential problems, once they have it. It is also true that organisations do not give accurate information for similar reasons.

This means that your information gathering and giving process needs to be as accurate as possible. We looked at interviews in the chapter on communication. In order to obtain accurate information about candidates, you should use more than one method, in the same way that you use more than one method when preparing the original job criteria; multiple methods give greater accuracy in matching the person to the job. The following list gives you a range of different selection methods, ranging from the most popular and least expensive to the least popular and most expensive. This is not to say that cost necessarily needs to be an important factor in choosing a selection method – expensive methods such as biodata or psychometric testing may be cost effective because of their perceived success rate in finding the right person to fill a job and because of the reduction in work required by the recruiter. However, selection effectiveness can be achieved without worrying about these issues.

1. Screening

□   □   □

Josh had said that once you'd got your pool of candidates the fishing process needed to begin with a filtering process. If you had eighty or ninety applicants, you could filter them by asking them to telephone and by having someone ask them pertinent questions about their experience or educatioanl qualifications. Of course, he'd said, you can also screen after shortlisting if you've got sufficient good candidates, by asking them to telephone for a brief chat.

□   □   □

Other screening processes could include using the type of information you already have as part of the selection process. If, for instance, you already have a group of good workers doing the same job, you could construct a profile looking at their education, experience, etc. and throw out anyone who didn't fit. There are large companies that sell these sorts of profiles based on information from several organisations. This is called biodata and seems to be a very good predictor of candidate performance.

2. Application forms

□   □   □

Sally thought again about how important creating the right impression was. She thought about some of the problems that they'd faced last year when they'd advertised Sue Sugarman's job while she was still in post. They'd used a box number then and asked for applications by CV. The resulting tidal wave of applications had been horrendous, trying to sort through 316 CVs in almost as many formats with widely varying levels of presentation. After Sally had waded through twenty handwritten or typed CVs, she'd completely lost interest in the selection process and consigned the rest to the bin.

□   □   □

After that experience she'd designed a standard application form, which they'd not used yet. It set out sections for

- knowledge, skills and attitudes;
- qualities required;
- experience;
- physical criteria; and
- other requirements.

3. Interview

□   □   □

Sally disliked the interview process, both as an interviewee and an interviewer. It was associated in her mind with too many refusals for further funding when the company had gone through a bad patch two years before. She also hated the lengths that people would go to to get the job. When she'd interviewed 'opportunistically', she'd had people telling obvious lies about gaps in their CVs.

Josh had laughed when she'd said how much she hated interviews, and had said that he thought that she was honest to admit it. He said that although the interview was the most popular form of selection, it was also the least useful in predicting the performance of candidates on the job.

□   □   □

Much of the reason that interviews are such a bad predictor is because interviewers simply don't like being in a face-to-face situation where people are asking them for something, or because they have a total misperception of the interview process.

Other problems with the interview included those people who were appointed to post on the basis of 'gut feelings' and those who brought their unrecognised and recognised prejudices to the process of selection. Josh had said that he'd worked with people who wouldn't appoint short people ('too pushy'), bearded people ('they have something to hide'), people who wear suede shoes ('unreliable') people who are too thin ('personality problems') people who are weighty ('personality problems') and people who are the 'wrong' star sign. It is, of course, against the law for even small business units above a certain size to discriminate against women or racial minorities.

Interviews were none the less an important method of exchanging information, but only if they were approached in the right way.

4. Group selection methods

When working with other people was an important part of the selection process, Josh had said that it could be useful to consider a group selection method. This could involve asking a group of candidates to carry out a task and to look at the ways in which they interacted. The task need not be particularly complicated. It could, for instance involve the group in designing and delivering a presentation on the changing nature of the world of work.

You could observe the group and look out for the people who seemed to demonstrate the sort of qualities which the job required: those who were verbally skilled, those who showed leadership behaviour, those who mediated when squabbles broke out.

It is important to tell people what sort of qualities you are looking for before you start such an exercise, as if you do not give clear goals, some potentially viable candidates may try to second-guess you and demonstrate completely untypical behaviours. Where clear goals exist, candidates may also try to show untypical behaviours, but this is very difficult to do successfully.

5. Realistic job previews

□   □   □

'It's a pity that you can't actually see them perform in a real context,' Sally said.

'Oh, but you can. There are few real reasons that you can't bring them into the plant or shop to see how they work out.'

□   □   □

Methods like this are time-consuming and there are serious issues of confidentiality, but if you can screen your shortlist down to two or three there's no reason that you shouldn't bring them in and give them a problem to handle.

You just need to make sure that the problem has a clear solution, preferably, it would be a problem that you've already dealt with.

The other thing about realistic job previews is that they can involve more staff in the selection procedure. People will tend to work well with candidates whom they have seen and had some say about.

6. Portfolios

Portfolios were something which were little used in the United Kingdom with the exception of specialist professions, such as photography or graphic design. The development of portfolios such as Records of Achievement seemed to indicate that this was something that would change. Growing numbers of employees, particularly in service companies, could develop portfolios of work including customer references,

7. References

☐   ☐   ☐

'Aha – references!' said Sally, 'The last lot of references that I got were rubbish – or rather they were wonderful and the person that I gave the job to was rubbish. I should have sued.'

'Recent studies seem to show that written references have some drawbacks. Just think why that last lot of references were poor.'

'Someone wanted rid.'

'That's certainly a possible reason.'

'I suppose poor references could be libellous – or slanderous, whichever it is.'

'That too,' Josh had said 'although one of the main problems is that people just don't know what you're asking for. The most accurate references are ones which come from face-to-face or telephone interviews with someone who has had direct experience of the candidate's work. Where possible, this should be a person that you know.'

'If you're writing, ask for a telephoned reply or say that you will telephone them. Where this isn't possible, enclose a copy of the information which you have collected about the job and ask the referee if the candidate is suitable for this job.'

☐   ☐   ☐

8. Other methods

☐   ☐   ☐

'Is that it, then?' asked Sally.

'Well,' Josh had said, 'here are a number of other methods of selection which you might want to consider. Other people use them, but they can be expensive in a number of ways.'

'Are they worth hearing about?'

'That's up to you. The most popular is psychometric testing, which offers actual tests in areas such as intelligence – you have probably been tested on the Wechsler IQ test at school and the same sort of issues that apply to school IQ tests apply also to selection IQ tests.'

'Other psychometric tests determine personality characteristics. These include Raymond Cattell's 16 PF Test, which broadly demonstrates candidates' emotional stability. The Meyers Briggs Test is reasonably user-friendly (it's short) and purports to identify people by personality characteristics such as extrovert v. introvert and thinking v. feeling. These characteristics are similar to those which we use when learning.

'Finally, there are selection methods which use samples of candidates' handwriting, their star sign or select through palmistry. There's not a lot of evidence to support these as adequate predictors of performance, although I try to keep an open mind.'

'So you think I ought to get Gypsy Rose Lee in, do you?' Sally said.

'I think you need to know what you want and to use processes that you feel comfortable with in order to select your candidate. From what you said to me, Gypsy Rose Lee was just as likely to select a suitable candidate as you were in your last round of interviews.'

Once you know what you want, and are comfortable with the selection processes that you have chosen, you can go on to look at the next stage of managing people for performance – development.

Checklist for selection by interview

1. Both I and the candidate both know specifically *why* we are there. If either of us doesn't, the interview isn't likely to succeed.

2. Both I and the candidate are adequately briefed, in writing.

3. The interviews will start on time.

4. There will be no interruptions.

5. The room arrangement and the lighting do not put the interviewee at a disadvantage.

6. The interviewee knows who the interviewer(s) is (are) and vice versa.

7. I have read my brief.

8. I will talk only 20 per cent of the time.

9. I control both the timing and the content of the interview, but do not dominate it.

10. I know enough about Equal Opportunities law not to breach it.

11. I am prepared to restate what the interview is for and, at the end, state what will happen next.

12. The interviewer should have a plan.

Summary

■ *Recruitment should not be confused with selection.*

■ *Recruitment is the process of developing the best potential pool of candidates for the job in question.*

■ *Selection is the process of filtering that group of potential candidates to 'fit' them to the job and the context in which the job is done.*

■ *The recruitment process is difficult without clear objectives. What does the job involve? What sort of qualities should the person have?*

■ *The selection process is ineffective without the same information.*

■ *There are a number of ways in which you can collect job information and translate it into job characteristics.*

■ *There are a number of ways in which you can collect information about the person in a way which will match job characteristics.*

■ *Using more than one method of collecting information will result in more accurate processes in effect.*

■ *Matching process is likely to involve managing relationships with the candidates and having clear objectives about the process.*

9 DEVELOPING PEOPLE

'You cannot teach a man anything. You can only help him discover it within himself.'

GALILEO GALILEI

The first part of the job contract is to give clear messages about the type of performance you expect from staff, the second is to ensure that they are helped to develop in line with the objectives of the organisation. Development is what helps an organisation move forward.

This chapter is designed to help you look at ways in which you can help staff develop and learn, as an asset both to themselves and to the organisation in which they work. It offers you:

► *an opportunity to consider your own attitudes to training, development, and learning;*

► *some techniques for making sure that training works for you;*

► *an opportunity to consider how you can take advantage of the training, learning and development which already exist in your own organisation.*

FAILING to develop staff adequately is like buying an expensive car, putting it on the road, running it for 40,000 miles a year and failing to maintain it. After all, you tell yourself, you pay to put petrol in it, you paid a lot of money for it, it's supposed to keep going for ever. There are lots of organisations like cars stood by the side of the road with black smoke pouring out from under the bonnet whilst the driver stands by, scratching his head, wondering what could have gone wrong and swearing at the manufacturer!

There are a number of clear steps in developing staff. These are:

- to gain an understanding of why development is important;
- to identify your own attitudes to development;
- to identify clear developmental objectives which link into organisational performance;
- to decide on the methods which you intend to use to help your people develop;
- to measure the effectiveness of these methods.

Why training and development?

□　□　□

It was 7.30 in the morning when Sally rang the direct line to Josh Slocum's office. For once he was at his desk, and Sally was bubbling over with enthusiasm.

'Josh, I just want to thank you for the advice you gave me on that recruitment problem we had. We've got this kid called Maggie Starling whose just come back from the States. Bright as a button, gets on really well with everybody in the team; she can really do the job. If it hadn't have been for you we'd have been floundering around again with somebody who just doesn't know what they're doing, I owe you lunch and . . .'

'Hold on a minute, Sal, thanks a lot, but what recruitment problem are you talking about?'

'You know, last month I spoke to you about Norham Road.'

'Yes, Sal,' said Josh, 'and I told you that you only had a learning problem that meant looking in the right place for what you already knew.'

'Yes, well, anyway, what I thought we could do is . . .'

□　□　□

Managers often have a problem with the whole idea of training and development. Some of the reasons for this are fairly obvious:

- There seems to be no discernable benefit in training for the 'bottom line'.

- Training and development seem to force admission of some sort of shortfall. 'We've been doing our work but you're saying that we need to train'.

- Development seems 'wishy washy' or 'soft'.

- There is a likelihood of poor pay-off investing in training and development, because you can't be sure that you'll receive the benefit – invest two or three thousand pounds in training someone and they could leave to go to a better paid job.

and others are more covert:

- If we develop staff they might overtake us, steal our ideas and take our place.

- I had to work my way to the top without help, why should anybody else have it?

Whatever reasons may be given for not developing staff, there are a number of more powerful and cogent reasons for doing so. We looked at Reg Revans' equation:

$$L \le C$$

in Chapter 2 on learning to learn. Let's turn now to the issue of staff performance. Most managers would say that performance is what they want from their staff, but how do they define it?

Performance can be defined as the added value created when the outputs of an organisation exceed its inputs.

$$\frac{\text{output}}{\text{input}} = \text{added value}$$

Performance from people can be seen as the same thing.

$$\frac{\text{outputs (as completed tasks, service provided etc)}}{\text{inputs (as reward, management time etc)}} = \text{added value}$$

People outputs consist of two elements. The first of these is an individual motivation or effort in carrying out the tasks. (We will look at motivation in Chapter 13.) The second is his or her capacity or ability to carry out the task.

Development is about increasing an employee's capacity to carry out a task. This might be a complicated task, such as doubling the number of service contracts completed by the organisation, or a simple one, such as assembling a cardboard package. Capacity should not be confused with motivation. It is all too easy to blame poor performance on lack of motivation when in fact the problem is lack of capacity.

New types of management and organisational practice, such as Total Quality Management, place an emphasis upon continuous improvement. Continuous improvement means developing the capacity of employees to produce better goods with less faults in shorter time periods, with new types of delivery. Without developing employees, this is impossible.

Development is perhaps more important to small organisations than it is to larger ones. The varying nature of work in a small organisation means that people have to be flexible in order to cope with these variations in task. Increased flexibility in production means making use of increased capacity by developing staff.

Finally, covert reasons for failing to develop should be analysed carefully. If a manager neglects employee development because they are concerned about their own position, it may be that this position, will no longer exist without employee development. Holding employees back from development cannot only create bad feeling, but it can actively hamper a manager's own personal development.

ASSESSMENT EXERCISE

It may help you to start off by considering your own attitudes to training. These vary widely among people, from those who think that it is likely to save the world to those who think that it is absolutely no use at all. Consider the following exercise.

Identify those with which you agree most strongly A, B or C.

1. A. Training is an important and useful way of improving business or organisational performance.
   B. Training is something which is necessary, but should be linked to defined training needs.
   C. Training is okay if it doesn't cost anything.

2. A. I believe training is good in all situations.
   B. I'd only train where staff performance needed bringing up to speed.
   C. Experience is what counts. All the training in the world doesn't make any difference.

3. A. Personal development is as important as vocational or management training.
   B. Training is about well qualified people giving instruction.
   C. Training's only use is in using new machinery or software.

4. A. It is very difficult to evaluate the effects of training, but you can see the benefits.
   B. Evaluation can be largely seen as justification.
   C. If you train your staff, they're likely to leave and go on so that other people get the benefits.

5. A. I would buy into new training methods if they seemed to work.
   B. Different methods of training should be used selectively, depending on the type of training which you carry out.
   C. Training is all about fads and fashions, none of which is better than any other.

Interpretation

Mostly **As**   Idealist: you have a somewhat idealistic view of training. You may wish to consider the degree to which training fits into your business needs.

Mostly **Bs**   Pragmatist: you have a pragmatic view of training which involves you in a practical view of it. You may benefit from looking at some of the unmeasurable benefits of training.

Mostly **Cs**   Cynic: you see training as unnecessary and a waste of time. You may wish to experiment with training in a framework of evaluation.

The results of the questionnaire should give you an idea of how you see training and development. Remember the systems view, however, that an organisation consists of money, capital equipment, premises, transportation systems, and people. If you try to develop one without understanding how it impacts upon others, you may have problems.

The developmental process

An essential part of developing an organisation is developing the people who work in it. Development is about learning and learning is about change. Before we go on to look at setting clear objectives in the development process, let's explore the idea of change a little further.

About 3,000 years ago, Plato, a Greek philosopher, identified three areas in which it is possible for individuals to change. The first set of possible changes are in knowledge. This is often seen to be the only job of training or education: 'We can offer Andrew a training course in running the new software. It's just knowing how to use the menus'. Knowledge isn't an inert component, however. Andrew will not only learn about software, he will also learn about his own ability, or lack thereof, to deal with new packages. Such knowledge will probably impact on other areas of life and work. Knowing about incidents in history, such as the Holocaust or the defeat of the Spanish Armada, will have an effect on the second area in which change takes place.

The second set of changes are about how we feel. This type of change is perhaps more subtle, since development is a personal process, which can impact upon values underpining attitudes. A great deal of work was carried out in the 1950s and 1960s in changing or helping people explore their values with the intention of changing attitudes affecting learning. Andrew's new skills in operating a software package will impact on his feelings of confidence, the way he feels about the people who have provided the training, and perhaps on how long he will consider staying with the company.

The final changes are the physical signs of changes in the other two areas. These might be called changes in skills or in what people do. Skill changes are often the only ones which are recognised in vocational training, because they provide hard evidence which can be measured to demonstrate the effectiveness or ineffectiveness of training.

Altogether this framework of knowledge, attitude and skills (KAS) will give you a starting-point through which to identify training needs and training objectives. Whilst each organisation will have unique training needs and need individual training objectives, the following list offers some which are common to all organisations.

KNOWLEDGE

1. Information about the customer needs and business

How the customer uses our product, our service, our information. What the customer's expectations are and how we meet those expectations. How our products and services help the customer grow. What we contribute to the customer's profitability.

2. Standards

Clear statements of our standards of excellence and achievement. Clear descriptions of our measurements of product quality, service quality and personal effectiveness. Clear statements of the way in which we evaluate performance.

3. Professionalism

Knowledge of what constitutes professional behaviour in your organisation. What the accepted practices are with regard to communication with managers/employees, colleagues, customers, suppliers. What rules relate to dress and what constitutes acceptable social behaviour at work.

4. Job information

What is the full range of job information required? Who should I go to for the information I lack and what can I expect the organisation to provide? What resources am I expected to use? What do I do if I can't find the information I need? What are the requirements of my job?

5. Organisational information

What is the business of this organisation? (You may surprise yourself by asking people this question.) What is its financial status? Where do I fit in? Where do I go or develop within the organisation?

ATTITUDES

1. Fairness

The need to treat other people fairly, and be treated fairly in relation to the way others are treated.

2. Openness

The need to deal with people openly, honestly and directly in order that they can do the best possible job.

3. Respect

The need to respect other people – employees, customers and suppliers – as fellow contributors to the well-being of the organisation. The need to receive respect.

4. Supportiveness

The need to receive support for work from administrative, technical and other staff whose jobs are interrelated with my job. The need to offer support in the same way.

5. Responsiveness

The expectation that my efforts will receive a response in terms of prompt and specific feedback and the resources needed to do the job.

SKILLS

1. Procedures

Step-by-step instructions or guidance on how to do a task or a whole job related to the way in which the organisation works.

2. Models

Representations of what is happening in the organisation which will help me understand what needs to be done.

3. Criteria

Standards of performance that tell me what I need to do and what constitutes acceptable work. Specific measures about quality and quantity. Measures related to skills I have.

4. Tools

Methods to communicate effectively. Ways of gathering data and processing it into an understandable and communicable form. Manual dexterity and methods for acquiring it. Methods to manage time and workload. Ways of making decisions. Problem-solving methods.

This checklist will help you identify some key areas which may benefit from employee development. The process of development as part of the job contract relies on the creation of an honest relationship between the employee and the manager. Development is not merely a process designed to benefit the employee, it also has to benefit the organisation. This can be done through a technique called key performance analysis.

KEY PERFORMANCE ANALYSIS

Key performance analysis is unlike ordinary training needs analysis in a number of important respects. Training needs analysis tends to look back and identify skill shortfalls. Key performance analysis looks forward to identify training needs which are linked to operational results. This involves a seven step process which involves looking at the following questions.

1. Why does the organisation need this person to occupy the position which they do? What is his or her core function?

2. What does he or she need to *do* to perform this function? What are the main activities which produce results for the organisation? What are the key result areas?

3. In each of these areas consider, how you know that the person is doing what they say and doing it well.

4. How can you tell whether the job is being done better or worse from one month to the next? What is the proof? This proof may be behavioural objectives, customer feedback, peer feedback, supervisor feedback, but it needs to be evidenced in a useful way. It's no use saying that Alan does a good job, because he has managed to do the job well and because he is liked. We need to know whether he met the criteria for the behavioural objective, to know how much positive customer feedback he receives over what time period and which deadlines were met for the amount of work processed.

5. Against the measures of how well the person does the job, how well is he or she actually doing? What is the current achievement level? You could record this for a month.

6. Is everyone concerned happy with the current achievement level? What steps does the individual employee need to take to improve this level of achievement in each of the key result areas?

7. If these steps are taken (and these could include training), how much could the employee improve on last month's achievement level? What would the objectives be?

You can turn this into an action plan for strategic training as in Fig. 9.1.

NAME			POSITION		
Function (Step 1)					
Key result areas **Step 2**	**Evidence of good performance** **Step 3**	**Measures of achieve-ment** **Step 4**	**Current achievement** **Step 5**	**Steps needed** **Step 6**	**Goal** **Step 7**

Fig. 9.1

Once you've decided what it is that you want your employees to learn – the content, the next thing that you need to consider is the process – how they are to develop the knowledge skills and attitudes that you want.

BLOCKS TO DEVELOPMENT

People tend to think that developing people is just about adding something to them – new knowledge, new skills, new attitudes. The thinking behind this is flawed: 'You've got a two and if you add two more you'll get a four. Unfortunately, people aren't numbers, and we may have to subtract something before you can get the sum right.'

Nancy Friday, an American writer on family relations, tells a story about a man married to a woman who always cuts the Sunday roast into two parts before she puts it into the roasting tray. He asks her why and she says that she's not sure, but that her mother always did it that way. The man, curious, goes to the mother who can't remember, but was sure that her mother did it that way. The man then visits the grandmother, who's still alive and asks her why she did it. The grandmother replies that she had only had a small roasting tin when she was younger.

Friday uses the story to demonstrate how we learn unconsciously from our parents, but we pick up learning unconsciously from all sorts of significant people. This sort of learning 'sticks'. It's very difficult to unlearn. The point is that to develop employees you might have to help them unlearn habits before they can learn new ones.

While everyone learns in different ways, there are some broad rules which you can obey when designing a developmental framework for employees:

1. Employees learn best when they are active rather than passive.
2. Employees learn best when the content of the learning is perceived as relevant and meaningful by participants and not only by the trainer – 'We want to know' rather than 'You need to know'.
3. Employees learn best when they are challenged rather than talked at.
4. Employees learn best when they are involved rather than observing.
5. Employees learn best when they are committed rather than detached.

Once you are aware of some of the blocks which may affect your training, you can decide how you are actually going to deliver in a way which overcomes these blocks.

DELIVERING DEVELOPMENT

In a small organisation you are likely to develop people informally on a regular basis. It can help you to consider what methods are available to develop employees before you integrate these into an effective overall developmental plan which links into the objectives which you have defined by using key performance analysis. Development can be achieved through four main processes

- informal training;
- one-on-one training – training between the manager and one member of staff;
- peer training – training between staff members;
- group training – this is training between the trainer and a group of employees.

Informal training

There are a number of useful ways through which you can develop employees informally.

- *Communication* We saw how changes in knowledge can develop people. Regular bulletins, team briefings, meetings etc will help develop employee knowledge. We talked about 'painting the big picture' in training and this is something we'll return to when we talk about leadership.
- *Delegation* We'll see in the chapter on delegation that it should be a developmental activity.
- *Project work or assignments* Giving someone a clearly defined project to carry through is risky but can pay dividends in development.
- *Modelling* If you show a positive attitude towards developing yourself and encourage development in key employees you will foster some positive attitude in other employees.

Formal and informal methods should be integrated. It can be damaging to give mixed messages about development by either giving someone a project and not meeting their request for further development in that area, or by developing them and not giving them the framework to practise the new behaviour.

One-to-one training

One-to-one training is perhaps the most common sort of training in smaller organisations. It can be effective if carried out properly. It is important, however, to avoid the production line syndrome. The production line syndrome is one where a new worker is given five minutes of instruction on working on a fast-moving production line and told, 'Now you do it and you'll soon get the hang of it'. The unfortunate employee is required to assemble unfamiliar objects passing by at speed when he or she has only just arrived in a new setting and where the information processing load is fairly high already – meeting new people, finding their way around, discovering the rules in the organisation. We may be hesitant in showing people what they need to do from fear of insulting them, but if we make clear why we are telling them, and ask them if they need to know, it is unlikely that anyone will feel insulted. All too often induction programmes involve meeting other people and being shown how the software works.

One-to-one training involves stepping out of your role as manager and into your role as trainer. Often these roles can be similar. As we will see later, one of the roles of a leader is that of developer of people, but it is important to be open about the change in role. To help support this role, it can be helpful for you to be rigorous about your objectives. Make it clear at the beginning of any session that this is a training session and stick to that.

BASIC STRATEGIES

Before you begin a training session you may wish to sit down with your trainee to talk about expectations. What sort of goals does he or she expect to attain through training? Once you have negotiated the goals of the training there are a number of basic strategies which may help to ensure that the training that you do is put into action and results in increased productivity.

1. *Present the big picture* Often people lose the relevance of their work to the overall aims of the organisation. This can happen in quite small organisations. You can remedy this by describing the way in which the job should be done, by describing the effects of the new practices or equipment, the benefits of doing something in a new way, describing what the organisation will look like if the new way works.

2. *Review the requirements* Be sure that your learner understands what the new task or situation requires. Take the time to prioritise, clarify and elaborate where the learner doesn't know. People like to know what the weather's like before they start a new trip and also where they're going. At this stage be careful of the person whose resistance to learning is so strong that he or she knows it all already.

3. *Fill in the gaps* Limit your gap-filling with information that is specifically relevant to the task.

4. *Take the learner from where they are* People will learn more comfortably and effectively if you start from their level of understanding. This is why the objectives setting exercise below is so important. Do not overwhelm your learner with demonstrations of knowledge or skill, unless it is to demonstrate how easy it is to learn a particular task. Don't presume that just because you learnt it easily, everyone else will. Show that you appreciate the knowledge, skills and attitudes that exist at present.

5. *Build your training around problem-solving* Individuals like to solve problems. It makes them feel useful and gives a sense of achievement. All learning is in some sense about problem-solving and a formal problem-solving approach will help to facilitate the communication between trainer and learner, as well as making the learning relevant.

6. *Try to demonstrate the outcomes* This is similar to describing the 'big picture' but is a smaller part of it. If, for instance, you're training someone to use a new machine show him or her the finished product from that machine. Make the outcome of training real.

7. *Provide feedback* We've already seen how important feedback is. Always give your trainee feedback in a form which they can readily understand.

8. *Plan for follow-up* Build into the training some suggestions for follow-up – a meeting after a week or some other sort of monitoring. Ask the learner for suggestions on follow-up.

9. *Provide a prop* Props in training – handouts, flipcharts, models – are all important. A short handout or description of the training content will define the session as a training session.

Remember that one-to-one training – or any sort of training – should not be too long: a one-to-one training session should not last more than thirty minutes. If you cannot get the information across in that length of time, you may wish to run two or more sessions back-to-back. Remember, however, that one-to-one training is very intensive and the session may break down into a general discussion. Thirty minutes (or even better fifteen minutes) helps maintain focus.

Each session should have a plan. A plan sets out the behaviours that you want to see as evidence that your training has been successful. Examples of behavioural objectives are:

- to sort
- to categorise
- to arrange
- to find
- to assign
- to connect
- to load
- to compare
- to calculate
- to select
- to reduce
- to restructure

Behavioural objectives are small and specific. If you train and expect to see a change in attitude, don't expect staff to be nicer to the customer as a result. Staff well may be nicer to the customer, but there are problems in evaluating what 'nice' means. McDonalds, the fast food company, have a large set of procedures dealing with staff–customer relationships but there is a considerable difference between 'Good morning, may I help you?' in a pleasant tone and saying the same thing in a dull or disinterested tone. When you evaluate, you will need to evaluate in a way which reflects the behavioural objectives you have set.

The other issue in planning a session is that the content of the session should have only around four items of content which you want to get across. Examples of content items might be:

- setting the machine up;
- safety procedures;
- overload signals;
- job timing.

More than four content items will tend to confuse the person being trained.

Peer training

When you don't have time to train, you can delegate the training task to someone else – a colleague or a peer. Peer training has many of the benefits which delegating any task will bring. It has other benefits, in that it can transmit information much more quickly.

Employees will tend to listen more carefully to other employees – after all, they see them all the time whereas they may see the manager only part of the time. Of course, this means that you need to be careful about choosing a peer trainer, because they can give the wrong sort of information.

A third advantage is the 'stickability' of the training. Training is associated in learners' minds with the trainer. If the learner is in constant contact with the trainer, they are more likely to find the learning is constantly reinforced.

The design of peer training is effectively the same as one-to-one training. Use the following exercise to consider how you might select a suitable peer trainer:

EXERCISE

1. He/she believes that every individual at work has the capacity to learn.

2. He/she feels that individuals learn at different rates and in ways which are unique to them.

3. He/she believes that adults learn best when they are involved and the learning is of some use.

4. He/she feels that training around agreed standards with measurable outcomes is best for the trainer and the learner.

5. He/she would give positive reward or reinforcement during a lesson.

6. He/she acknowledges that adults like to tell you how they learn best and what they need to know.

7. He/she likes to share what they know with other people.

8. He/she takes a pride in their work.

9. He/she has a good relationship with fellow workers.

10. He/she shows patience when presenting information.

You can train your peer trainers by using the guidelines on key performance set out above.

Group training

The final method is group training. Group training is generally perceived as the only form of training, because of our early classroom experiences. Group training has a lot in common with presentation. If you marry the principles of employee learning to the skills of presentation, you will need to take control of the session through effective planning and to encourage activity, challenge and participation in the group that you are training.

PREPARATION

It will help you to consider the following issues in the approximate order given as you prepare to train a group.

How to assess needs and prepare

Ask yourself the following questions. What information do you have on participants' work environment, age, sex, race, religion, etc?

● What are the participants' expectations re the workshop?

● Has any pre-course work been carried out?

● What further information do you need to obtain at the beginning of the programme?

● What can you anticipate from the participants in the way of mood, willingness to volunteer, readiness?

Where you have already set broad goals for the training programme, you will also need to consider specific issues around the people whom you intend to train. As we've seen, people will bring all sorts of differences in attitude, learning preferences, and expectation to the learning arena. Tailor your training to your audience.

How to set training objectives and prepare your audience

This stage involves you taking action which will prepare your audience. You may wish to negotiate or set the goals for the session and establish your own responsibilities as a leader or trainer. Above all, be explicit about the values of the session, the methods to be used and the ground rules.

How to assess resources and skills

This third stage involves deciding the tools that you will use. Above all, you should be comfortable with the methods which you decide to use. Consider your own special interests and skills as your enthusiasm will help get the message across. Make a list of the resources you need and the resources available to see if there are any gaps.

Stating the objectives for each session

Ideally, the objectives should be specific and measurable: 'by the end of this workshop you should be able to . . .'. Objectives should be set through discussion and negotiation with the staff. Remember that you should present the objectives to the participants at the start of each session. If participants have clear goals, this will help them to learn more readily.

Predicting the time schedule for each element

This should be specific: introduction, 10 minutes; forming groups and giving instructions, 5 minutes; working on the task, 40 minutes; etc. On a larger scale, review the schedule to see if sufficient time is available for what is planned, for each element. Try to remember to provide 'fillers'. Is more time available than the work will consume? Avoid planning so much that the participants feel hurried.

Allocating responsibilities

If you decide to use other tutors, remember to make sure that the responsibilities are clearly defined and that everyone knows what they are supposed to deliver. No matter how good a trainer is, he or she cannot read minds. If you don't specify what you want, you will not get what you want, and you will have nobody to blame but yourself.

Assessing logistics

Make sure that you have enough space: large rooms, small rooms, comfort, convenience. Make sure that you have your toolbox ready – materials such as handouts, pencils, flip chart paper, nametags, workbooks, masking tape, 'blue tac', markers, reference materials, tape recorder and tapes, video recorder and tapes, etc. Remember housekeeping details: breaks, meals, special needs, and socialisation. The socialising effect of training can be very useful – don't discount it.

Provide for evaluation

Consider how you will integrate the evaluation process into the programme and into your overall development strategy. Unused training can be lost or wasted training. Have you made arrangements to put it into action ?

DOING IT

After designing and preparing the group and the material the final issue is actually to deliver the training.

This checklist is designed to offer you some ways which may help you keep the attention of a group in a 'pure' training situation. Other methods of securing audience participation are outlined in the chapter on communication.

- Focus the group's attention on yourself from the very beginning.
- Tell the group what they will be able to do by the end of the session.
- Use each group member's name. Have people introduce themselves or use name cards.
- Praise group members when they do something right.
- Keep the pace lively by using problem-solving exercises.
- Reward the group with breaks after lectures or difficult problems.
- Don't lecture for more than ten minutes at a time.
- Move around the room.
- Vary pitch and tone in delivery.
- Use humour – share horror stories and funny incidents.
- Repeat important points. Write them on flipcharts or black/white board.
- Don't use jargon.
- Use analogies and metaphors to get complex ideas across.
- Use visuals.
- Break the group up into smaller groups and let them work on problems or share information.

Training, one-to-one or in groups, is something which will become more effective and more natural with practice. Training is about effective communication with groups.

AFTERWARDS

Evaluating development

Once you have actually carried out the training, the final step is to evaluate it. Training without effective evaluation is worthless. Evaluation is necessary for two main reasons. The first of these is that evaluation will give you feedback on the effectiveness of your training.

Try to remember the worst teacher that you ever had. He might have talked to class after class of children five days a week for 30 years without getting feedback except through exam results. He never changed his style or his material, just plugging away as the needs of his audience changed and his listeners slowly disconnected.

Now try to remember the best teacher you ever had. She probably listened to you when you told her that you didn't understand and this is the benefit of feedback. People whom you train may give you feedback consciously or unconsciously, but they will need to see responsiveness to the feedback they give. If ignored, they will turn away and your training will be ineffective.

The second reason for evaluation is that it will give you information about the way in which your business is going. We will see in Chapters 10 and 12 on appraisal and delegation how these skills will give you information about your business. Development is one of the ways in which you can gain information on the capacity of your human resources. When you evaluate you will probably need to consider two main issues: the effectiveness of the content of your development, i.e. what you are training, and the process of your development, i.e. how you have delivered it.

Evaluating effectiveness of contents

We've already looked to some degree at preparing for tactical evaluation. Tactical evaluation is an evaluation of the small steps which are seen in the behavioural objectives which you've set. In your 15-30 minutes' training session you can expect to achieve up to three behavioural objectives. These may be:

- to set up the new laser printer;
- to load the postscript cartridge;
- to load fonts on to disk.

You can evaluate the effectiveness of training these objectives by actually seeing them carried out. This gives you evidence of the skill. You can also check on the learner's knowledge by asking questions such as:

'What would you do when . . .?'
'When would you . . .?'

Unfortunately, this evaluation is subjective. It rests upon your own interpretation of adequate or good performance. This can vary from day to day, depending on any number of factors. It may be more helpful to set measurable standards of achievement for each behavioural objective. Examples of standards for behavioural objectives include:

- with 90 per cent accuracy;
- with zero defects;
- with a maximum of three errors per page;
- in fifteen to twenty minutes;
- so that it is level;
- at A equals 440 pitch;
- within 0.05 microns;
- with increase of customer satisfaction to 6 on a scale of 1–8 (where 8 is high).

Once you've set standards for your behavioural objectives, you can measure the content effectiveness of your training much more easily.

Evaluating effectiveness of process

The other type of feedback available to the tactical trainer is feedback on process. Generally speaking, your training works if you achieved the standards set for your behavioural objectives. You can enquire to see whether you can improve the process by either designing a learner feedback form or asking questions such as:

- Were the objectives realistic? (Ask for specifics.)
- Did I cover everything that needed to be covered?
- Did the training help you learn? (Ask for specific suggestions for improvement)
- Did I present the information clearly enough? (How could presentations be improved?)

Remember that, when you ask for feedback

- You should make sure that the learner knows that you want him to be honest. Dishonest feedback is useless and damaging.

- Accept feedback as feedback. Don't defend your position or explain. Try to think why.
- Raise probing questions to clarify.
- Don't let the feedback giver get carried away.

Once you have evaluated the effectiveness of your development in terms of process and content, you will need to consider how to relate this to your overall business objectives. Overall, this can be seen as strategic evaluation.

STRATEGIC EVALUATION

In order to carry out a strategic evaluation, we need to go back to the key performance analysis which we saw earlier in the chapter. The second step in this process involves identifying the key areas which produce results for the organisation.

At the beginning of this chapter, we identified the performance of an employee as being:

$$\frac{\text{input}}{\text{output}} = \text{performance}$$

Obviously, 'input' and 'output' can be measured in a number of ways. Some common ways include:

$$\text{Profits per employee} = \frac{\text{Gross profit}}{\text{number of employees}}$$

$$\text{Output per employee} = \frac{\text{Units produced or processed}}{\text{number of employees}}$$

$$\text{Value added per employee} = \frac{\text{Value added (sales revenue-cost of sales)}}{\text{number of employees}}$$

In order to evaluate strategic training effectiveness, we need to relate employee performance through one of these measures (or any other measure which you want to apply) to training evaluation.

□ □ □

'So what are Presteign's strategic objectives?,' asked Josh.

'Well, we want to open a new distribution depot in Manchester, increase our turnover by 50 per cent over the next two years and keep production costs at their present level.'

'Okay, Sal, let's just look at one of those. You want to increase turnover by 50 per cent in a two-year timescale. That's pretty specific. Most people respond to that question by saying to be the best widget production company in the West Midlands what do you need to do to achieve that aim?'

'Take on more sales staff, reach different markets, produce more.'

'And what sort of knowledge, skills and abilities are your staff going to need to do that?'

'I suppose they'll need sales management training, marketing training, training in new production techniques.'

'Okay, break it up using the key performance analysis framework we talked about earlier.'

Sally took out her pen and started to write, then looked up.

'Who should I do it for?'

'Who is your key salesperson? asked Josh.

□   □   □

Each organisation will relate key performance areas to strategic objectives in a different way. The important issue in the development of employees and the relationship between the employee and the manager is that there are clearly defined links between individual and organisational performance. In the next chapter we will look at the way in which this relationship can be formalised.

Checklist for employee development

1. I can identify a framework for developing employees.

2. I can identify clear objectives when developing employees.

3. I can develop staff using a variety of development methods, including one-to-one and group training.

4. I can integrate formal and informal training.

5. I can identify peer trainers and help them develop employees.

6. I can evaluate training tactically.

7. I can evaluate training for my organisation strategically.

8. I can manage the development of employees.

Summary

■ *Developing people is a necessary part of developing an organisation. It is also an essential part of the job contract between the manager and employee. When people have a clear path to development, they will feel more fulfilled and motivated.*

- *People's perceptions of development and its benefits will differ and this will affect the way that they develop in their organisations.*

- *Development is about helping people change in order to meet changes in their work environment. Ultimately, it is about equipping them with the knowledge, skills and attitudes through which they can change themselves.*

- *There are a number of ways in which a manager can develop his or her employees.*

- *These include formal methods such as one-to-one, peer and group training.*

- *They also include informal methods like assignments, project work and effective delegation.*

- *The most effective development strategy is one which integrates formal and informal methods.*

- *Development should always be evaluated in terms of clear objectives.*

- *Strategic evaluation is about linking development to business objectives.*

- *Development can be evaluated tactically or strategically*

- *Tactical evaluation is about identifying the effectiveness of the development itself.*

10 PERFORMANCE APPRAISAL

'People are so overwhelmed with the prestige of their instruments that they consider their personal judgement of hardly any account.'

F. WYNDHAM LEWIS

In considering performance appraisal as part of the job contract, we need to consider once again the nature of the relationship between the manager and his or her employees. In the context of a good relationship, appraisal is easy, providing you have an appropriate framework through which you intend to appraise.

The objectives of this chapter are:

► *to help you identify your own appraisal strengths and style;*

► *to help you consolidate and build on these strengths;*

► *to help you systemise an appraisal system.*

PERFORMANCE appraisal is the human system's equivalent to a compass for checking direction or perhaps the automatic pilot of an aeroplane. It is designed to ensure that your aeroplane is on course and that it has not strayed into dangerous territory. Without an effective automatic pilot, you may not reach your intended destination or, even worse, fly into a mountain-side.

Effective appraisal involves taking a number of steps and using some of the resources which we identified in the first section of this book. The steps are

- deciding what it is that you are appraising;
- deciding how often you will appraise;
- choosing the best information source for appraisal – who should appraise;
- deciding on a structure for the appraisal;
- being aware of the problems;
- carrying out the appraisal.

□ □ □

Sally was due to meet Josh for their monthly lunch date. She was twenty minutes late, but wasn't too worried, because Josh had always been late when they'd been at college. To her surprise, he was sitting at a table in the local crêperie drinking his coffee.

'Sorry I'm late, Josh,' Sally said, sitting down, 'but I've been talking with some Germans about new plant and I was waiting for a fax.'

'That's okay, Sally,' Josh said, smiling pleasantly. 'It's given me a chance to look at the paper. How are things with you?'

'Not bad,' said Sally. 'Things have been a lot better now that we've got the new people in at Norham Road and Bill, Dave and I have been doing some training down there so the atmosphere is a lot better. The performance figures have gone up a bit, but the staff still seem to be doing what they like and it's really annoying me.'

'What sort of control system have you got in place down at Norham Road, Sal?', asked Josh.

'Well, the supervisors are pushing things along and of course we're monitoring the budgets and production figures pretty closely.'

'Are you sharing information on performance with the staff?'

'I'm not sure what you mean. I suppose so. Why?'

'I just wondered how you were setting targets for staff and monitoring how they were meeting those targets?'

'You mean appraisal?'

'I suppose so,' said Josh, 'although you don't have to call it appraisal. The appraisal process is often fraught enough. You could call it 'Review and Action Plan.'

'Why should we worry about appraisal, Josh?'

□ □ □

What use is appraisal anyway

Many managers who work in organisations adopt appraisal systems because other successful organisations have them, or perhaps just because it is the right thing to do. This can mean that the organisation ends up with an appraisal system that does not fit its needs. In addition, people are often unclear about what it is that an appraisal actually does. For most managers and staff who have had experience of appraisal, it is linked inextricably with problematic issues such as pay awards or specific problems in staff performance. Perhaps this contributes to the confusion which they feel. Very few managers are 'naturally' good in appraisal.

Appraisal can be used for a number of purposes and with a number of intended consequences:

1. *Evaluation:* this is designed to give some idea of individual performance and to share out pay and benefits according to the differences in performance. In practice, of course, this rarely happens because of other issues such as status or length of time within the organisation.

2. *Audit:* this is designed to discover the work potential of individuals and groups working in the organisation.

3. *Training needs analysis:* this is designed to ascertain individual and group training needs. We saw, in the last chapter, some of the problems with standard training approaches, but appraisal and development are inextricably linked, in that identifying a performance shortcoming will mean offering a path through which it can be remedied.

4. *Motivation:* appraisal can be used to give information and praise to motivate and reward staff for good performance.

5. *Development:* this is an intended consequence of 'good' appraisal in that reward can be used in a number of different ways. One of these is to allow them to develop their own autonomy, something which we will develop further in Chapter 12 on delegation.

6. *Planning:* effective appraisal will give an accurate picture of staff capacity and an idea of whether you will need to take on more staff or can manage tasks with existing staff.

7. *Control:* this is, of course, the underlying reason for all work systems. Without control, there are unlikely to be satisfying outcomes from work. Without control, staff and managers will be running around working part of the time on mutual projects and part of the time on individual projects and part of the time on projects, the purposes of which are unclear even to them. This isn't to say that control has to be external. In fact, in many smaller work units it is internal, with all members of staff sharing a similar set of purposes.

Seven sets of objectives, some of which overlap, and some of which may contradict, are unlikely to lead to clear processes within the appraisal interview. People participating in the interview are unlikely to feel comfortable without clearly defined objectives.

Broadly, we can say that the seven sets of aims set out above can be translated into three groups.

The first of these relates to the management of people through the distribution of rewards. As we will see in the chapter on motivation, there are a number of different types of reward available to the manager. These range from money through to status, autonomy – even the key to the executive toilet, a marked car parking space or a new job title can be used as rewards. Because the whole subject of reward is such a sensitive one, it impacts strongly upon the other two groups and should always be kept separate from them. We can call this type of appraisal *reward appraisal*.

The second group deals with the potential of the particular person being appraised. This group attempts to answer the question of the future needs of the organisation in which you work. This may include asking what sort of skills and attitudes the organisation will need in future, how the person involved wants to develop either in their existing job or a new one, whether he or she is realistic in their expectations and how the whole organisation is likely to benefit from such development. This type of appraisal can be called *development appraisal*.

Development appraisal can leak into the final group, with which we will concern ourselves here. This is the group which addresses issues such as an individual's actual (present) performance over a particular period and in connection with particular projects or work. We can call this type of appraisal *performance appraisal*.

A performance appraisal system is designed to add to staff capacity in the same way that development does, although by a different route. Development is about adding to the capacity of employees by giving them the tools to do the job. Performance appraisal is about adding to that capacity by identifying and measuring the ways in which those tools are used.

INDIVIDUAL AND TEAM PERFORMANCE

Performance appraisal or review is often considered to be about individual process. There are, however issues which relate to team performance in that no one works in a vacuum. All our work depends upon, and supports the work of, other people. This means that an individual may be unable to perform adequately if he or she is working as part of a team which is failing to perform.

Questions about the accuracy of performance appraisal may seem to be largely academic, but it is important to recognise that work is not carried out in a vacuum, and that group, team or departmental performance may impact upon individal performance just as individual performance will impact upon group team and departmental performance.

□   □   □

'The trouble is,' said Sally, 'that appraisal seems like such a formal process. Dave used to work for a bank and he talks about formal appraisal interviews that he used to have and they sound like a nightmare.'

'Appraisal doesn't have to be a formal process, Sal,' Josh said. 'As part of the relationship between a manager and an employee, it's better as a discussion rather than an interview.'

'Every time you ask an employee how he or she is, how they are doing, how they can develop, and what help they might need, you've carried out an appraisal.'

□   □   □

How often?

Before you actually embark on the process of achieving increased capacity from a performance appraisal, you may need to consider both the frequency and the framework for the review.

The first point to consider is just how often should a performance appraisal take place. Larger organisations will often hold performance appraisals once or twice a year, and unfortunately many smaller organisations follow this practice. Larger organisations, which were once able to work in stable environments, with work which did not change on a day-to-day basis and staff who carried the work out in a familiar manner, only needed appraisal once or twice a year. Smaller organisations, that work in rapidly changing environments in which staff workload is never the same twice, may need a different type of appraisal system.

Let's look at putting this into action. Organisations tend to hold reward appraisals once a year. This ties in with budgets and for many people is the only type of appraisal which is important. Reward appraisals will involve both parties in the sort of negotiating behaviour outlined in Chapter 7. Because of the way in which budgets are set, it is unlikely that a reward appraisal will take place more than once a year.

The second type of appraisal which we identified was the development appraisal. Developmental appraisals can take place quite often, perhaps four or more times in a year. A developmental appraisal may be nothing more than a check to see how the needs of the employee are fitting in with the work that he or she is carrying out on behalf of the organisation.

The final type of appraisal is that of performance. This type of appraisal may also take place formally once a year, but it is one which goes on constantly. If it does not go on all the time, you may well have problems. The formal 'appraisal interview' may be the only time that the manager and employee get together to talk about the issue of performance, but you may wish to ask yourself if this is appropriate for your business.

Adequate performance appraisal over a whole period is a much more accurate indicator of your business performance than financial information, because it comes back as quickly as financial information and it can be much more enlightening. People generally know when they are not performing to their best capacity, and will, if asked properly, tell you.

Before we go on to look at what should actually be appraised, let's look at who could appraise. Who would be likely to have, or be able to obtain, the best information about performance?

Who will appraise?

Once you've decided how often appraisal will be carried out the next important question is, 'Where is the best information likely to be found?' It is easy to assume that the supervisor or line manager is the best judge of performance. This may not be true. Good information about performance is likely to come from all sorts of sources – line manager, supervisor, the employee, the employee's colleagues, production figures, etc. A really effective appraisal system will make use of as many of these information sources as is practicable.

The best source of information about an employee's performance may often be the employee him- or herself. Obtaining employee information can be done jointly with the supervisor or manager in a formal or informal interview, or it can be done solely by the employee. It may be that employees are not completely honest about their own performance, so managers tend to doubt employees' ability to rate themselves. This may be reluctance on the part of the manager to give up perceived authority, which carrying out an appraisal can bestow. Research seems to indicate that employees who self-appraise without input from managers do so accurately when pay is not linked to performance, and when employees are not asked to compare themselves with others. Where self-appraisal is carried out jointly, you will need to use the communication skills which we looked at in Chapter 3. The next source of performance information is peer appraisal. Peer appraisal by work colleagues is potentially more accurate in that peers spend more time with the person being appraised than do managers. Relationships between peers, however, may mean that such information is not accurately presented. Peers may either be afraid of being seen as 'grassing' on their fellow employees or – where relationships are poor – will give inaccurate information for reasons of their own.

Finally, where employees are in contact with customers and suppliers, the best form of performance information may well be from those individuals with whom staff come into contact. This may take the form of customer service enquiries or customer feedback documents.

As in the collection of job-related information, the collection of performance related information is likely to be more accurate when collected from a number of sources.

A structure for appraisal – How to appraise

Once you have decided how often you are going to appraise and where the best information on performance is likely to be found, the next thing to consider is how you are actually going to carry the appraisal out.

There is little difference between the process of a selection interview and that of an appraisal interview. There may be a shift in focus but the structure of a selection interview, i.e. beginning – middle – end, is reflected by a similar model involving appraisal: setting the performance step – checking understanding – reviewing the last step.

Setting the performance step means identifying ways in which employees can improve their performance to meet your organisational objectives. Checking understanding involves making sure that the performance step set is agreed and understood by the people involved.

SETTING THE PERFORMANCE STEP

The rules for selection interviews also hold true for appraisal – social and perceptual scene setting, etc. This means that you should take time to prepare for setting the step. A pro forma which you may find useful is outlined at the end of the chapter. Remember the focus of an appraisal interview should primarily be on the future performance of the employee rather than the past. This is particularly important in the opening, as this will set the tone of the whole interview.

Broadly setting the performance step involves two types of activity. The first is to gather information about the person's capacity to perform. It is useless setting a performance step unless the employee is able to carry it out. This involves establishing an agenda which doesn't just focus on particular tasks. The primary issue in the early stages of the review is to gather information. This means that the person appraising needs to initiate conversation and listen actively. The conversation should focus on the wider world of work – relationships with other staff members and career aspirations. This will help develop a whole picture of the individual's needs and potential.

We have seen that relationships are vital in the process of managing people. When setting the performance step, you should attempt to maintain your relationship with the person being appraised. This emphasis on mutuality ('We are going to have a problem next year with the new Health and Safety regulations') will thus keep the focus on the relationships and thus avoid appraisal as something which is done 'to' the employee. If you don't feel, however, that your relationship with the employee is a good one, try to avoid this. When a manager has spent twelve months telling an employee that 'you've done this and you haven't done that', the latter will not welcome the proverbial arm around the shoulder on the one day of appraisal.

Where a poor relationship exists between the employee and yourself, try to improve it outside of the appraisal context. Where this isn't possible, try to appreciate their agenda. Try to tap into the appraisee's interests, and foresee what they might want from the interview. This first stage is to encourage them to talk about their work as they see it. Whilst you may not see it in quite the same way, their perceptions are true for them.

The final emphasis on the relationship which you can make at this initial step is to acknowledge that performance will be a result of the relationship between you and to ask for honest feedback about your own performance as a manager. This does not mean tacking a forlorn, 'What more can I do as your manager?' on the end of the interview. The emphasis on 'your manager' may be sufficient to block feedback. It does mean asking honestly for feedback and dealing honestly with it when it comes.

Once the relationship issues have been dealt with, the second type of activity involves tackling actual aspects of performance.

DEALING WITH PERFORMANCE

When addressing work issues, you should plan effectively. We've seen how formal interviews, and indeed all communication, needs a structure. Without adequate preparation in an appraisal interview, important topics may be lost. In fact, formal interviews are likely to lose such topics because formal processes tend to structure communication and it becomes less wide-ranging.

The main issues with regard to performance at this stage of the process are that you should always talk about performance, responsibilities, and accountabilities, rather than individual tasks. As we will see when we look at delegation as part of the job contract, an effective manager needs to set objectives, targets and results, not methods or means.

In setting a performance step, you should bear in mind that it is not merely enough to agree the steps, but also to take some action to make this happen. Since you have initiated the appraisal, this is to some degree your responsibility, although it is also the appraisee's. A step should never be identified and responsibility not allocated. This may mean writing down what was said and highlighting agreed action and responsibilities. Many organisations record appraisals, although when an appraisal has little to do with day-to-day performance this may be merely an exercise in covering one's back. The performance step should, however, be recorded and shared.

The performance step should always be a realistic one (preferably measurable and timed, too). It is possible to have such a positive relationship with an employee that plans can get out of hand. By agreeing something within an appraisal interview, you are making a promise. If you fail to keep your promises, your relationship with staff will suffer. It is far better to agree a small performance step and the action which it will need to be supported by than a large one and forget about it – your work will have been wasted.

CHECKING FOR AGREEMENT AND UNDERSTANDING

The first rule in checking for agreement is to listen more than you talk. If you don't listen, the appraisal may well, from the best of motives, become a one-way exercise in communication. It is often the case that a manager may be full of ideas about helping staff develop and visions for the future of the organisation. This enthusiasm may overwhelm the appraisee.

Remember at this point also that appraisal is a focused discussion leading to an agreed action or set of actions. Some people may not have a lot to say at appraisal. Checking the step involves using communication skills in both good and poor relationships.

In checking the step you will also need to use probing and open questions to encourage people to speak freely, to make thorough and honest self-assessments, and to elicit agreement with regard to the nature of the step.

In this part of the process, you should also encourage the appraisee to speak first. Encouraging the appraisee to set their agenda for the interview establishes equality in the relationship and shows that you value the employee by putting them first.

Examples of questions that you could use when checking the performance step are given on the following checklist.

Checklist for future performance

Introduction

- How do you anticipate that your job could (should) develop or change in emphasis over the next year/time period?

- How would you like to see your working relationships (with me or colleagues) develop?

- What can be done to improve things or make things better?

- How would you prioritise the things that you've identified.

Job/relationships

- What can you do to help things happen?
- How would you go about doing that?
- What help would you need from others/me?
- What do you see as appropriate objectives for the next year/period?
- How could we measure success?
- What would be likely to block success?
- How could we overcome these blocks?
- What alternatives do we have?

Developmental issues

- What additional training, development, special projects would be useful for you?
- What sort of responsibilities would you see as taking on?

Personal

- How do you see your future career progressing?
- How do you see your long term future with this organisation?
- What do you see as the next steps in your personal development?

Conclusion

- Is there anything that you'd like to talk about?
- How do you feel about what we've discussed?
- What do you see as the main targets that we've discussed?
- When should we meet again to review progress?

Once you've identified agreement to the next performance step, the next part of the process is to check the last step.

CHECKING THE LAST STEP

This is often the most sensitive point of an appraisal process, in that it deals with issues of potential failure in performance and/or the nature of the relationship. As we've seen, looking backwards is useful only in discovering the causes of potential failure so that they can be put right for the future. Managers often spend 90 per cent of the time in an appraisal considering past performance, and 75 per cent of that time in concentrating on negative aspects of that performance. This means that only 10 per cent is spent looking forward and 25 per cent looking at good performance. It is hardly surprising that neither managers nor employees look forward to appraisal.

Reviewing the last performance step should concentrate on average performance over the course of the period being reviewed. We will see in the section on what can go wrong that we tend to pick out the peaks or troughs of performance rather than overall performance. In checking the last step, it is much more useful to concentrate on those elements of performance which are currently acceptable and identify ways in which they can be improved.

In checking the last performance step, remember to ask them what has gone right before you ask what has gone wrong. Equally, once they have identified what has gone wrong, listen and use probing questions before you begin to give feedback on performance.

Examples of suitable questions for use in checking the last step are given below.

Checklist for past performance

Introductory

- What are your expectations of this point of the appraisal?

- What particularly would you like us to cover?

- How do you feel about the last year/period?

Job

- What do you see as the main purpose of your job?

- How has the job developed over the last year/period?

- Which aspects of your job do you find least/most interesting?

- Which aspects of your job do you see as most challenging?

- Which areas do you feel happy about?

- Which areas were most frustrating?

- What has caused these successes?

- What has caused these problems?

Relationships

- Who are your main work contacts?

- Who impacts on your performance most?

- Who do you effect most in your work?
- How do you feel your relationships are with colleagues, staff, me?

Development

- What do you think are the key skills you need to do your job?
- How do you rate yourself in these terms?
- What skills do you feel you have that aren't being fully used?

Personal

- How do you feel about the problems we've identified?
- What would you say you've learned from this?
- What would you do differently in looking back?

Conclusion

- Is there anything else you'd like to raise?
- How do you feel about this assessment?
- How can we take this forward?

Once you have explored the reasons for either positive or negative performance, you can then give them feedback on that performance. Feedback is one of the ways in which you communicate with people to help them change or develop. Consider the following exercise to help you think about giving feedback either in appraisal situations or in any others.

FEEDBACK EXERCISE

'Feedback' is a communication to a person (or a group) which gives that person information about how he or she affects others. Feedback helps an individual consider and alter his or her behaviour and thus better achieve his or her goals.

Below are eight criteria for useful feedback. Rate the feedback that usually occurs in your organisation by circling the appropriate number on each of the eight scales. You may also want to make some notes for each criterion, such as particular group occurrences.

1. Useful feedback is descriptive rather than evaluative. It merely describes the sender's reaction, thus leaving the receiver free to use it or not. By avoiding evaluative language, it reduces the need for the receiver to respond defensively.

| Descriptive | 1 | 2 | 3 | 4 | 5 | 6 | Evaluative |

Comments

2. It is specific rather than general. To be told that one is 'dominating' will probably not be as useful as being told, 'Just now, when we were deciding the issue, you did not listen to what the others said, and I felt forced to accept your arguments or to face attack from you.'

| Specific | 1 | 2 | 3 | 4 | 5 | 6 | General |

Comments

3. It takes into account both the needs of the receiver and the giver of feedback. Feedback can be destructive when it serves another giver's needs and fails to consider the needs of the receiver.

| Takes needs of both into account | 1 | 2 | 3 | 4 | 5 | 6 | Does not take needs of both into account |

Comments

4. It is directed towards behaviour the receiver can change. Frustration is only increased when one is reminded of a shortcoming over which one has no control.

| Directed towards modifying behaviour | 1 | 2 | 3 | 4 | 5 | 6 | Directed towards non-modifying behaviour |

Comments

5. It is solicited rather than imposed. Feedback is most useful when the receiver himself asks the question which those observing him can answer.

| Solicited | 1 | 2 | 3 | 4 | 5 | 6 | Imposed |

Comments

6. It is well timed. In general feedback is most useful when given as soon as possible after the observed behaviour (depending, of course, on the person's readiness to hear it, on support available from others, etc.).

| Well timed | 1 | 2 | 3 | 4 | 5 | 6 | Poorly timed |

Comments

7. It is checked with the sender. For example, the sender can rephrase the feedback he has received to ensure clear communication.

Checked   1   2   3   4   5   6   Not checked
with sender   with sender

Comments

8. It is checked with others in the group. In a work group particularly, both giver and receiver can share their feedback; is it only one person's impression, or is it shared with others?

Checked   1   2   3   4   5   6   Not checked
with others   with other

Comments

Giving feedback is important in terms of increasing the subordinate's awareness of self, particularly with regard to strengths and weaknesses. If properly given, feedback results in greater rapport between the manager and employee. Feedback is effective when the manager ensures that it:

- is descriptive rather than evaluative;
- is focused on the staff member's behaviour rather than the staff member as a person;
- concerns behaviour that is open to change;
- is specific and based on information rather than general and based on impressions;
- provides information from the owner manager's experience;
- reinforces positive new behaviour and what the subordinate has done well;
- suggests rather than prescribes avenues for improvement;
- is continual rather than sporadic;
- is based on need and is listed by the staff member;
- is intended to help;
- satisfies the needs of both the manager and the subordinate;
- is checked with other sources for verification;
- is well timed; and
- contributes to the rapport between the manager and the subordinate and enhances their relationship.

You might want to discuss the characteristics of effective feedback with the employee before any appraisal session begins. No one likes nasty surprises and it does seem to help if the manager can signal as much as possible about what is going to happen before the interview to reduce the employee's uncertainty. It might also be helpful to discuss possible reactions with the employee. The employee should be encouraged to view the feedback in terms of exploring ways to improve his or her performance. Of course, if your relationship with your staff is poor, they are unlikely to see feedback in this way. This could result in defensive reactions such as;

- denying the feedback, instead of accepting responsibility for the behaviour being discussed;
- rationalising, instead of analysing why the behaviour was shown;
- assuming that the manager has negative feelings about the subordinate, instead of trying to understand the manager's point of view;
- displacing (expressing negative feelings when the manager may not fight back), instead of exploring the feedback with the manager;
- accepting automatically and without exploration, instead of listing more information in order to understand the feedback and the behaviour;
- taking an aggressive stance towards the manager, instead of seeking his or her help in understanding the feedback;
- using avoidance techniques such as displaying humour, instead of concern for improvement;
- exhibiting counter dependence (rejecting the manager's authority), instead of listening carefully to the feedback;
- showing cynicism or scepticism about improvement, instead of accepting the feedback and planning to check it with other people; and
- generalising, instead of experimenting with alternatives for improvement.

Providing you use effective communication and feedback, you will generally be able to manage defensive reactions. Additional behaviours which may be useful in managing defensive reactions include the following:

- The 'you–we' technique involves using 'you' to compliment or reward the person being appraised and 'we' to designate a need for improvement. 'You are doing a great job down on the pontoon but we have a problem.' The 'you–we' technique shifts the focus away from blaming the employee and making him or her defensive.
- The second-hand compliment involves relaying a compliment from a third party. 'Dave says you have done a great job.' This again rewards the employee, but reinforces that reward in that the second-hand compliment is a compliment from two people.

- Advice request is one which can be used where communication is threatened and the employee is so defensive that he or she won't listen to your feedback. You may then ask the employee for his or her suggestions and advice with regard to the performance issue at hand.

□ □ □

'Okay,' said Sally, 'I can see why we need to appraise and have to go about it although I think it's complicated.'

'All I've offered you, Sally, is a structure for dealing with appraisal interviews, if that's the way you want to go. I think that the formal appraisal interview, is only an expression of what you should do all the time. You will or won't build your relationship with staff all the time. An honest relationship which gives honest feedback is most of what appraisal needs to be.'

'What else does it need to be?,' Sally asked.

'Well', said Josh, 'we need to do two things. First, we need to be careful about our own judgement. We go blithely through the world believing that we've got perfect judgement about people when it's generally poor. Second, we need to identify clear links with performance. Unless an employee can see clear links between his performance and the organisation's performance, the appraisal process is a sham.'

'Hold on, what do you mean poor judgement? I'm a good judge of people . . .'

'Like Steve,' Josh said. 'The wonderful thing about people is that they don't realise how bad their judgement is.'

□ □ □

WHAT CAN GO WRONG

Because of the potential quality of the information which you can gain from accurate performance appraisal, you should be aware that there are two sets of traps which you can fall into with regard to the whole process. The first of these pertains to the ways in which human beings acquire and process information. The second pertains to the skills of the person acquiring information.

Human information processing capability is huge, but limited in a number of ways. The first of these is the fact that people will tend to see what they expect to see. The second is that people tend to perceive what is 'vivid' or immediate. This leads us into two main issues.

The first of these is the so called halo or horns' effect – appraisers will tend to rate people with one noticeable good quality as being generally good. Of course, this tendency also works in the other way, leading us to believe that one noticeable 'bad' quality means that all aspects of their performance are bad.

A similar effect is that we tend to put too much emphasis on recent behaviour or performance. In this sort of situation a poor performance from someone who is generally good, or a good one from a poor performer, will stand out and may colour the whole of the interview. This is called the 'recency' effect and may leave employees feeling either that they have been unfairly judged with the resulting loss of motivation or – perhaps worse – that the person appraising is gullible and can be easily fooled into accepting poor performance.

Research has shown that different people reach different conclusions on the basis of the same data because of differences in values, likes and dislikes. Different 'frames' will lead to different judgements about a person. People who like women may tend to give a better rating to a female member of staff for doing a job less well than a male member of staff, or vice versa.

The second group of problems relate more to the attitudes of the individuals involved in the appraisal process. The first of this group of problems is called 'central' tendency or leniency. It is a natural human tendency to avoid extremes because we are averse to risk. Extreme behaviours are likely to make us stand out from the crowd and make us more visible and thus potentially more at risk. Appraisals can be potential areas of conflict, particularly when they involve sensitive issues such as pay. We may find it difficult to handle conflict and appraisals can turn into a 'warm bath' where both appraiser and appraisee avoid extreme judgements, even when they are appropriate.

In addition to the problems of leniency, there is often a problem with rigour in the appraisal process, because human behaviour is multidimensional; that is, it has many aspects. 'Good' behaviour or performance in a job is made up of many factors. When appraising, we can attempt to measure a number of factors which are not related to actual performance. We may fail to realise what it is that we are attempting to measure, with confusion resulting for appraiser and appraisee alike.

Once you know about the things that can go wrong, you can identify paths to put them right. Proper questioning and feedback giving is important. The next stage is to identify the ways in which you can link performance appraisal and organisational performance. The link here is generally the manager himself or herself, but apart from mistakes in identifying the links there can be blocks in making the link.

LINKS TO PERFORMANCE

This exercise is designed to help people identify different types of feedback and to evaluate the type that they give most regularly. Once you have looked at implementing a structure or framework and dealing with the poor performer using effective feedback techniques, you may wish to consider examining the links between organisational and individual performance.

Look at the following exercise on links between organisational and individual performance.

Consider the following statements.

		True	False
1.	I can identify clear production or service delivery outcomes for each of my staff or each of my managers.	True	False
2.	I have a clear set of job descriptions which place emphasis on results to be achieved rather than duties to be carried out.	True	False
3.	I have clear feedback systems in place which interface with all of my customer groups and provide me with the type of information against which I can assess departmental and individual staff performance.	True	False
4.	Every one of my staff knows what their production or service delivery targets are.	True	False
5.	I tend to think about people by job title or duties rather than their capacity or capability.	True	False

If you can honestly answer 'True' to more than three of these questions, you have a clear framework for appraisal. It is more likely, however, that you cannot honestly answer 'True' to any of them. (You may want to go out and ask an employee what his or her production targets are and how they fit in to the organisation objectives – the answer may surprise you.) This means that you have a gap between your organisational and individual performance targets.

Creating links

Links between organisational performance and individual performance are an essential part of the honest relationship between the organisation's manager and his or her employees. Where such links are unclear, the manager's job becomes much harder.

So far we have looked at the ways in which you can develop this relationship at every opportunity – recruitment, selection, employee development. In many organisations the symbol of the relationship between employee and manager is the job description. We touched on the shortcomings of the job description in Chapters 8 and 9.

Most job descriptions fail because of the acceptance of the job description as:

1. a description of activities to be pursued, rather than results to be achieved;
2. a permanent document, which does not change to meet changing conditions and personalities;
3. containing no provision for continuous improvement;
4. containing no way of measuring the results mentioned above.

Many managers see the job description as either a supplement to the job advertisement or as a basis for disciplinary action. The job description can be much more than this. It is not merely a part of the recruitment process. It can be developed to represent formally the performance contract – the relationship – between the manager and the employee.

To do this, the contract needs to contain five elements:

1. agreement on the scope of the job (responsibilities);
2. agreement on the specific results the job holder is to achieve, (accountabilities);
3. agreement on the way in which the timings will be agreed, (scheduling);
4. agreement on the means needed to measure performance and reporting relationships, (control and feedback);
5. agreement on level of authority.

The key issue in the development of a contract which will enable you to appraise effectively is to determine the difference between responsibility and accountability. Some of the differences between responsibilty and accountability are set out in the table below.

Responsibility	Accountability
Is usually assigned with no opportunity for negotiation.	Is negotiated.
Is impersonal and job-related.	Is personal and related to the post-holder.
In general, is saying what the work is.	Is specific in saying what must be done.
Only loose control is possible (I'm happy with your performance to date).	Tight control is possible (you've not achieved the targets we agreed last week).
Specific authority is not set.	Specific authority must be set.

Responsibility	Accountability
Performance measurement is almost impossible.	Performance measurement is qualitatively and quantitatively possible.
Poor basis for reward beyond basic salary.	Equitable basis for performance-related pay.
Staff development is difficult to identify and general.	Staff development is specific.
Poor for motivating staff (what should I do?)	Effective for motivating staff ('I've got three thousand units to get out by the end of the year').
Expressed as activities to be pursued.	Expressed as objectives to be achieved.

Once you understand the differences between responsibility and accountability, you can incorporate this into a formal contract which should reflect an honest relationship between the manager and the employee and which will have clear, measurable targets for performance, which link into overall organisational objectives.

Job Title   Sales Manager
Scope/Content: Is responsible for company sales in the North of England. Responsible for six sales representatives. Responsible to the director of Marketing. Responsible for advertising and promotion, market research, sales training, customer relations.
Timescale: 1994–5
Key Results Areas 1. Sales forecasting and planning 2. Gross sales margins 3. Sales costs 4. Marketing channels 5. Sales staff development 6. New marketing channels
Timescale: 1994 ——>

Objectives

1. Achieve total sales volume and gross sales margins within plus or minus 5 per cent of budget.

2. Increase own label sales by 15 per cent from 1994 levels without loss in total sales volume.

3. Recruit and develop five new sales representatives to develop North West of England.

4. Develop North West of England market by June 1 so that sales volume increases by 28 per cent at total development costs of £140,000.

5. Complete market research and testing of new product by 1 April. Submit recommendations to board by 15 May.

6. To be completed by 1 April 1995.

An example of a job contract for a sales manager is given below.

Resources allocated

Budget	Salary	100,000
	Travel and accommodation budget	30,000
	Staff development budget	1,000

Development key performance document

Timescale: 1994–5

Levels of authority

Reporting systems to consist of monthly budget and monthly sales report. Staff development reports every three months. Weekly telephone conversations on progress.

This type of document will make appraisal much easier. It sets out from the start what you expect from an employee and what you can offer. It therefore makes the relationship a clear and honest one, with agreed measurable objectives. You may feel that setting all this down in documentary form is unnecessary. Not doing so, however, can lead to misunderstandings and jeopardise the relationship which enables you to appraise effectively.

If you intend to use this process, it may also be useful to use the following form to help the appraiser and the appraisee prepare for the performance review.

Preparation for review

1. **The job**
   (a) What are the main accountabilities of your job? (Please refer to the job contract and note any significant changes.)
   (b) Which areas have you found most satisfying and which have gone particularly well since your last review? (Please say why this is.)
   (c) Which areas of work have you found most challenging and difficult since your last review? (Please say why this is.)
   (d) How would you anticipate that your job could develop or change within the next (*time period*)? (How would you prioritise these?)

2. **Relationships at work**
   (a) Who are your main contacts? Please indicate other people within or outside this organisation who most directly affect or are affected by your job.
      – affect my job
      – affected by my job.
   (b) What support and assistance do you give and receive from others at work. Please note where this is useful or less than useful.
      – support from others
      – support to others
   (c) How would you like to see your working relationships develop over (*time period*)?

3. **Your career with** (*name of organisation*)
   (a) How do you feel in more general terms about your job?
   (b) How do you see your future with this organisation? (Please indicate any expectations or ambitions you may have.)

4. **Other issues**
   Are there any other points which you might wish to raise which have not yet been covered?

Checklist for appraisal

1. I have clear objectives in mind when appraising.

2. I am aware of the limits of my own information-processing capacity.

3. I can identify and use a variety of different information sources about employee performance.

4. I can develop a clear structure with agreed agendas for appraisal.

5. I can communicate effectively with people being appraised.

6. I can deal honestly with difficult behaviour.

7. I can control this appraisal.

Once you have further developed an honest relationship with employees by being clear about the performance that you expect, you can go on to consider the next stage in the relationship. This is one which is central to the job contact – motivation

Summary

- *Appraisal can be used for a number of purposes which fall into three broad groups:*
  - *reward*
  - *development*
  - *performance*

- *When appraising, you need to be clear about what it is that you are appraising.*

- *Performance appraisal is a joint process which requires two-way communication to develop the relationship between appraiser and appraisee.*

- *Performance appraisal is also an information-seeking process which can utilise a number of information sources.*

- *In order to avoid confusion, appraisal needs to be carried out in a clear framework.*

- *One framework involves identifying a performance development step, checking this step with the appraisee and checking the last step.*

- *Within this framework, emphasis should be placed on the mutual, relationship-building nature of the process.*

- *Difficulties do exist in appraisal because of assumptions and limits in human information-processing.*

- *Once reasons for performance have been identified and a performance step jointly agreed, the next step involves linking the individual's performance to the organisation's objectives.*

- *This involves the development of a job contract.*

- *Once the job contract has been developed, it can be reviewed by means of an appraisal scheme.*

11 MOTIVATION

'And no one shall work for money, and no one shall work for fear,
But each for the joy of working.'

RUDYARD KIPLING

In considering motivation, we can stretch the motor-car metaphor that we looked at in Chapter 10 a little further. Whereas development is about maintaining your vehicle and appraisal is about steering it properly, motivation is about putting the fuel in the vehicle. Without fuel, all your work will have been in vain. You may have chosen a BMW, maintained it regularly and be the best driver in the world, but without the fuel of motivation your shiny car is not suitable for its intended purpose.

An understanding of motivation is necessary to help you understand why people do the things that you want them to do and why they sometimes do things that you don't. Motivation is the study of the determinants of all human behaviour. It is the search for underlying reasons as to why people behave in the ways that they do.

There are a number of major frameworks which are used to explain why people act in particular ways. Some of these involve the idea of needs and their achievement. Others see people as doing things because of the expectancy that they will pay off in rewards, or not doing things because of the perceived difficulty of the task. Because some of these frameworks conflict, there is a process which can help you motivate staff effectively. This will involve:

- developing an understanding of the main framework which attempts to explain human behaviour;
- personalising these to meet your own management situation;
- developing a range of behaviours which will motivate a range of different staff in a range of different situations.

The objectives of this chapter are:

➤ *to help you understand how to motivate both staff and self to improve performance;*

➤ *to help you develop a structured and consistent attitude to motivation;*

➤ *to consider how you may integrate a number of motivational theories to provide a practical solution to motivational problems.*

SALLY had spent all day on the workshop floor. She'd had to cancel two important meetings and she'd not finished the scheduling for next month's production run.

Maggie and Jonathan had shaken their heads sadly when they'd told her about half the staff being off 'sick' with mysterious stomach ailments after Sandy's engagement party. Jonathan had looked like a dejected bloodhound, shaking his head and saying, 'You'd have thought that after all the time we spent on training they'd have been anxious to work.'

Sally had thought that the training and the new appraisal system would have made a lot of difference. Production had gone up and absenteeism had gone down for about a week after they'd been introduced.

She wasn't prepared to keep on spending money and time on something that didn't seem to be working and the other night she'd gone out for a drink after work with Dave who'd given her an hour and a half's worth of horror stories and 'I told you so' about consultants in general and Josh in particular. All she'd been able to say was that they'd not had to pay anything for his advice.

She'd just finished getting Mike and Dave, two of the forklift drivers, to set up the machines when her bleeper went. Cursing, she ran back across to the office where a call from Josh was waiting.

'Hi, Sal, how's it going?'

Sally was reluctant to say anything at first, but she remembered what he said about feedback and told him about the problems and the fact that she felt he was in part responsible.

'I'm sorry that you feel that way, Sal,' Josh had said. 'I told you when you started this whole process that it would impact upon a lot of other stuff. Systems planning doesn't mean doing half the job by putting appraisal or development into your organisation. What you need is a formula to help you get your staff team moving.'

□   □   □

For a manager, motivation is about providing people with the means to achieve their goals and also about ensuring that the individual's goals and the organisation's goals are aligned to some degree. As such, motivation is something which concerns the interplay between people and organisations. Many theories in the world of work psychology see people's skills, knowledge, energy, creativity and commitment as an organisation's most important resource. Organisations may, however, be so alienating, dehumanising and frustrating that these critical resources are wasted with the resulting cost in human terms.

In many ways, larger organisations seem to be either ineffective or oppressive and inhumane. Such organisations are presented as being dominated by insensitive and selfish managers who care only about power and profit. Such a view portrays people as pawns who are at the mercy of the organisations and who can only hope to protect themselves or exploit the organisation before it exploits them.

What does this mean for smaller organisations? Can small organisations also be seen as uncaring and dehumanising? Will people working in smaller organisations also react to those organisations in the same manner as people working in larger organisations – by withdrawing labour and commitment or by actively sabotaging the organisation's effort? One of the classic stories of people's reactions to work is that of the workers at the sweet factory who were so fed up with their job that they set up the rock machine to put an obscenity through eleven miles of Blackpool rock.

There is little research evidence which indicates that smaller organisations differ from larger organisations in the question of motivation. At the bottom of this issue there are several core assumptions;

- Organisations exist to serve people.

- Organisations and people need each other.

- When organisation needs and people needs don't fit, one or both will suffer – either people will be exploited or people will take advantage of the organisation.

- A good 'fit' will benefit both people and organisations.

Central to this way of looking at organisations is the issue around organisational needs and human needs. As we've seen, the whole question of motivation is driven by the concept of human needs.

We are generally so used to saying, 'I need . . .' that it comes as a surprise to note that the whole concept of need is seen as suspect by some writers. People who look at organisations may find that need is difficult to define or observe, and that the way in which human beings behave is so influenced by other factors that the whole idea of need is of no help in explaining this. As we've already said, the concept of human need drives all our work. Unless we can understand staff needs or our own needs, how can we satisfy them? Furthermore, how do we understand the consequences for failing to do so?

The idea that people have needs is, of course, buried deep in our common sense. People talk about needs all the time, but the meaning of the word is often blurred and ambiguous. What is a need?

A need can be defined as something which people have to have in order to survive and develop. So basic human needs are things such as air, food and water, because without these things people will not survive. More complex is the idea that people have basic psychological needs as well, so that apart from a need to provide food and shelter, people have an inbuilt need for love, companionship and security.

One point of view states that these psychological needs are present in everyone at birth. Another states that human needs are so coloured by environment, socialisation and culture that it is pointless to talk about general human needs. This is, of course a version of the nature/nurture debate which has long been a subject of controversy in the social sciences and elsewhere. The nature party states that all human characteristics are 'inbuilt' by genetic and biological factors, whilst the nurture party believes that human characteristics are a result of learning and experience.

Such a debate can become heated when the stakes are high for a nature supporter. Inbuilt factors which create undesirable behaviour may need to be treated with drugs, whilst for a nurture supporter these undesirable behaviours may need to be addressed through changes in school or social systems.

The nature and nurture argument is misleading in these extreme forms. We do not need degrees in psychology or biology to know that some people are different because they were born with different characteristics, or that people are capable of enormous amount of learning and adaptation and that what they learn is influenced by what goes on around them.

At present, a consensus is emerging in the social sciences that both the nature and the nurture arguments are true. People's innate abilities are determined by genetic patterning, but these abilities and needs are subject to enormous and radical change through what they learn (are taught) by their surroundings.

If we accept the nature/nurture interaction, we can define need somewhat more accurately. A need can be defined as a predisposition to prefer some types of experience over others. Needs energise and guide the way that we behave and they vary in strengths at different times. Because of a phenomenon called habituation, the continued satisfaction of needs will result in that satisfaction becoming debased or devalued and people will develop new needs.

What does it mean?

This may seem irrelevant when you attempt to work in a small organisation and your next concern is how to buy the next lot of stock or how to pay the next wages bill. None the less, it has a central impact on how we all live and work.

If you have a need to become a successful manager and feel that this book can help you, you will learn a lot from it. If, on the other hand you don't want to be a manager and you think that the sections on needs is a lot of gobbledygook you are unlikely to learn much from it.

We can say three things for certain about needs.

1. People who tend to try to satisfy their needs become unhappy when these objectives are frustrated.

2. They learn things that satisfy needs but don't learn things that don't.

3. People develop in environments where their needs are satisfied and become psychologically frustrated in situations where their major needs are frustrated.

MASLOW'S NEEDS

If we agree, then, that all people have needs and that some of those needs are the same, what needs do people have in common? Abraham Maslow[1] developed one of the most influential theories of human needs. He started from the point that humans have a variety of needs, some of which are more fundamental than others. He noted, for instance, that the need for food was paramount to the hungry, but that people who had sufficient food had different needs.

Maslow grouped his needs into five basic categories and arranged them in a hierarchy from higher to lower. The strategies to satisfy lower needs dominated behaviour until these needs were satisfied, then strategies to satisfy higher needs took over.

In Maslow's view, lower needs were what he called 'prepotent' and had to be satisfied at least in part before humans went on to the satisfaction of higher needs. Maslow's ideas have had an enormous impact on the thinking of managers and social scientists. If we accept these ideas, it means that an employee's and a manager's behaviour will vary in accordance to the satisfaction of need. It means also that systems designed to motivate – pay, benefits, etc. – must adapt because of the change in the way in which people meet their needs.

In organisational terms, Maslow's theory means that we must constantly upgrade the way in which we manage staff. Pay may be enough to help them satisfy their lower level needs, but we will then need to introduce job security to offer safety needs, team-working to offer belonging needs, job redesign and authority to offer needs for esteem, and training and development to needs for self-actualization.

A variant of Maslow's hierarchy of needs even offers transpersonal needs above self actualization needs. Transpersonal needs would deal with spiritual or religious issues. Although Maslow's ideas may seem plausible, they have never been proved valid. Equally, they have never been proved to be invalid. A number of researchers have tried to prove Maslow wrong or right, but needs are so hard to measure that the theory has been unproven to date.

So, if we accept Maslow's hierarchy, we can see that the motivation of staff and self is about designing work so that it meets the needs of staff and self.

[1]Abraham Maslow, *Motivation and Personality*, Harper and Row, 1954.

Putting Maslow to work

Frederick Herzberg[2] tried to put Maslow's theories into action in a different way. He carried out a number of surveys in which he asked employees to talk about the times when they felt best and worst about their jobs. The dominant theories in 'good feelings' stories were achievement, recognition for performance, responsibility, advancement and learning. The 'bad feelings' stories were about things such as company policy, administration, supervision and working conditions.

Herzberg called those aspects of work that produced job satisfaction 'motivators' and those that produced job dissatisfaction 'hygiene factors'. In effect, Herzberg took Maslow's hierarchy and cut it in two with hygiene factors including physiological, safety and belonging needs, and motivators including needs for self-esteem and self-actualisation. Herzberg's hygiene factors all dealt with the environment in which the work was carried out, whilst the motivators concerned the work itself. He argued that all the methods used to motivate staff – better pay, better fringe benefits, training, etc. – were variants of what he called the KITA approach to motivation, the belief that the surest and quickest way to get something done was to kick them in the backside. In Herzberg's view, KITA approaches do not motivate – they may get the person to move, but not necessarily in the right direction, and they will soon need another kick to get them to move again.

Herzberg argued that the idea of job design and enrichment was central to motivation. He saw job enrichment as being the process of 'vertical job loading'. This is done by adding to the job factors which gave the worker more autonomy, more freedom, more challenges and more feedback about their performance. We will return to Herzberg's theories when we look at how we put motivational factors to work.

Another theorist in the field of motivation was Chris Argyris.[3] Argyris saw a basic conflict between the human personality and the ways in which organisations work. Although he did not base his idea directly on Maslow's, his views were similar. He argued that human beings have 'self-actualisation' trends which develop in specific directions as they mature from infancy to adulthood.

1. They move from dependence on others to higher levels of independence.

2. They move from a narrow to a much broader range of skills and interests.

3. They move from a short-term perspective, where interests are quickly developed and quickly forgotten and there is little interest in the future, to a longer time perspective.

4. Finally, they move from a low level to a higher level of self-control and self-awareness.

[2]Frederick Herzberg, *Work and the Nature of Man*, World Books, 1966.

[3]Chris Argyris, *Integrating the Individual and the Organisations*, Wiley 1964.

Argyris felt that organisations were incompatible with this drive to maturity because of the way in which they were structured. Organisations meant that tasks were specialised and this defined tasks to an extreme degree.

> *'Michelle will assemble the box and Mavis will staple it and Sandy will stick the label on and Ethel will fill it with packing and Denise will put the widget in and Sonya will seal it.'*

Task specialisation requires a chain of command to co-ordinate the efforts of the individuals working. The chain of command means that people at higher levels have to direct the work of people at lower levels. This direction means that people will become passive and dependent on being told what to do. This means that their drives to self-actualisation will be frustrated. Argyris called this psychological failure: employees become unable to define their own goals (identify their own needs) or identify how they might action them.

This basic conflict between people's drive to maturity and the way in which organisations treat people as children would lead to a number of possible ways of behaving for the employees concerned:

1. They could withdraw from the organisation through continued absenteeism, or simply by leaving.

2. They might withdraw psychologically by being apathetic towards their work.

3. They might actively sabotage the organisation – remember the Blackpool rock.

4. They might try to gain promotion, but this is difficult as the number of jobs decreases as one climbs the hierarchy.

5. They might create organisations such as trade unions to redress the power imbalance.

6. They might bring their children up to believe that work is pointless and unrewarding.

□   □   □

'So you're saying that the people at Norham Road are withdrawing from the work and that the approaches which we're using at the moment – giving them training or appraising them properly are KITA approaches.'

'Not quite,' said Josh. 'There are a number of ways of explaining motivation and it's as well to have a theory base before you put them into action. What you've got at the moment is inconsistency in your approach. When you give people messages by giving one minute and taking away the next, you've got problems. It's like being kissed and slapped at the same time, or being greeted warmly one minute and ignored the next.'

'Anyway,' he went on, 'Maslow's, Herzberg's and Argyris' theories all saw people as having a drive to maturity or fulfilment. There are other ways of looking at it.'

□   □   □

Not everyone agrees that people have a natural tendency towards 'growth and development'. Consider the following exercise.

THE X-Y SCALE

Part 1

Directions: The following are various types of behaviour which a manager may adopt in relation to his staff. Read each item carefully and then put a tick in one of the columns to indicate what you would do.

My approach is to:	A Make a great effort to do this	B Tend to do this	C Tend to avoid doing this	D Make a great effort to avoid doing this
1. Closely supervise my staff in order to get better work from them.	☐	☐	☐	☐
2. Set the goals and objectives for my staff and sell them on the merits of my plans.	☐	☐	☐	☐
3. Set up controls to assure that my staff are getting the job done.	☐	☐	☐	☐
4. Encourage my staff to set their own goals and objectives.	☐	☐	☐	☐
5. Make sure that my staff's work is planned out for them.	☐	☐	☐	☐
6. Check with my staff daily to see if they need any help.	☐	☐	☐	☐
7. Step in as soon as reports indicate that the job is slipping.	☐	☐	☐	☐

8. Push my people to meet schedules if necessary. ☐ ☐ ☐ ☐

9. Have frequent meetings to keep in touch with what is going on. ☐ ☐ ☐ ☐

10. Allow staff to make important decisions. ☐ ☐ ☐ ☐

Part II

Directions: Read the descriptions of the two theories of management below. Think about your own attitudes towards your staff, and locate on the scale below where you think you are in relation to these sets of assumptions.

Theory X Assumptions

1. The average human being has an inherent dislike of work and will avoid it if he can.

2. Because of this human characteristic of dislike of work, most people must be coerced, controlled, directed and threatened with punishment to get them to put forward adequate effort towards the achievement of organisational objectives.

3. The average human being prefers to be directed, wishes to avoid responsibility, has relatively little ambition, and wants security above all.

Theory Y Assumptions

1. The expenditure of physical and mental effort in work is as natural as play or rest.

2. External control and the threat of punishment are not the only means of bringing about effort towards organisational objectives. Man will exercise self-direction and self-control in the service of objectives to which he is committed.

3. Commitment to objectives is a function of the rewards associated with their achievement.

4. The average human being learns under proper conditions not only to accept but also to seek responsibility.

5. The capacity to exercise a high degree of imagination, ingenuity and creativity in the solution of organisational problems is widely, not narrowly, distributed in the population.

6. Under the conditions of modern industrial life the intellectual potentialities of the average human being are only partially utilised.

Indicate on the scale below where you would classify your own basic attitudes towards your subordinates in the terms of McGregor's Theory X and Theory Y. A '10' would indicate that you strongly practise Theory X management – a '40' would indicate that you strongly practise Theory Y management.

Theory Y _____ **Theory Y**

| 10 | 20 | 30 | 40 |

Part III

Now score yourself on Part I as follows:

Items 1–3 and 5–9 scored like this:

(Column)	A	B	C	D
	1	2	3	4

Items 4 and 10 are scored like this:

(Column)	A	B	C	D
	4	3	2	1

Compare this score with the score when you located yourself in the X-Y scale. You will then have a crude index of the extent to which your assumptions match those of the two theories.

Douglas McGregor[4] took Maslow's theory of motivation and added another dimension. McGregor felt that the perspective of the manager would determine their response to work. McGregor, writing in the 1960s, suggested that most managers subscribe to Theory X. This theory proposes that managers need to direct and control subordinates. According to Theory X, employees are passive and lazy, have little ambition, prefer to be led and resist change.

There was a wide variance in Theory X assumptions ranging from 'soft' Theory X to 'hard' Theory X, which suggested that managers need to coerce, threaten, control and punish staff. 'Soft' Theory X, on the other hand, is a persuasive style which tries to help everyone get along. 'Hard' Theory X was, in McGregor's view, able to produce low productivity, antagonism and sabotage. 'Soft' Theory X, while likely to produce superficial harmony, will in the long run cause apathy and employees who expect more and more while giving less and less. Theory X tends to create self-fulfilling prophecies and general signs that both variations of the theory are correct and that more Theory X management is needed to cope with workers 'who just don't seem to give a damn any more' or who 'are never satisfied'.

[4]Douglas McGregor, *The Human Side of Enterprise*, McGraw Hill, 1960.

McGregor argued that evidence from the behavioural sciences, though inconclusive, seemed to indicate the need for a new theory – Theory Y. Maslow's needs hierarchy was the foundation of the theory which argued that managers need to behave differently. McGregor's key proposition in Theory Y was that 'the essential task of management is to arrange organisational conditions so that people can achieve their own goals best by directing their efforts towards organisational rewards'. It is the job of management to ensure that the interests of the organisation and the interest of the staff coincide.

Forms of motivation

We've discussed motivation being about the satisfaction of needs and looked at some of the ways in which we might look at individual needs. Let's now look at some of the ways in which a manager can satisfy needs in a manner which helps his or her organisation to reach its objectives.

PAY AS A MOTIVATOR

One of the major elements in giving people the things that they can use to meet some of their needs is pay or reward. Clearly, if you give someone ten or fifteen or thirty thousand pounds a year, you are giving them a powerful tool in reaching a state where some of their needs are met. Pay will enable them to buy food, drink, shelter – even, perhaps, some social and psychological needs.

It is dangerous, however to see money as being the sole or even the best motivation for the type of behaviour that you need. It also is important to ensure that when you pay to help satisfy someone else's needs, you are motivating the right sort of behaviours.

□   □   □

'Pay is quite an interesting subject, Sal,' Josh had said. 'People seem to think that pay is about exchanging money for time or effort or bright ideas or even being nice. The problem with pay is that it is such a received idea. Everybody knows that when you go to work, you get paid. Everybody knows that in order to get people to go to work, you've got to pay them, although if you ask people what they are paying for you'll get two different groups of answers.

'The first of these is the generally accepted maxim of a fair day's pay for a fair day's work; the second is that we pay for performance.'

'I think that it's a bit more complex than that. If we are only paying for four days' work, we're paying for time – $37\frac{1}{2}$ or $39\frac{1}{2}$ hours a week. This means that we might have employees who start at 9, finish at 5.30 and don't do a lot in between.'

□   □   □

If we pay for 'performance', we need to decide what our output measures are. Performance standards in many organisations measure anything but performance but even so, as we saw in Chapter 10 on performance appraisal, accurate performance assessment is difficult, which is why most people find it easiest to pay for time.

Let's consider some of the things which we could be paying for.

- time;
- productivity;
- customer service;
- creativity and new ideas;
- new skills development;
- vision;
- commitment;
- flexibility;
- ability to work as part of a team;
- ability to work on own account.

We can subsume all these into one heading of 'performance,' but if we're unclear about what it is that we're paying for, we can unwittingly give the wrong messages to staff and find that we're paying for something that we don't want.

Look at the following statements and ring the number that corresponds most closely with your understanding of pay.

	True	False
1. Pay is about giving people what the job is worth.	1 2 3	4 5
2. Pay should be clearly linked to identified outcomes.	1 2 3	4 5
3. Pay will depend on length of service.	1 2 3	4 5
4. You can't pay less than the minimum wage for a job.	1 2 3	4 5
5. Everybody gets paid for the time they spend at work; you can't change that.	1 2 3	4 5
6. A skilled worker should always be paid more than an unskilled worker.	1 2 3	4 5
7. A manager should always be paid more than a manual worker.	1 2 3	4 5
8. Pay is what makes workers work.	1 2 3	4 5

Scoring

Tot up the total of the circled numbers and assess yourself on the scale below:

30–40 Your attitude towards pay isn't stuck in the old paradigm of a fair day's work for a fair day's pay. You probably use your pay systems in a flexible way.

20–30 You seem to be able to look at some aspects of pay with a fresh eye but still have some preconceptions.

10–20 Your organisation may be working but it is unlikely to be performing effectively.

under 10 You may be paying people for very little. Consider carefully your pay structures and what your staff are delivering.

The other thing that you need to ensure is that you are paying enough to get the right sort of person for the job. Pay doesn't only impact on motivation, it also affects recruitment. High-calibre staff are invariably in short supply; they will know how much they are worth and will expect corresponding rewards. Any reward system will need to be attractive and competitive.

Pay needs to reflect performance. We have seen the danger of being unclear about what performance is and of confusing rewards, developmental and performance appraisal. This does not mean that you should not reward performance, as failure to do so will result in demotivation and a decline in the performance which you value.

The third issue in reward is not only to ensure that you are rewarding the right sort of performance, but that there is some equity in reward between people at lower reward levels in an organisation and those at a higher level. Too great a gap between levels of an organisation may also be demotivating.

☐   ☐   ☐

'So you can see that reward and motivation are difficult subjects to tackle. The other problem is, of course, the extent of secrecy in your organisation. Many people feel that pay is a confidential matter. If you want to use reward as a motivator to get better performance from your staff you will need to make sure that the targets are open and that pay and pay differentials are known by everyone. If reward is kept in the dark, it is not as effective a motivator as other factors which we shall look at later.'

'But you've used reward and pay interchangeably here. Is pay reward?'

☐   ☐   ☐

Pay is part of reward and part of a reward's strategy, A reward strategy is about developing and integrating a whole range of management tactics to ensure that staff perform. These can include appraisal, evaluating, strategy needs in order to meet eight objectives:

1. Ensure that the organisation can recruit the quantity and quality of staff it needs to meet its performance targets.

2. Develop the 'fit' between organisation and people.

3. Provide rewards for good performance and incentives for further performance improvement.

4. Make sure that similar jobs are paid similar rates (this is a legal requirement).

5. Make sure that the different character of different jobs is recognised.

6. Create flexibility to ensure that the system can accommodate particular needs (for instance, if a company needs an 'expert' who would be paid more than the Head of Department).

7. Be robust – this is simple to explain, operate and control.

8. Be cost-effective.

In order to achieve these objectives you will need to gather relevant information before you put your strategy into action.The first step is to know the nature of the market. Without a knowledge of the market you will find it difficult to 'set a price' for the type of employee you are seeking. Most managers will actively scan the recruitment sections of the newspapers to gather information on pay scales for the sort of employee they seek. Some organisations also sell these types of data. Incomes Data Services and the 'Pay and Benefit Bulletin' published by Industrial Relations Research Services offer survey information about pay and benefits.

Using advertisements will only give you an approximate picture of the sort of salaries, so you should be aware that:

- Recruitment information may not be reliable, as it is designed to attract rather than inform.

- There can be a wide variety of job types within a job title – 'Business Development Manager' can be paid across a wide range.

The essential elements of effective pay systems are balance and linkage. **Balance** means that a pay system should never be allowed to get out of control. Pay should reflect the levels of performance which the individual worker produces. **Linkage** means that there should be clear and recognisable links between pay and performance. Because of the way in which funds are transferred now, people can lose sight of the links between pay and performance. Numbers appear in their bank account at the end of the week or the end of the month, with no apparent connection to performance at work.

We looked in the Chapter 10 on appraisal at the way in which accountabilities are a central feature of the job contract. It is part of the manager's job to make sure that there are links between these accountabilities and the pay system. We will look at how this can be achieved later in the chapter.

MOTIVATING THROUGH WORK DESIGN

Apart from reward, there are a number of other ways in which we can motivate staff. The first of these takes us back to Herzberg and his work on 'job enrichment'.

As we've seen, Herzberg believed that the nature of the job was central to motivating employees. If jobs are narrow, fragmented and restrictive, it is possible to redesign work to make them more appealing. Herzberg argued for what he called 'vertical job loading', on which the employee is given increased authority and challenge within the job together with more feedback. This means that people in the packing department of Presteign would be encouraged to take on more responsibility in, let's say, ordering the disassembled packs and designing the way in which work came into the packing department. They might also be encouraged to be involved in the way in which work was planned.

Herzberg's work has been criticised heavily, largely because he relied purely on what people said about the work in which they were involved. Individuals tend to attribute unpleasant factors to influences outside themselves or in some cases outside of their organisations, whilst claiming personal credit for good factors.

Job design

Hackman[5] and his colleagues extended Herzberg's theories and argued that three factors were necessary to ensure that job redesign experiments were successful.

1. They needed to see their work as meaningful and worthwhile. This means that where Sandy is stamping box after box, she needs to know why she is doing this and how her task fits into the overall functions of the organisation. On a day-to-day basis, it is all too easy to lose sight of the purpose of work. This holds true for both managers and employees, and many methods have been tried to help retain that sense of purpose and commitment, some of which we will look at later in this chapter.

2. They need to feel personally accountable for the work that they do. Working in organisations can often contribute to a loss of identity. When work is carried out by Presteign Limited, it is not perceived as being the responsibility of Tanya, school-leaver/trainee. Again, efforts have been made to ensure that

[5]J.R. Hackman and G.R. Oldham, *Work Redesign*, Addison Wesley, 1980.

people are accountable for their efforts by the use of individual production targets, progress charts, etc.

3. The above is unlikely to be effective without the third component, which is that of effective feedback. We have looked elsewhere at the need for feedback for managers and staff. Without knowledge of progress, it is difficult to feel motivated about work.

A number of job characteristics which will contribute to the motivation of staff come out of Hackman's work and the work of others. These characteristics are likely to result in an increase in the three factors which lead to feelings of accountability, meaning and feedback:

- *Variety* in the job, the tools used, the place where the job is carried out and the people whom the employee meets. An employee who sits in place at a production line carrying out the same task repetitively with the same tools and seeing the same people (like Charlie Chaplin in the film 'Modern Times') is unlikely to feel any sense of meaning or accountability.

- *Autonomy* in the way the task is performed. If Neil tells Sandy that he needs 300 boxes a day to be assembled and that the assembly has to be done in a particular way, Sandy is unlikely to feel that her job has any meaning.

- *Responsibility.* Jobs are often designed to operate within authority structures and, as Argyris pointed out, this tends to reduce the employee's sense of responsibility for the task. We will look later at the question of delegation, but many managers tend to become swamped with enquiries about 'how to do' the task when they feel that they have already demonstrated this. Unfortunately, there is a variant of Parkinson's Law which states that the availability of a factor will ensure its use. If someone is available to solve problems on people's behalf, it is unlikely that they will easily learn to solve problems on their own behalf.

- *Challenge.* The degree to which the job presents an opportunity for growth and development is a factor which contributes to the meaning of the job. Solving problems and overcoming difficulties also gives a sense of achievement.

- *Interaction.* This is the way in which people holding a job meet and respond to other people. A retail sales job is likely to have a high degree of low-quality interaction with customers, while a flexible manufacturing cell, built around a high performance team, is likely to have a high degree of high-quality interaction. Where sales staff are in constant contact with customers who do not seem to care for them as people, a manager will need to introduce better quality interaction by allowing staff to develop as a team.

- *Task significance*. This again gives meaning to the job. Hackman notes that a person whose job it is to tighten nuts on an aircraft engine will be more likely to deliver a high performance than a person whose job it is to fill boxes of paperclips. The aircraft fitter will see his or her task as significant.

● *Goals and feedback*. Without clearly defined objectives and feedback on performance, staff will be in a position where they are like blindfold people, trying to find a pin in a darkened room. Without clear, accepted goals or objectives, nothing is very likely to succeed.

Job redesign seems to work. It may be ineffective in some cases, as both McGregor and Argyris note, that many workers have been trained to accept Theory X assumptions and will resist a move towards more responsibility. It does, however, tend to produce an increase in the quality rather than the quantity of production, because workers will get more satisfaction out of doing a job well than from doing more work. It also tends to increase staff flexibility, i.e. the way in which jobs can be moved around amongst staff as the need arises, and makes it easier to attract and retain staff.

□　　□　　□

'So I have to completely redesign the jobs in the plant. It would cost a fortune,' Sally said.

'You don't have to completely redesign anything, Sally. I've already said that you use the bits that are useful. What elements could you redesign?'

'Well, I suppose I could paint the big picture in the same way that I did with Neil.'

'Fine, what else?'

'Well, if it's about symbolic rewards and objectives I suppose I could put up some coloured charts which will show how well or badly the Norham Road site is doing and how it fits into the total effort.'

'That would be pretty good, Sal, that's a powerful simple message.'

'And I could have a wine and cheese party once a month for the best department . . . and –

'Okay, okay, Sal, I think you've got the idea.'

□　　□　　□

Other issues which are designed to better the 'fit' between the worker and the organisation by matching needs are participation, and self-managing work teams.

MOTIVATION THROUGH PARTICIPATION

The worker participation movement is a result of Elton Mayo's work, based upon experiments carried out in the Chicago factory of the Hawthorne Electric Company and in other factories in the United States. A classic example is described in William Whyte's book *Money and Motivation*. In this, he described a group of staff – all women – who were responsible for painting dolls in a toy factory. The women worked a new system whereby each women took a toy from a tray, painted it, and put it on a hook passing by on a belt. The women received an hourly rate, a group bonus and a learning bonus.

Management expected no trouble with the new system, but production declined dramatically. Staff morale was very low. They especially complained about the heat in the room and the speed of the belt. Reluctantly, the supervisor followed advice to meet the staff and an agreement was ultimately reached to put fans into the workshop, although the industrial engineer who designed the system doubted that these would help. The fans led to a significant increase in morale and further talks led to the women making a radical suggestion – that they be allowed to control the speed of the belt. The industrial engineer resisted this because he'd calculated the 'best' speed for the belt, but reluctantly the supervisor agreed to try it out.

The staff worked out a complicated schedule in which the belt ran fast at some times and slow at others. Morale shot up. Production exceeded the engineer's targets and began to overload other parts of the plant. Pay shot up and the women's production bonuses meant that they earned far more than many 'senior' staff members. As a result, the experiment was discontinued. Production dropped, morale plummeted and most of the women left.

None the less, the experiments had proved that employee participation in designing some of the elements of their job improves both production and morale. These experiments were 'discovered' again in the 1970s when the work of Joseph Juran and W. Edwards Deming and Quality Circles became popular.

Quality Circles were groups of people from the same work area who met voluntarily to focus on issues of product quality. These circles were initiated by management asking for volunteers and then training their volunteers in problem-solving techniques and the way in which groups develop and work. Group members are not given pay for their involvement, although it is recognised in other ways – ceremonies, T-shirts, publicity within the organisation, etc.

Participation may, however, be problematic if it is not implemented honestly. Managers tend to believe in participation for themselves rather than for staff. This is because managers are reluctant to 'trust' and are ambivalent about their own attitude to power and control. Consider the following exercise.

Examine the following statements and place a ring around the letter which you believe corresponds to your own attitude towards power.

	Very strongly		Not at all
1. I need to control what's going on around me.	A	B	C
2. I need to be involved in everything	A	B	C

3. I find it difficult to delegate	A	B	C
4. I don't like uncertainty	A	B	C
5. I prefer games of skill to games of chance	A	B	C
6. I generally trust other people's ability to do a job	A	B	C
7. I don't like asking for favours	A	B	C
8. I don't like crowds of people near me when I've got work to do.	A	B	C

Scoring

For questions 1–5 and 7–8 score 3 points for every A, 2 points for every B and 1 point for every C. For question 6 score 1 point for A, 2 points for B and 3 points for C.

16–24 points You demonstrate a high need for control. You are unlikely to accept the idea of worker participation at all.

8–16 points Your need for control is lower but your attitude towards worker participation is likely to be a token one.

under 8 points You probably already involve workers in all elements of the organisation's operation (or you lied!).

Stemming directly from Quality Circles came the idea of Self Managing Work Teams and organisational democracy. (We will look in more detail at the issue of work teams in Chapter 13.) The idea was to give a team responsibility for a whole product, service or project and to provide its members with enough autonomy and resources so that they could be responsible for their own output. Teams met regularly to discuss scheduling, assignments and current problems.

The work of individuals like Einar Thorsrud, who developed the production teams at Volvo in Sweden, seems to show that self-managing work teams do 'work'. A number of major firms such as Cummins Engine, General Motors and Shell Oil have experimented with this work format. In some cases, incentive schemes have been changed to base workers, pay on the range of different tasks that they can perform. In Sweden, and particularly in Norway, the social aspects of work have been given a great deal of attention and worker participation or consultancy has been legally mandated in many firms.

Organisational democracy is to some degree an acknowledgement of the work of a group of British social scientists based at the Tavistock Centre. These scientists stated that all work was a result of the interplay between the social and the technical systems in the workplace.

One of the basic problems with all of these participative methods of motivation for managers working in smaller organisations is the extent to which they consider the business to 'belong' to them. If you feel that the business belongs to you and that the people who work for you are tools to get 'your' organisation from point A to wherever you want to go, such methods will be pointless.

MOTIVATING THROUGH TARGETS

We've looked at length now at the way in which motivation can be a response to needs. There are a number of other ways of looking at a needs-driven approach. Broadly, these can be broken down into two groups: the first group are Expectancy Theories and the second Gestalt Theories.

The perception of need

Expectancy theories concentrate on the links between goal achievement and performance. Needs theories state that if you offer an employee the methods to meet his or her needs, they will behave in a manner which ensures that these needs continue to be met.

The links between behaviour and goal achievement may not, however, be so simple. First, individuals have different goals and second, they will only achieve these goals if they feel they have a realistic chance of obtaining them. So if Dave and Carol are given a job to do, which seems to them that they have no possibility of completing, and Sam and Tracey are given the same job, but are given more resources to do the job, Dave and Carol will not expect to complete and will be unlikely (all other things being equal) to expend much effort on it; Sam and Tracey on the other hand will be likely to work harder to complete the task.

Expectancy theories of motivation are linked to attributional and instrumental theories in that they do not portray people as passive reactors to their needs. In these theories, individuals can make informed choices about likely pay-off and likely causes of behaviour. In this model, human beings make judgements about the likelihood of success or failure in achieving their goals through completing a task. They will take action to achieve success and to avoid failure. In the example above, Dave and Carol will try to achieve their goals in other ways, unless they perceive that the likelihood of success is zero.

One of the interesting implications of individuals as 'judges' is the phenomenon of learned helplessness. This is a situation where individual employees see no links between their behaviour and the presence or absence of a stimulus. They may become apathetic and withdrawn.

Expectancy theory teaches us that targets can be set to motivate: 'If you sell 1,000 units by the end of the month, there will be a bonus of £500, i.e. if you satisfy the organisation's needs or my needs, you will also be satisfying your own needs.'

These targets do, however need to have a realistic chance of success; otherwise individuals will either seek other methods of fulfilling their needs, or abandon the task, psychologically or spiritually.

MOTIVATING THROUGH COMPLETION

The final group of theories in this are Gestalt theories. Gestalt is a school of psychology which attempts to interpret motivation as an attempt to make our world orderly, simple and stable. Gestalt psychology sprang from a number of experiments carried out in the 1920s which concentrated on explaining the processes of human perception. Gestalt theories involve four main principles, which are about the ways human beings organise perception and interpret the world.

These principles state that people are motivated by a desire to produce order, simplicity and stability in their environment. Whilst this is not the place to dwell deeply upon Gestalt theory, it is an approach which is being adopted more commonly, particularly in learning theory. The principle of closure is demonstrated in the figure below.

We will generally see this figure as three incomplete circles rather than two back-to-back semicircles with a spare at each end. We tend to demonstrate a need to complete incomplete figures. In wider terms, this means that we need to 'complete' incomplete situations. Where we are frustrated in completion, we will find other ways of trying to 'achieve closure'. We are all faced with incomplete situations at work and in life generally. The Gestalt school sees much of our behaviour as an attempt to achieve closure in other ways.

Gestalt theories of closure have relevance in the workplace in terms of work design and the need to complete a task, once it is started. Gestalt may well be the reason for Volvo's production successes in dedicating one team to build a whole motor car or significant elements of a motor car, instead of splitting up

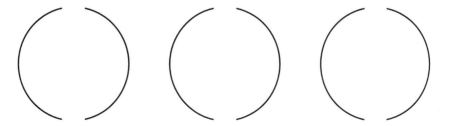

Fig. 11.1 The principle of closure

tasks and leaving employees without the opportunity for closure. As we can see, motivational theories start off simple, a way of managing behaviour to meet needs, and become more complex. The next section looks at how we can practically use these theories in a small business unit.

□   □   □

'Okay,' said Sally, 'I can see how complex it all is. How do I make sense of it? I mean, my head's buzzing, I don't know whether I should motivate people by organisational democracy, job redesign, pay or whatever.'

'It is complex, Sal,' replied Josh, 'but a single accurate theory of motivation would explain why people do what they do. It could also explain how to make people do what you want them to do.'

'That's what I want, Josh, I want to know how to make people do what I want them to do.'

□   □   □

Needs theories aren't, then, simply about making sure that people get paid on time. There is an issue with regard to the environment through which needs are met. Employees are very sensitive to the messages in their environment and if they don't feel that there is a direct link between their behaviour at work and the rewards which they receive and which enable them to reach their goals, they will become confused and behave in a way which managers find frustrating and puzzling.

Before we go on to look at the sorts of messages which employees might receive, let's look at what you might need to do to assure motivated and best performance from employees.

Within the framework of what we've seen, there are a number of behaviours which you can develop to help motivate your staff. These fall into three areas:

- reward systems;
- job design;
- expectancy.

Pay systems

Managers should design pay and reward systems so that:

- Desired performance is rewarded. Do not reward undesirable or neutral performance.
- The relationship between performance and reward is clear. Whatever rewards (pay, promotion, the best parking space, a new job title) are offered should be clearly and explicitly linked to performance throughout the whole of your organisation.
- They are balanced within your organisation.

Job design

Managers can influence motivation in the way that jobs are carried out in terms of the seven areas which Richard Hackman identified:

- *Job variety* Provide opportunities for people to do several jobs/combine jobs
- *Autonomy* Give people responsibility for designing their own working systems.
- *Responsibility* Give people responsibility for quality control.
- *Task Significance* Inform people of the importance of their work. Establish relationships with customers and suppliers
- *Interaction* Form natural work groups or teams
- *Challenge* Show people how their work fits into the picture
- *Feedback* Establish relationships with customers and suppliers. Open feedback channels

Expectancy

In motivating staff it helps to remember that motivation is an individual process. People are motivated by different things. This means that the final step is to individualise the motivation process by:

- finding out what particular outcomes or rewards are valued by each employee;
- being specific about the behaviours which represent good performance;
- ensuring that the levels of performance which you decide (targets) are realistic;
- making sure that there is a direct link between targets and rewards, i.e. that performance leads to outcomes – without a clear link motivating expectancies will not be created;
- checking that there are no conflicting expectancies, i.e. that levels of performance are linked to different outcomes elsewhere;
- ensuring that changes in reward are large enough to influence performance – trivial rewards will result in trivial changes in performance;
- making sure the system is fair.

Checklist for motivation

1. I understand the concept of motivation through need.

2. I understand the concept of motivation through expectancy.

3. I can design pay and reward systems to motivate staff.

4. I can design jobs to motivate staff.

5. I can ensure linkage between performance and reward.

6. I can help employees take responsibility for their jobs.

7. I can help employees gain autonomy in their work.

8. I can paint the big picture to demonstrate challenge in work.

9. I can establish relationships between staff and customers/suppliers.

10. I can control motivation in my organisation.

Summary

- *Motivation is the study of the determinants of human behaviour.*

- *Motivational theories are largely based upon the idea of people doing what they do in order to meet needs.*

- *The concept of need is slippery and difficult to define.*

- *People have a range of needs from basic – food, shelter, etc., through to psychological – need for fulfilment, love, etc.*

- *A manager needs to develop 'fit' between an organisation and employees so that they satisfy their needs by satisfying organisational needs.*

- *Because of the nature of organisations, this is difficult.*

- *Managerial attitude and assumptions will also colour the motivation process.*

- *Some methods of improving motivation include re-arranging reward systems, increasing employee participation and job redesign.*

- *These can be augmented by developing an honest and consistent relationship with employees and communicating with them adequately.*

12 DELEGATION

'It's a working principle of the Head Bureau that the very possibility of error must be ruled out of account. The ground principle is justified by the consummate organisation of the whole authority.'

FRANZ KAFKA

Delegation completes the job contract as a function of the relationship between the manager and employee. Recruitment, development, appraisal, motivation and delegation are the key elements which make up the cycle of managing for performance.

The final element – delegation – is perhaps the most difficult one to manage. Delegation completes the performance cycle by allowing the manager to control processes through other people. Delegation is essential because a manager can't do all the work. If you want your organisation to function properly, you must delegate. Unfortunately, as we shall see, there is a considerable difference between delegating and delegating well.

The objectives of this chapter are:

▶ *to help you consider why you should delegate;*

▶ *to help you identify some of the signs of poor delegation;*

▶ *to offer you some paths to delegating effectively;*

▶ *to look at the way in which delegation forms part of the job contract.*

'I DON'T know,' Sally said, 'maybe I need some discipline. I really found myself in difficulties when I was handling Jim's disciplinary. I don't want that to happen again.'

'It sounds as though you need to learn to delegate, Sal', said Josh.

'But I already do delegate! I give Neil and Karen jobs all the time.'

'Sal, everybody delegates. You couldn't do your job if you didn't delegate. The major issue is how effectively you delegate and how comfortably you delegate.'

□   □   □

The process of delegating effectively and delegating comfortably will involve a number of elements:

- identifying your own attitude towards, and style of, delegation;
- learning to give up responsibility for a task whilst retaining control;
- practising the type of behaviours which demonstrate trust;
- selecting and matching the task to the employee;
- clearly setting out the contract within the process of delegation.

Consider the following exercise.

EXERCISE. Are you happy delegating?

You are the production manager of a small company making a range of construction tools. The five person management team has decided to introduce a new product, a battery-powered impact driver. Production schedules need to be set up. The development of a pilot production cell needs to be designed and carried through. You already have your hands full with the training of statistical Process Control teams and you decide to delegate the task to Dave Peachtree, the senior production assistant, who has only worked with the company for six months.

Consider the following statements and answer 'yes' or 'no' to those statements which agree actions and attitude.

Actions

1. I would clearly explain the task. YES/NO

2. I would set clear deadlines. YES/NO

3. I would identify guidelines and make sure that my door was always open. YES/NO

4. I would check that Dave understood his instructions. YES/NO

5. I would regularly check on progress. YES/NO

Attitudes

6. I am happy to give such an important task to a relatively new worker. YES/NO

7. I am clear whether I am motivating, delegating or appraising. YES/NO

8. I feel a little guilty at giving the job to Dave because we've all been so busy. YES/NO

9. Dave is very capable. If he does well, I'm going to look poor in comparison. YES/NO

10. I don't think that you can trust anyone, really. YES/NO

Scoring

Action: If you answered YES to questions 1, 3 and 5 score one point for each answer. If you answered NO to questions 2 and 4 score one point for each answer.

Attitudes: If you answered NO to questions 6–9 and YES to question 10, score one point for each answer.

If you have scored over 5, you may be unhappy with your delegating skills. You've probably never been shown how to delegate. You are an unhappy delegator.

□　　□　　□

'But why shouldn't I feel that way? 'Sally asked indignantly. 'It's my business, I worked hard at it. I don't see why I should give it up to someone who hasn't put in the same effort that I have.'

'Sure, Sal,' Josh said. 'Calm down. We have already looked at some of the reasons that people don't put the same effort in and some of the problems caused by expecting them to do things that they have not been properly trained for. Delegation is an essential part of the job contract.'

'So far you have picked the right people, you have integrated them into your business by developing them, you have set them targets to motivate them and you have checked progress through appraisal. Surely you are going to actually give them the job to do?'

'Is that all it's about then, giving them the job to do?', asked Sally

'Let's look and see what the dictionary says, shall we?'

Josh walked over to the bookshelf in the corner of the room and pulled down a tattered copy of the *Concise Oxford*.

'"Delegate = v.t. depute(person); send as representative(s) commit (authority, powers, etc.) to or to agent."'

'So it's about giving up authority or power to someone else. We have already seen how you feel about that so I suppose we really need to make a case as to why you should, before looking at how we can do it.'

□　　□　　□

Why delegate?

There are a number of good reasons for delegating. First, as we've seen, you can't do all the work. Inasmuch as this is true, it is amazing that managers don't spend more time learning to delegate.

Second, it is one of the methods that we have already looked at to develop staff. Development is something which employees must learn to do for themselves.

Third, it is a way in which employees can avoid demotivation. It is very demotivating to be selected and trained for a job, only to be told that you cannot do it or that you are not trusted to do it unless you are being watched all the time. This gives messages about trust and the self-fulfilling prophecy shows us that if you show people that you don't trust them, they become less trustworthy.

Fourth, there are issues about the management of time, location and organisational product diversity. If an organisation is going to grow, it is likely to take up more of all of these. One person will simply not have the time to do, or even to check, all of the tasks that need doing. The organisation may open other branches or sites which will cut in on time resource because of travel time. The organisation may offer more products or services as it develops, and this diversity means that delegation must be practised because one person or group of people will not be able to carry out all of the core tasks which the organisation requires.

□　　□　　□

'But I keep telling you, I am delegating. I told Bill to go and see Nexus the other week, when that staff meeting came up. I know that I cannot be in two places at once,' said Sally. 'You know that I am snowed under at the moment. All this stuff that you are asking me to do . . .'

'I am not asking you to do anything, Sal,' said Josh. 'You said you had got problems. Sorting them out may not be easy, but they're your problems. Anyway, if you are snowed under you are not delegating properly, look for the signs.'

'What signs?'

□　　□　　□

ASSESSMENT EXERCISE

Consider the following exercise which is designed to look at some of the signs of poor delegation. Consider the following statements and answer 'yes' or 'no' according to whether they are true for you most of the time.

1. I have to give frequent and detailed instructions to employees.
2. I hold staff meetings constantly.
3. I never bother with staff meetings.
4. I always take home a 'fat briefcase' at night and at weekends.
5. I feel under constant pressure.
6. I tend to criticise my employees face-to-face and/or to friends or colleagues on a regular basis.
7. I don't have any written procedures.
8. I have a complete procedure manual for every eventuality.
9. Employees know exactly what their objectives are.
10. Liaison-making with my organisation tends to be slow.
11. There is often conflict about decisions being made by the wrong people.
12. Large numbers of people report to me.
13. There are clearly defined levels in my organisation and people know their place.
14. Only a small number of people in my organisation can spend more than a small amount of money.
15. I find myself exasperated at the number of little problems I have to handle.
16. Employees seem to quote me a lot.
17. I don't know all the details of what's going on.
18. Everything is top priority in my organisation.
19. Employees get information on a need to know basis.
20. Co-ordination of activities often tends to break down in every organisation.

Scoring

Score one point for each 'yes' answer with the exception of questions 1, 9 and 17 which score one point for a 'no'.

If you have scored over 16 points, you have got real problems with delegation. You have got no time for anything other than work and you probably mistake 'busyness' for performance. You need to learn to delegate effectively.

If you have scored 10–16 points, you are a hybrid doer and manager. You probably think that you delegate effectively but still wonder where the time goes.

If you have scored under 10, you are moving towards effective delegation

---

The exercise above will have given you some idea of the degree that you suffer from the symptoms of poor delegation. The next step is to look for underlying causes.

The causes of poor delegation

These can broadly be defined in three areas:

- roles
- relationships
- control

ROLES

In small organisations roles tend to be ill-defined. As we will see in Chapter 13 on team building, both formal and informal roles are important in an organisation. *Formal* roles involve issues such as job title and nature of the work carried out. *Informal* roles are likely to involve personal characteristics and the way in which a person fits into the group. Let's look, for a moment at what we mean by 'role.' The word role originally meant the part which an actor plays. It broadened to include a person's function or the part they were expected to play in a group or an organisation.

Roles are not only the part we play, however. They are about messages which we send to ourselves and others about who we are. Roles are given and received by behaviour; for instance, your role as a manager will be defined to a large degree by the way in which other people defer and ask you for advice.

Small organisations are prone to uncertainty. People who work in small organisations may not have a clear vision of the future and the present can be problematic. Small organisations are uncertain because their information-gathering apparatus may be inadequate. Poor information leads to uncertainty, which contributes to poor role definition. In a larger organisation, people's roles can be stable and well-defined: 'Fred has been the sales manager here for twenty years.' In small organisations, a high level of uncertainty means that people switch roles very rapidly, moving from project manager to personnel manager to sales manager in a very short space of time.

Instability or poor role definition can create difficulties in relationships. If people cannot identify a clear formal or informal role for a person, they may find it difficult to build a relationship with that person. They may also find it difficult to delegate where roles are unclear, or where they have previously held a role and a new 'role holder' comes into post. For instance, when a manager has previously acted as financial controller but work pressure forces recruitment of a new finance controller, the manager may find it difficult to delegate because he or she is unable to relinquish the role; ultimately, this might lead to role conflict.

RELATIONSHIPS

The second group of causes which lead to poor delegation are connected to the quality and nature of the relationship in which the delegation takes place. Roles have a major effect on relationships. You might be prepared to delegate to the tea boy, but you might find it difficult to delegate to the sales manager, particularly if he or she seems knowledgeable and confident.

Delegation is all too often seen as something that has to be done downwards. This perception of delegation comes about because delegation involves the tasks that a manager does not want to do. We will look later at the problems caused by delegating only the bad tasks.

Delegation is about giving up power and authority. An effective manager will manage his or her relationships within the organisation so that he or she can delegate upwards, sideways as well as downwards. When relationships are effectively managed, delegation becomes the norm rather than the exception.

Whilst delegation is about giving up power and authority, it is not about giving up control.

CONTROL

It is a commonly accepted belief that relationships happen naturally in a passive process which involves people coming together. It is also commonly held that relationships are about 'good' things such as support, help, mutual recognition and not about criticism or challenge. An honest relationship will involve all these elements and more. An honest relationship within the context of a delegated task or responsibility involves:

- retaining control whilst giving up authority and power;
- adapting controls to the task or responsibility in question.

Retaining control

Retaining control involves giving up, within limits, responsibility for the process of the task or group of tasks whilst retaining responsibility for the outcome. In delegating, control is about the information that you need to ensure that the task is progressing within agreed limits.

Thus if Sally delegates a task to Neil by saying, 'Could you do this?', she will need to put in place a framework which will ensure that:

- time checks are made. ('Could you let me know how it's going by Wednesday?')
- status checks are made ('Could you let me know how many have gone out by Friday?')
- objectives are set. ('We'll need to get this lot out by the end of the month.')
- fallbacks are implemented. ('If you've got any problems I'll be around all week.')
- checks are made. ('You're sure that you've got what you need?)

This is very similar to the steps introduced in Chapter 11 on motivation. All of these elements involve the job contract and effective delegation can be very motivating in that it increases employee participation and authority.

Adapting controls

It is important, when you consider the subject of controls, that the controls are appropriate for the delegated task. Again, in the chapter on motivation we saw the effects of inappropriate measures on performance. In order to delegate effectively, the manager needs a clear set of objectives. Without clear measurable objectives, delegation is likely to fail.

There may be a gap between what we say we want employees to do and what we actually ask them to do. General objectives such as 'being the best widget-making operation west of Cheam' are little use in delegating specific tasks. Equally, specific objectives such as 'improving defect rates by 1 in every 5 units' will be ineffective for a more broadly based, delegated task. Reporting methods and procedures should also be appropriate to the task.

This means that control mechanisms – reports and objectives setting – should be tailored to the nature of the task. Remember that individual tasks need individual solutions. Standard controls tend to interfere with delegation.

□　□　□

'Okay, okay,' Sally said, 'I still think that you are just a control freak.'

'Without controls, Sal, you have not got an organisation. It's not organised. You might have a playground or a public relations service or a place to go when you want to feel needed, but you don't have an organisation which is going somewhere.'

'You have persuaded me that I need to learn to delegate and that delegation is more than just telling my staff to do something, but if it is more, how much more is it?'

□　□　□

The delegation process as a contract

We have seen how roles impact upon relationships as part of the delegation process. It may be helpful to think about the delegation process as a contract. There are contractual duties on behalf of both the delegator and the delegatee.

Broadly, the first contractual duty of a delegator is to control the delegatee flexibly. Control should be broad enough or subtle enough not to stifle initiative. The second is to let other people make mistakes. The third is to give authority to those who can make best use of it and the fourth is to give the other person's ideas the opportunity to be tried out.

Within these four core propositions there are a number of specific behaviours which will help build an effective delegatory relationship. These can be broken up into behaviours before, during and after the delegation.

USEFUL BEHAVIOUR BEFORE THE DELEGATION

The first of these takes us back to selection. You need to select the right person for the task that you want to delegate. Clearly it is no use delegating a complex new task to someone who does not learn quickly and has not the verbal, manual or conceptual skills to carry on the task.

- *Delegate both the good and the bad*. It is a natural human desire to save the good stuff for yourself and give the bad stuff to someone else. If you can accept and deal with this, you will be able to reward effective delegation with enjoyable or important tasks. Remember that in Chapter 11 on motivation we saw some of the problems which stemmed from giving 'good' people 'bad' tasks and poor performers easy tasks.

- *Delegate gradually*. Delegation is not merely taking the contents of an 'in tray' or action file and handing them over to someone else. Test the water and start off by delegating small tasks before you go on to more complex and difficult ones.

- *Delegate in advance*. If you wait until a problem develops before you delegate, you are giving messages to employees which may lead to their feeling that 'the only time I get the job is when he is in trouble'. If you delegate in advance, you have got more time for planning and development. Prepare before you have to.

- *Delegate for specific results*. It can help here to differentiate between the words 'accountability' and 'responsibility'. In the process of delegation responsibility is the scope of a job – what must be done to carry out the tasks that the job involves. Accountability is the results which must be achieved within the scope of the job. Delegate on the basis of accountability.

- *Avoid gaps and overlaps*. Make sure that only one person or group is accountable for performance in one particular area and make sure that they know that. Where accountability gaps or overlaps occur, delegation can fail because either it 'was not my job' or 'it was the other person's job'.

- *Communicate constantly*, unless the delegatee knows what is required delegation is unlikely to be successful. This involves issuing communication skills to give the delegatee a clear picture of the limits of the assignments, results expected, time limits involved and the method of reporting on the progress of the task assigned. This communication should go on throughout the delegated process.

The more perceived influence over the task that the delegatee has, the more likely he or she is to be motivated to carry the task through, and the more satisfaction will be found in its completion.

USEFUL BEHAVIOUR DURING THE DELEGATION

- *Delegate the whole of a task to one person or to one team.* This makes one person or team specifically accountable and minimises the likelihood of confusion and mistakes. It also gives a clear and positive trust message to the staff involved.

- *Define responsibilities and targets clearly.* Tell people what you expect from them, it saves a lot of trouble later on.

- *Be consistent.* Delegation should be carried out consistently. Unless you intend to carry the delegation through, it is best not to start. Delegating sporadically, or revoking a delegation for no good reason, will cause confusion and threaten the delegatory relationship.

- *Give support* Support when the delegatee is right contributes to the trust relationship. It will also help the delegatee to manage the delegation if he or she runs into problems with other staff or customers.

USEFUL BEHAVIOUR AFTER THE DELEGATION

- *Delegate credit, not blame.* One of the most difficult parts of the delegation process is the issue of credit and blame. If a delegated task is completed successfully, the delegatee and not the delegator should, and will, be given the credit. When a delegated task fails, the delegator and not the delegatee should accept the blame.

- *Delegation involves responsibility without power* and as such needs mutual trust within the contexts of a good working relationship. Delegators who try to claim credit or apportion blame to where it is not due will not be able to preserve a good working relationship.

- *Review results, not methods.* A common belief is that there is 'one best way' to complete a task. Delegating the task means accepting different methods for task completion. The important question is whether or not the task results have been achieved, not the manner in which they have been achieved. Attempts to influence approach will lead to overcontrolling and give poor trust messages. Once the delegation has been made, the person should be left to carry out the task within the controls you have put in place. He or she should be free of anything but carefully tailored support.

Finally, there are *some tasks which should never be delegated*. These include problems in relationships with staff who report directly to you – appraisal, reward, discipline, counselling and coaching are best done by you if you want to maintain an effective relationship with the employee in question, and with other employees who might see and interpret the issues themselves.

We have already seen the need to know the compatibility and capacity of the delegatee and to match this to the task. We have also seen the need to develop by delegating varied tasks which stretch the individual. Taking on this role is the equivalent of making an offer to contract with the delegatee. The other element of the contract is the role of the delegatee.

□   □   □

'But how can I check out whether the other person is prepared or able to contract,' said Sally.

'There are some behaviours which you can look for both before and during the delegation', said Josh.

'But surely, by the time the delegation is going on, it is going to be too late?'

'Hey, Sally, managing is about taking risks. If you cannot take risks, you should think about your position as a manager.'

'All right,' said Sally reluctantly. 'What are these behaviours?'

□   □   □

BEHAVIOURS TO LOOK FOR IN THE DELEGATEE

It can be useful to think of the delegation contract as being a customer–supplier relationship. The behaviours which we saw above constitute an offer to tender. Relationships aren't one-way processes and as such there are some things which you can expect in your 'suppliers':

Initiative

The delegatee needs to agree to take the initiative. People who take the initiative are generally easy to spot. Delegation is not a one-way process.

Suggestions

The first thing you can expect is that the person delegated will take responsibility for recommending the job results rather than having them defined. In our customer- supplier metaphor, this would be the equivalent of walking into a garage and telling the mechanic that you have a problem with your car.

We expect the mechanic to ask us what the problem is and not to wait for us to tell him or her what it is. We also don't expect to have to explain why the problem has occurred. The mechanic is an expert, we're not. When delegating, the delegatee is the expert.

Openness and trust

The second thing that you can expect is an adequate level of openness and trust with the delegatee. Relationships are risk-taking processes. If your openness and trust don't seem to be reciprocated, don't delegate to that person.

Disagreement

A 'good' delegatee will feel able to disagree with the delegator about the realistic nature of the goals, and whether they fit in with the personal objectives of the person delegated. As we saw in Chapter 11 on motivation, motivating people is about ensuring a degree of fit between personal objectives and organisational objectives. Effective delegation includes the same thing.

Self-development

The effective delegatee should be actively looking for opportunities to develop him or herself as well as actively seeking new assignments. Where an employee or colleague is looking for training or new developmental activity, he or she is likely to be an effective delegatee.

Carrying out the delegation

The final sign of an effective delegatee is one who has completed delegation adequately in the past. 'Completed' means precisely what it says. In the delegation contract, we have seen that there is a tendency for the delegator to interfere in the task when it is half-finished or stand at the shoulder of the delegatee. Equally, there is a tendency, particularly when the delegated task is problematic, for the delegatee to turn to the delegator at every stage to check. It is much easier for the delegatee to ask for answers from the delegator. This must be discouraged. Unless the delegatee is prepared to take on the whole task and provide answers for the delegator, the contract is flawed and your delegation will cost you more than you can perhaps afford to 'pay'.

What stops you in the delegation process?

We've looked so far in this chapter at how to define delegation, why we should delegate and what sort of skills are likely to be useful in developing the delegation contract. None the less, your approach to delegation will be dictated by a number of factors – need for power, need for achievement, interest and emotion. The emotions which a delegator feels will impact upon the delegation process.

Let's take a snapshot of the sort of feelings which a delegator may have about the delegation process.

- *Guilt* The person delegated might already be snowed under with work. You may feel guilty about giving even more. Delegation, however, isn't only something that managers do to employees. The delegatee can also learn to delegate and if the delegation is properly carried out within the framework of an open, supportive relationship, he or she can refuse.

- *Fear* Fear is a powerful feedback. It's so powerful that we immediately shy away from its implications. 'I could lose the whole order, then I couldn't meet my loan repayment, then I'll be forced to cease trading and I'll be unemployed and my girlfriend will leave me or my children will starve.' If your delegation is realistic and you've adapted the controls, your fears may be unrealistic. Consider your fears in context and if they are realistic, do the task yourself.

- *Envy* This is one reason which many people don't acknowledge. We've seen that delegation is about giving up power. It's also about giving up praise whilst retaining responsibility. The key questions here are whether or not the delegatee might do the job better, and if they get the praise from it, how the delegator feels. Delegation seems at one level to make a delegator unnecessary and this produces envy and uncertainty. If you're envious, consider the costs of not delegating.

- *Anxiety* Uncertainty is about loss of control. It is closely connected with anxiety. Research in the 1950s shows that a degree of uncertainty or anxiety tends to create a 'vigilant' problem-solving attitude, which actively searches for information in order to reduce anxiety. A higher degree of anxiety will lead to 'hypervigilant' behaviour, which gathers information in a sporadic manner and which merely adds to the uncertainty of the problem-solver. This block can be overcome by knowing your people and putting adequate controls in place.

- *Distrust* Distrust is a chronic form of anxiety which is directed at other people. Because we've been 'burnt' in the past, we'll not trust people again. If you don't trust the people with whom you're working, you're unlikely to achieve much anyway. Trust is about the nature of the relationship between the people that you manage and yourself. Work at building that relationship.

- *Conflict* Delegation is also about mediating between the demands of the task and the capacity of the delegate. Sudden changes in the demands of the task need to be negotiated into revised objectives. Where openness and trust exist, conflict can be managed into negotiation and into new work targets.

All of the above are likely to have undesirable effects upon the nature of the relationship between the delegator and the delegatee. Open, honest relationships which facilitate the delegation can be encouraged by effective communication, as we saw in Chapter 3. It can also help to recognise and acknowledge the feelings you may have about delegating or about the relationship. Whilst delegation is the core of managerial activity, you will only delegate effectively within the context of a good relationship if you feel happy delegating.

The job contract

The final section of this chapter looks at delegation in the context of the overall job contract. We have seen how we can develop formal job contract as a reflection of the relationship between the employee and the organisation. We've looked at the setting of objectives and accountabilities within the job contract and also the ways in which these can be monitored. Incorporating delegation into the job involves deciding and agreeing delegated authority levels before writing these into the job contract.

An aid to developing authority levels can be found in a method of structuring delegation developed in the United States in the 1970s. This structured approach to delegation is called MBE, or management by exception. MBE is a process whereby the whole task is given to a subordinate and zone parameters are set as in Fig.12.1.

The steps for delegating through MBE are:

1. The manager determines beforehand the types of condition or performance which will require his or her attention and those which will not. In effect, the manager says, 'As long as things are running according to plan, don't bother me. But, if they exceed or fall below such-and-such a limit, let me know, and I'll take over.'

2. Surveillance is maintained over the activity or process, either by personal observation or through an agreed reporting system. If the reporting system is a financial one, a variance reporting mechanism will be required, e.g. 'If turnover falls below £6,000 a week, I need to know'.

3. As long as performance is within the agreed limits, the manager should pay no further attention to the activity. As soon as performance falls outside the agreed standards, the manager can take corrective action.

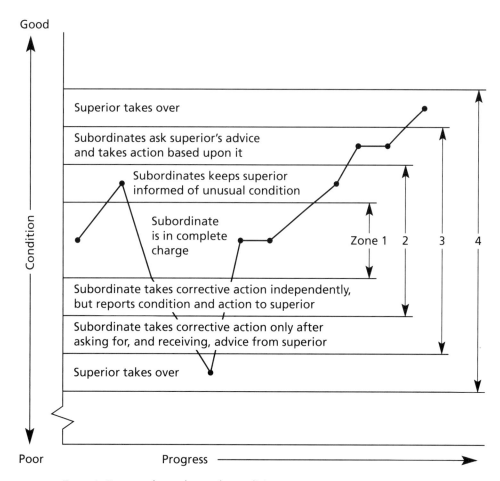

Zone 1: Expected, or planned, conditions
Zone 2: Unusual, but acceptable, conditions
Zone 3: Undesirable conditions
Zone 4: Vitally disturbed, or unacceptable, conditions

Fig. 12.1 Management by exception

Once you've decided your delegated authority levels you can then incorporate them into the job contract, as follows.

RESPONSIBILITY LEVELS

- The jobholder will have discretion over budgets of up to £500 per week providing cash returns are completed weekly.

- The jobholder will manage the sales force whilst sales are rising at a minimum of 1 per cent per month or as long as sales do not drop by more than 2 per cent per month, allowing for seasonal fluctuations.

- The job holder will carry out staff training, providing proper evaluation systems have been linked to the organisation's strategic objectives, to an agreed budget of 1 per cent of departmental turnover.

- The jobholder will be solely responsible for business development for all customers within his or her geographical area whose turnover is less than £800,000 p.a. He or she will be jointly responsible with the sales director on all businesses with a turnover between £800,000 and £5m.

Checklist for delegation

1. I can identify my own attitude towards delegation and manage myself when delegating.

2. I can perceive the need for effective and comfortable delegation.

3. I can identify my own role as delegator and use a range of behaviours to transmit that role.

4. I can identify the behaviours which are likely to indicate a good delegatee.

5. I can adopt controls within the delegation process

6. I am comfortable delegating.

7. I can control the delegation.

Delegation completes the performance cycle as it relates to the manager's relationship with individual employees. Within the workplace, however, the employee has relationships with other employees. These can often outweigh the relationship between the manager and employee and the manager must often intervene in these relationships to ensure that he or she is managing for performance. This is where team management comes into its own.

Summary

- *Most managers feel that they delegate effectively, although many may not be happy delegating.*

- *Ineffective delegation impacts on the work-load and management style of a manager, and vice versa. There are a number of signs which may indicate ineffective delegation. These signs are caused by problems in one of three areas: the nature of role; the relationship between the delegator and delegatee; and the amount and type of control in the relationship.*

- *Effective delegation follows a number of rules which concern the context and relationship within the process of delegation.*

- *This process can be considered as a contractual relationship, which involves risk and exchange between the roles of the delegator and the delegatee.*

- *A number of behaviours in both of these roles are essential for fair exchange.*

- *The core issues with regard to the process of delegation can be incorporated into the job contract.*

13 TEAM BUILDING

Coming together is a beginning; keeping together is progress; working together is success.

HENRY FORD

Previous chapters have dealt with the manager's relationship with his or her employees. As we mentioned in the last chapter, however, employees do not merely have a relationship with their manager. They also have a relationship with each other, which can in some ways far outweigh the relationship with the manager.

There is no one particular path which will guarantee that your employees will work together. There are a number of methods or approaches which will help you intervene in employee relationships. Team building is about using a range of approaches and techniques to build relationships amongst employees. Effectively, it is about relationship building for other people.

The objectives of this chapter are:

► *to look at some of the advantages of team building;*

► *to look at some theories which underpin the way groups function;*

► *to look at the drawbacks of team building;*

► *to develop ways of building teams based on the experience of a successful team.*

THERE are a number of steps which can help you to develop teams within your own organisation. These involve:

- understanding the purposes that team working fulfils;
- understanding some of the processes involved in developing relationships in groups;
- understanding the nature of role relationships and communication in groups;
- using communication to develop relationships and define roles;
- understanding the drawbacks of team working.

☐   ☐   ☐

The situation at Norham Road had really improved out of all recognition, thought Sally, since they'd brought the new supervisors in and tied in appraisal, pay and the big production charts. Since she'd been delegating according to Josh's checklist, she'd also found she'd had more time, but she'd resisted the urge to go down to check. It still felt risky, but results were paying off.

The only problem was that there seemed to be a lot of bickering amongst staff about the production targets and the bonuses which had been negotiated. None of it seemed to be directed at management, but Maggie had had to send two girls home for having a slanging match in the canteen on Wednesday.

Dave had been down and although he'd been full of praise about the way production was climbing, he'd made an off-the-cuff remark about people running to teacher. She'd asked him to explain and he'd said that it had been like a playground down there, with everybody stabbing everybody else in the back and then running to one of the supervisors for approval.

She'd rung Josh and he'd said that it sounded as though relationships with the supervisors were strong, but that relationships between staff were breaking down.

'Of course, Sal,' he'd said, 'some people like it that way, lots of managers think that keeping people at each other's throats will make them safe and more able to manage effectively. "Divide and rule" is their motto. I think it diverts a lot of time and effort from organisational goals.'

'Production is still up', Sally said.

'Oh yes,' Josh replied, 'but there's always room for improvement.'

'But why teams?', Sally asked.

☐   ☐   ☐

Why teams?

Human beings are social animals. They live and work in communities of people. Upbringing is in small groups – family, classrooms, gangs – and people learn early to be comfortable in small groups. This helps them to develop commitment to a team, which they might not have to a large organisation.

This social cohesion gives us strength. Most tasks are beyond individual human beings. Growth and development comes through interaction within groups, as does the completion of any major task. Groups also offer continuity. A group can continue work on a task when individuals leave or take a break.

This cohesion and continuity mean that well organised groups – teams – can improve productivity in the organisations in which they work by between 8 and 11 per cent. Teams can give 'more bang for your buck'. Teams can also contribute to the improvement of working climate, because of the improved relationships which they should engender between employees.

It is important, however, to look at what team working involves, before you consider implementing team building within an organisation.

WHAT IS YOUR TEAM FOR?

It is important to know *why* you are organising for team working or building a team before you begin. Team building has been one of the many popular 'fads' in management practice, and consequently people may adopt the idea of team building as a good one in all cases. Management fads are like the hula hoop or the skateboard. They pass in time and can do more harm than good. Where team working is inappropriate, it can do more harm than good.

There are a number of considerations with regard to whether relationship building amongst employees is appropriate or necessary. These can be offered in the form of indicators.

- The first thing that will indicate whether teams are appropriate is the nature of the work itself. Teams tend to perform better when they are involved in carrying out tasks which have clear short or medium range objectives. Where the work can't be broken down in this way, teams can be destructive.

- The second indicator for team performance is the nature of the work environment and the management style, which is accepted. A 'strong' management style, where the team leader needs to *tell* people or where the leader is very influential, may not assist in team development. Leadership in a small group may have very different characteristics to the generally accepted model of what a leader or manager does. If you are unhappy to relinquish power to a group in the fashion that we've looked at in Chapters 11 and 12 on motivation, and delegation team building may be inappropriate.

- The third indicator is the individuals who make up the team and the way in which they communicate. Teams do not need to be made up of similar individuals and diversity can be an advantage in developing high-performance teams. Where the work requires little communication between employees, there is little reason to develop teams.

- The final indicator is the nature of the environment. In an organisation which is structured by departments or where individuals concentrate on individual tasks with little relation between employees, it may be inappropriate to consider team building.

There have been many explanations of the processes which take place in teams, and before we look at actually putting teams into action, we can examine these theoretical bases to try to obtain a picture of the way teams work.

WHAT SORT OF PROCESSES ARE INVOLVED?

One of the more influential methods of looking at the way in which teams 'work' involves the type of people who make up the team. These 'types' or informal roles have been classified and scales developed to identify them. One of the most popular of these was developed by Meredith Belbin,[1] who identified a number of 'traits' or characteristics in each potential team member, as follows:

- high intelligence *v.* low intelligence
- high dominance *v.* low dominance
- extroversion *v.* introversion
- stability *v.* anxiety

These traits combined with a number of secondary measures, determine team 'type' or role. Belbin identifies eight types or roles as being appropriate or useful in team work

Team types

Chairman   Focuses on objectives; establishes the work roles and boundaries for other team members. Shows concern to use human resources effectively. Clarifies and sets agendas. Summarises and makes decisions when necessary – a good listener and communicator.

Shaper   High nervous energy. Full of enthusiasm and drive. Continually looking for opportunities for action from ideas. Heavily involved in team's action and successes. The task leader of the group.

Plant   The creative ideas person; tends to bring new insight and imagination to the group. Concerned with basics, not details. Tends to criticise. May withdraw if ideas are rejected.

[1] R. Meredith Belbin, *Management Teams – Why They Suceed or Fail*, Heinemann, 1981.

Monitor Evaluator	Objective and serious. Concerned with idea analysis rather than idea generation. May lack motivation, but skilled in analysis and decision-making.
Company Worker	The practical organiser. Concerned with order and feasibility. Methodical, efficient and systematic. Does not respond well to innovation or lack of structure. Pragmatically focused; may be inflexible, but responds to direction.
Resource Investigator	Friendly and sociable; enthusiastic and positive. The member who goes outside the team to explore and obtain new ideas and information. Enthusiasm may fade quickly; tends to be stimulated by others.
Team Worker	Sensitive, aware of feelings and emotions in the group. Tends to weld the team together. A popular and supportive member; uncompetitive and dislikes friction. A good listener and communicator.
Completer Finisher	Concerned with details and order, tends to worry over possible mistakes; communicates a permanent sense of urgency. May get bogged down in detail, losing sight of the main objective.

For Belbin, a balanced team needed to be made up of a full range of these roles and a missing role, or more than one person within the team occupying the same role, would weaken the team.

This approach involves managing relationships within the group by selecting compatible people, or people who occupy compatible roles. Whilst some research has shown this approach to be effective, roles are unstable. They will change, depending on the nature of the task and the environment. People can be shapers in one area and monitor evaluators in other areas.

ASSESSMENT EXERCISE

Whilst roles shift, we may find that we have 'preferred' roles. What role do you feel that you occupy in Belbin's typology? What role might you wish to occupy? If you work in a group, what roles do others fulfil? Consider how your role might change in different circumstances and how you might develop new skills to fit new roles.

We can see role-based approaches to team building as involving selection and matching people so that their relationships 'fit' from the outset. This can be seen as a 'true love' approach to team building, which interprets the answer as finding the perfect partners.

Given that selection is important, relationships still need to be worked at: 'true love' may end in 'divorce', with catastrophic results for the work group. The next approach which we'll consider is the work that can be carried out to maintain the relationship within the group. In the chapter on motivation we looked at some of the preventive maintenance that a manager can carry out to link reward and performance. This approach also looks at maintenance.

Task and maintenance

Douglas MacGregor carried out research into the characteristics of effective and ineffective teams by looking at the way in which they worked. He found that in order to create effective work groups, a number of different criteria need to be met. Broadly, these can be split into two types: the first of these he called 'content', and the second 'process.'

1. *Content* is essentially concerned with 'what' the team are doing – nature of task, needs for particular skills or information. When considering content issues for your team, it can also help to consider how these might impact on the team's motivation.

2. *Process* needs are concerned with 'how' the group work together as a group. Process skills can be further divided into task and maintenance activities.

Task process activities are concerned with the way in which the group focuses on task and may include activities such as:

- *initiating* putting ideas forward or starting new activities;
- *asking* collecting information or views;
- *giving* volunteering information and ideas, making suggestions;
- *clarifying* helping interpret, asking for explanations;
- *summarising* bringing ideas together;
- *testing for agreement* checking on the readiness of the team to take action.

Maintenance process activities are involved with the way in which a team 'holds together' in its work and may include such activities:

- *harmonising or smoothing* bringing others together, exploring and reconciling disagreements;
- *gatekeeping* bringing everyone into the activity, allowing everyone to participate;

CHARACTERISTICS OF EFFECTIVE TEAMS	CHARACTERISTICS OF INEFFECTIVE TEAMS
Underlining goals	
Task or objective of the group is clearly understood and accepted by members.	It is difficult to understand from what is said exactly what the group task is, or what the groups objectives are.
Member contributions	
There is a lot of discussion in which everyone participates but it remains pertinent to the group task.	A few people tend to dominate the discussion. Often their contributions are way off the point.
Listening	
Members listen to each other. Every idea is given a hearing.	People do not really listen to one another. Ideas are ignored and over ridden.
Conflict resolution	
There is disagreement. The group is comfortable with this, and shows no signs of having to avoid conflict or keep everything sweetness and light.	Disagreements are not dealt with effectively by the group. They may be suppressed by the leader, avoided or buried.
Decision making	
Most decisions are reached by a type of consensus which make it clear that members are in general agreement and/or willing to go along	Actions are taken prematurely before the real issues are either examined or resolved.
Leadership	
The group leader does not dominate it, nor do group members defer unduly to him or her.	Leadership is clearly in the hands of the group leader. This may be strong or weak but the leader always 'sits at the head of the table'.
Self evaluation	
The group is conscious of its own operation. It will frequently stop to evaluate progress or what is interfering with task process.	The group tends to avoid discussion on its own 'maintenance'.
Organisation of task	
When action is taken clear assignments are made and accepted.	Action decisions tend to be unclear. No-one knows who is supposed to do what.

Fig. 13.1 Characteristics of effective and ineffective teams

- *encouraging* agreeing, building, supporting;
- *listening* showing understanding;
- *standard setting* surfacing feelings and beliefs, bringing things out into the open.

Each of the above is a way of acting in a group. Groups and teams with a balance of task orientation and process orientation will tend to be 'successful' both in completing their tasks and in maintaining their environment; that is to say, they will be both productive and happy in their work. McGregor identified what he termed 'effective' and 'ineffective' characteristics of work teams by looking at some of these factors in actual performing teams (Fig. 13.1).

ASSESSMENT EXERCISE

How well do the groups with which you are involved rate on the above characteristics? How do these task 'teams' evaluate themselves? Are team members clear about objectives? Does one person tend to dominate the team and what effect does that have?

Examine your own and others' behaviour in the group. What behaviour do you display most of all? What types of behaviour do you find most difficult to deal with? How do you propose to develop your skills to bring more effective behaviour to the team?

MacGregor's characteristics of effective and ineffective teams depend upon the actions of the individual team members and the way in which they contribute to the communication and processing of information. In this model the group members can actively work to develop their relationships within the team.

Group dynamics

Another approach to the way in which teams work takes a more passive set of processes as its model. In this approach the group members are likely to pass through a number of stages, because of the information-processing needs and the communication issues in the group.

These stages can be represented as follows:

Forming

This stage is characterised by 'testing' behaviours such as greetings and welcomes. People check out the rules or 'norms' of the group and begin to plan unconsciously what roles they might take on and what the purpose of the group might be. This stage might also be referred to as preparation for negotiation.

Storming

This stage involves competition for role and purpose. This competition can be difficult to recognise, as it can be hidden as well as being open. At the storming stage, people might attack others within the group, withdraw, try to create alliances or dominate others.

Storming is a time when group members test the rules and boundaries which they've identified in the first stage and prepare for the next stage. This stage might also be called negotiation or conflict as people come to terms with each other's needs from the group.

Norming

The norming stage is one where the rules begin to be accepted. They 'harden' and people have dealt with, or contained, conflict. Group members here begin to take on responsibility for their roles and accept the group's collective purpose. Rules on norms are the accepted processes which guide the nature of the relationship.

Performing

This stage is where, internal issues having been dealt with, the group turns outwards to perform its task or meet its goals.

Mourning

Mourning is the stage when the group's internal or external purpose no longer exists. Internally, relationships are accepted and possibly static. Externally, the task may have been completed. Group members will tend to exclude themselves from the relationships and roles which they formerly held. Often there may be a reluctance to face the fact that the group is ending and it may be that one or more members will need to end the group on a positive and celebratory note.

TAKING STOCK

Consider the groups in which you may take part or manage. How does this staged model help you map the way they work? At what stage are these groups? Have they missed out any stages? What can you do to help the group work through these stages?

So far, we've looked at three approaches which might help you in working with groups. The first of these emphasises the informal roles within the group and managing relationships through selection. The second emphasises maintainence processes and the sort of behaviours which can help maintain the relationships within the group. The third emphasises the nature of the relationships within the group, but states that relationships need to pass through certain stages in order to work properly.

Let's look for a moment at what group process can mean in practice by looking at the work of high-performance teams in practice. A good example is that of the Eagle groups.

Looking at high-performance teams

There have been two Eagle teams. The first was a group of Special Force troops in the Second World War. This group outperformed any other Commando group by reacting and destroying apparently unreachable targets with the lightest of casualties possible.

A team of researchers was assigned to the group and they found that the reasons for its success was the fact that it could change its structure to meet different circumstances or environments. For instance, in the planning stage everyone would chip in with suggestions and information. There were no leaders during the planning stages and all suggestions were treated equally. This structure changed when the group went into action. At this time, the group adopted a formal, almost rigid structure, with every member having a clearly assigned and agreed responsibility which had to be carried out with strict timing and precision.

This ability to change its structure to fit the circumstances provided the best of both worlds. The participative structure in planning allowed all group members to contribute and thus increased the creativity of the group. The group in action took on a form where authority and roles had to be clear and communication was clearly defined.

The second Eagle group was a research group within Data General, the large American Computer group. This Eagle group created a new, 32 bit computer in record time, with fewer resources and less support than any other division in Data General.

Strangely enough, the group never received any special arrangements or extra resources. For a year the group members jeopardised their health, their families and their careers. Nor was the group guided to any particular 'shining vision'. The group leader Tom Watson observed that 'not everything worth doing is worth doing well' and the group seemed to feel that if it worked – even if it was quick and dirty – then they should use it. Group members seemed to be unusually confrontational and direct which, one presumes, helped push past communication barriers. One of the team, David Peck said to his engineer that he was an idiot. When ordered to apologise by his boss, Peck approached the engineer acting sheepishly and said, 'I'm sorry you're an idiot.'

Borland and Deal[2] identified a number of points about the development of effective teams from Kidders[3] book about Eagle Group. The first of these is that the way in which someone becomes a group member is important. The Eagle Group recruited in a way which elicited commitment from its workers. They put up barriers to entry, demonstrating how hard it was to get into the group, then they allowed the applicant in. This created a cohesiveness or sense of belonging to an elite group which engendered that elusive quality, 'team spirit'. We saw in Chapter 8 on recruitment and selection that whilst selection is a two-way information-gathering process, there may be a 'ritual' element. It is important to remember that the information-seeking process is as important as the ritual.

Example holds a group together better than command. If people in the team see the leaders operating or behaving in a particular way, they will tend to behave in that way also. This is a fairly basic psychological mechanism called 'behavioural modelling'. If, however, the leader is seen as directing rather than doing – not being congruent – the group will tend to ignore that person.

Diversity gives a team competitive advantage. We may want to surround ourselves with people who are 'just like us', but this will reduce the amount of creativity which we are likely to generate through conflict. As we saw in the last chapter, conflicts can have a useful function as well as a destructive one.

Specialised language tends to grow up easily amongst technical specialists, but it also comes about in other small groups, too. In the Eagle group a 'Kludge' was a mess, something to be avoided, a 'canard' was anything false. The teams within the project became 'the Hardy Boys' and 'The Microlads' and the prototype computers became Trixie and Woodstock. This sort of shared language binds a group together and is a visible sign of group membership. It also sets the group apart from outsiders and reinforces its identity as a group.

Stories within a group, about reputation or compatibility, reinforce the sense of group identity. Groups also tend to need some superordinate threat and or goal, that is, something outside the group to work for or to avoid. In the case of Eagle group, this superordinate threat was the senior executive team which they would mock and play practical jokes on. Their superordinate goal was to build the best 32 bit computer in the world.

A element is that of humour and play. Groups can focus singlehandedly on the task in hand, but in the longer term, effective teams working in high pressure environments tend to use joking and banter as a way of relieving tension and developing creativity. Borland and Deal give surgical teams and aeroplane cockpit crews as two examples.

[2]Lee Borland and Terence Deal, *Reframing Organisations*, Jossey Bass, 1990.
[3]Tom Kidder, *Soul of a New Machine*, Little Brown, 1981.

Use rituals in communication: the leaders of the Eagle Team met regularly, but their conversations were not limited to work. The group's official leader, Tom West, always made himself available at a particular time to anyone who wanted to talk to him. In addition to these rituals in communication, the two sub-teams within the Eagle group were very dependent upon each other and would hold 'ceremonies' every so often to provide praise and mockery for achievements and failures in the project. The team were given, and took, opportunities to celebrate their achievements.

The final ingredient is the way in which group members made contributions to the overall aims of the team. People were not put in 'boxes' with assigned roles. Instead, group members often made contributions well beyond what was expected. For instance, Rosemary Seale, the secretary, carried out far more than normal 'secretarial duties' because she felt that she was 'doing something important'.

In summary, the secret of Eagle group's success was the way in which it integrated all of the team frameworks into one in an informal 'culture,' which underpinned enjoyment and creativity The Eagle group became a team in the best sense of the world.

□ □ □

Josh shifted in his seat. 'Of course, this is the upside of team building,' he said. 'There is a downside as well.'

Sal stared at him. 'Eagle Group sounds like a nice place to live'.

'Yes,' said Josh, 'but you need to be careful. Remember to question all of your assumptions. Just because somebody like me comes to sell you a team building course or a residential weekend does not mean that you should buy it. Over the last few years we have seen a whole industry grow out of team building. Mostly it borrows examples from large manufacturers and bleats "team build good – departments bad" to prove that teams improve productivity.'

'Well, don't they?', asked Sally

'Yes, they do – in some large manufacturing and service companies – but at Norham Road you have got a series of specialised teams which are aimed at a particular product area. Let's look at what can happen.'

□ □ □

WHAT CAN GO WRONG?

Groups in organisations can take many different forms – project teams, production teams, committees, quality circles, statistical process control teams, working groups, to name only a few. Whatever they are called, they often frustrate and confuse their members. One of the oldest jokes about groups is that a camel is a horse designed by a committee.

Organisations large and small are full of people who hate working in groups because groups are invariably confused, frustrating and inefficient. They are also threatening and stressful or at least potentially so.

This attitude is common in small organisations, where much of the achievement has been directly linked to the effort of one person. Small organisations can reflect this 'single person' culture. Certainly this is what has happened at Presteign, which is more of a conglomeration of single-person small businesses than an organisation.

Yet, as we have seen, groups have obvious advantages over individuals. They are more diverse, have greater knowledge and more time and energy. Groups can be a good way of improving communication. Nevertheless, groups can over-respond to social pressures or individual domination, and personal goals can frustrate group purposes. As well as being productive, inducing commitment, developing people and creating excitement, groups can create stagnation, imprison people, induce conformity and leave people feeling frustrated, worthless and unproductive.

This section offers a way of looking at groups which uses a particular framework to identify central issues in group process. Where task issues will concern themselves with formal roles, formal processes, timetables and resources, relationship issues will concern themselves with informal roles, informal processes, agendas and conflict.

ROLES

A role is a position defined within a group that is defined by expectations and needs. The person who occupies a particular role is expected to behave in ways that reflect the role and also because they need to behave in that way.

For instance, a manager will be expected to tell people what to do, be confident and take the initiative. Staff are supposed to obey the rules, work hard and support the manager. Politicians are expected to promise that things will get better if they are elected, and voters are expected to respond sceptically but vote anyway. Roles in an organisation can be defined by titles and job descriptions, for instance the 'Head of the Packing Department' will create certain expectations about appearance, behaviour, etc.

In teams, the roles can be much more informal. Every small group (which meets for a length of time) will have a network of informal roles. This informal network will have a strong, subtle and pervasive influence on the team. We have already seen that the personal characteristics of team members will affect the nature of the task. Different people have different skills and needs that they will bring to the task. Groups will, as we have seen, do better when they structure themselves to take into account differences in skill and preference among team members.

In addition to the roles which are negotiated or imposed because of task needs, there are other sets of roles relating to personal needs which are quite unconnected with the task. Consider the packing department of Presteign. The staff group consists of Neil, Karen, Sally and five packing staff: Anne, Doris, Kirsty, Sandy and Michelle. For these purposes, there are two groups in the packing team: a management group and a staff group. In the management group, for example, Sally may only feel comfortable when she is feeling influential; Neil may only want a quiet life and Karen may find it hard to take part in the group's tasks unless she feels needed. As the group meets, members will send signals to each other about the roles that they want. These signals are often unnoticed as signals by the group members, but their message is taken on board. Sally will jump in and take the initiative, Neil only speaks when spoken to and Karen smiles and expresses the hope that everything will go well.

As long as these informal personal roles are well matched, the team will get along well. But let's presume that another member joins the team. Let's call him Terry. Terry always likes to be in charge and he and Sally will come into conflict. This will have a spin-off effect on the team and people may take sides, with the conflict becoming widespread and ultimately affecting the team's productivity.

Few teams have an unlimited amount of resources or an unlimited number of compatible individuals. They have areas of both compatibility and conflict. Many teams never address the role issues which need attention. Some teams see them, but refuse to talk about them for fear of offending others. We saw in Chapter 3, the difference between constructive and disruptive conflict. Avoiding such issues can mean that they reawaken, particularly when the group is under pressure.

Potential conflict of this sort should be surfaced and dealt with.

INFORMAL GROUP PROCESSES

The second issue which can lead to poor team performance is that of the rules or norms which govern the processes within groups. Each team – as with the Eagle group – will develop its own 'rules' about how they do things. Often these rules can be so team-specific that they exclude other groups. The sense of cohesion that this gives the group can be very useful. It can also be problematic in that some teams will develop one, two or even three sub-groups.

Presteign's packing department management group and its staff group have thus separate sets of team rules about dress, approach to work and so forth. When these two sub-groups are to work together, they may not communicate sufficiently to perform adequately.

Remember that just because a 'team' is called a team does not mean that it has to be a team. Watch out for the real team within teams; these will be defined by norms of dress, sense of humour, language and one hundred and one other things.

HIDDEN AGENDAS

A hidden agenda is an objective which the individual may not reveal to his or her team mates. If everyone in a team has a hidden agenda, then the confusion and opportunities for conflict will increase dramatically.

In our management packing team, for instance, Sally may be out to make a name for herself with fellow directors, Neil may want to make life easy for the staff and Karen may be looking for another job. These hidden agendas will all impact on the team performance and can destroy performance capacity altogether.

CONFLICTS

We have looked at the uses and problems of conflict in Chapter 4. Potential conflict underlies all group processes. If Sally and Terry fail to agree about their respective roles, or if Sally and Neil fail to negotiate about their respective agendas, or if Neil thinks that Karen is going off looking for other jobs, this conflict can become real, with a resulting series of problems and loss of productivity.

We have seen in Chapter 4, some strategies for dealing with conflict in one-to-one situations. In group conflicts there are a number of simple guidelines to help deal with conflict. Teams need to:

1. *Agree on the basics*   That is, identify their own rules or norms and roles; only if all members are equally comfortable with both the informal rules and roles will the teams develop commitment. Remember also that formal titles and processes will impact upon informal roles and rules.

2. *Agree on the common ground*   A team will need to continue to search for, and identify, issues in common. Emphasising common issues will tend to shift attention away from hidden agendas and towards a common purpose. Common purpose should not be confused with common attitude. As we have seen, one of a team's major strengths is its diversity.

3. *Experiment*   Where conflict is intractable, it is best to try out new solutions. In the example of the packing team, Terry and Sally both wanted to lead the group. The team could experiment with one leader one week, another leader the second week, and perhaps no leader at all for the third week. Experimentation is a powerful tool for obtaining more information where conflict is intractable. It gives the information upon which the group can make a decision to resolve the conflict.

4. *Doubt their own infallibility*   There can be times when a team can turn into five leaders in search of a follower. When this happens, it can help if one of the group at least asks, 'What is going on here? Are we sure we are right?'

5. *Treat differences as a group responsibility*   In the event of conflict between Sally and Terry, it will be a temptation for the other group members

to step aside and avoid the conflict. As we have already seen, though, a group is like a car: if it careers off the road, all its constituent parts will suffer. It is the responsibility of all the group to resolve differences. Even if an issue seems to be entirely personal, it will spill over into the group's ability to work effectively.

☐   ☐   ☐

'So,' said Josh, 'you can see that groups or teams are both satisfying and awkward – even dangerous places to live. If you get it right, you will increase productivity between 7 and 11 per cent, without any added resources. If you get it wrong, you might cut productivity by the same amount.'

☐   ☐   ☐

ASSESSMENT

We've looked above at another approach which attempts to consider the nature of roles which we saw in Belbin, typology and the nature of relationships which we saw in MacGregor and the 'forming storming' model.

Consider the following exercise to analyse the functioning of a group in which you might have taken part recently.

1. **Task Role**
    (a) How was the task identified?
    (b) Who planned for the task?
    (c) Was a leader identified?
    (d) How did this happen?

2. **Process Role**
    (a) Who suggested, brought in new ideas?
    (b) Who mediated?
    (c) How was conflict dealt with?
    (d) Who was involved and who was excluded?

3. **Relationships**
    (a) Did everyone know what was going on and what was expected of them?
    (b) How were sub-tasks delegated?
    (c) How did personalities 'fit' together?
    (d) What processes contributed to the continuance of relationships?

4. **Communication**
    (a) How did the team communicate?
    (b) Was communication two-way or one-way?
    (c) How was negotiation carried out?
    (d) Was communication task-oriented or process-oriented?

List four main strengths that you feel your approach to the task demonstrated:

1 _____   3 _____

2 _____   4 _____

List three major weaknesses

1 _____

2 _____

3 _____

Using the above categories, write out an action plan as to how you would carry out a similar set of tasks again.

_____

We can see that within a team there are a number of crucial issues, each of which impacts upon others. Roles impact upon relationships, which impact upon communication, negotiation and dealing with conflict, which in turn again impacts on roles.

We saw in the work of the first Eagle group that flexibility in all of these is important to teams, but that the flexibility needs to be channelled and focused and may need to become rigid to carry out the task. We saw in the second Eagle group that there are certain 'rules' which will help foster team performance and developments.

Let's look at two practical tools which can underpin team development. The first of these is a way of looking at communication processes and will involve the sort of skills we saw in Chapter 3.

Developing a small task group involves using a wide range of communicating behaviours. One way of looking at this is the TORI model developed by J William Pfeiffer[4]. This involves four factors, each of which is a function of communication.

1. *Trust* confidence in other team members' ability and attitude. *Key questions*: Do the other team members do what they say they are going to? Can you believe in them? This factor reflects the idea of congruence that we saw in Chapter 3.

2. *Openness* the free flow of information, ideas, perceptions and feelings. *Key questions*: do we share information about the task? Do we share information about our own feelings? This factor involves self-disclosure.

3. *Realisation* self-determination, role freedom. *Key questions*: What choice do I have in this group or task? How much freedom do I have to develop?

[4] J. William Pfeiffer, *A Handbook of Structured Experiences*, University Associates, 1985.

This factor impacts upon the nature of the relationship in which the communication takes place.

4. **Interdependence** shared responsibility, reciprocal influence. **Key questions**: How much does my job depend on others in the team? How much do others depend on me? This factor also impacts upon the nature of the relationships.

You can use these four factors to build your own team within the vision you have developed and shared. Trust will come about when you yourself demonstrate your own trustworthiness and trust others. Openness will develop as you share information and feelings in a positive way. Realisation is about the amount of choice which you give to other team members and interdependence is about a shared vision of a common future.

Another way of considering the process of team communication involves the channels through which communication takes place. Whilst the TORI model assumes that everyone can 'talk' to each other, this may not be so. In the diagram below, we can see five methods in which a team can communicate information.

We need to devise a communication structure which meets the needs of the task. Remember that a one-boss structure will involve the boss in dealing with lots of issues with the concurrent expenditure of his or her time. Where tasks are complex and open to interpretation, this load can be too heavy.

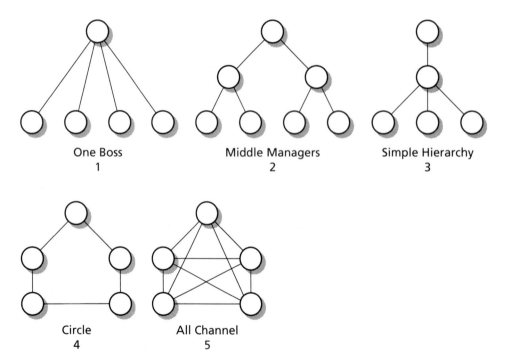

Fig. 13.2 Team communcation

A second way of looking at the communication process would be to introduce 'middle managers' who would filter the information to and from the boss. This could reduce the load on the boss (although it may not), but it will also increase the amount of time it takes to get things done. Team performance could be dependent upon the skills of your 'middle managers'.

A third option is to put one 'manager' between the boss and the rest of the team. This design tends to be more efficient than the previous one, but fewer team members will have access to the team leader and the power invested in the one manager may be considerable, leading to confusion about who is 'boss'.

A fourth option is to pass information sequentially around the network. This has advantages in that it involves all team members, but again, information passage is slow. In fast-moving business situations, this may not be helpful.

A final option is to consider a 'star' or all channel network which allows each member to talk to everyone else. This design is useful where tasks are complicated and ambiguous, but bears the risk that people may get left out of the information loop. If your team members are good at communication, enjoy participation, can tolerate uncertainty and do not have too many conflicts, this may be the model to use.

RESPONSIBILITY CHARTING

We saw that in the Eagle commando group, roles were flexible until the mission was actually carried out. Responsibility charting is a way of formally structuring roles so that no time needs to be lost negotiating or 'storming'. Similarly, as sports teams which have to function in uncertain situations have clear responsibilities and communication channels: the members of a soccer team will have clear roles and responsibilities and communication rules are clearly designed. This is not to say that before the match, the team would not be free to suggest strategies or change positions in a 'kickaround'. Responsibility charting assigns:

R Responsibility given to an individual in a group and outlines how that person will relate to others.

A Do some people in the team need to have their actions approved?

C Are there individuals who need to be consulted?

I Are there people whom the responsible persons need to keep informed?

ROLES

In looking at a team of four people within a retail clothing shop – Jill, Jean, Joanne and Sam, we have come up with the following:

Tasks	Sam Assistant	Jill Display	Jean Display	Joanne Manager
Display		R	R	
Stock order	C	R	I	I
Customer complaints				
Cleaning stock	C	C	A	R
Checking	C	C	R	I
Sales	R	R	R	R

Once you have sorted out roles and communication patterns within the teams that you manage, you will have a foundation for performance. Remember, though, that team building involves building the power of relationships within the team. As relationships become more powerful within the team, you should expect to lose some of the power of your relationships. Relationships will become more 'equal'. If you find this difficult to accept and need a special relationship, then you should not consider team building. Bear in mind, though, the penalties in time and effort resource which this is likely to involve.

It may help you to consider your own attitudes to teams by completing the following exercises.

HOW DO I FEEL ABOUT TEAMS

The style and tenor of a group's approach to problems, and of its internal processes, can often usefully be related by the use of a slogan or an aphorism, such as 'We work hard and play hard', 'We're good losers', 'We enjoy chatting.'

Usually there are also hidden, inadmissible slogans which may provide a bitter face to the group. These have been likened to T-shirt messages with the overt message printed on the front and the twist on the back. (e.g. 'We share our work fairly' on the front and 'except for the nasty jobs' on the back). Further, individuals may carry messages on vests underneath the T-shirt (e.g. 'And I do as little as I can').

Can you identify these messages for your group and its members? Ask yourself what would be a good epitaph for your group. Perhaps 'They did a good job', 'They tried hard', 'They ran out of time'. Seeing what is written on the tombstone of your efforts can be a salutary experience!

In closing this chapter, it is important to remember that whilst the internal mechanisms of a team are important – roles, relationships, etc., so is a team relationship with its task. High performance teams will need tasks which are consonant with their abilities. As we've seen, teams tend to work more effectively when involved in finite, measurable projects, which involve the whole team and which they have the opportunity to complete.

Developing teams can be very useful. Teams tend to get things done. Team building is not, however, a partial process. Done properly, team building can release much of the energy locked within the organisation. A partial process of team building can either not release the energy, in which case you've wasted your own time and effort, or release it in ways which you find hard to control.

Teams need to expend the energy which is generated by bringing them together. If you don't have anything for the team to work at, it will waste that energy on backbiting and politics or on completing the wrong task.

Releasing the energy in relationships allows teams to perform much more effectively than groups.

Teams can produce	**Groups produce**
– total involvement	– partial involvement
– voluntary effort	– involuntary effort
– decisions	– recommendations
– a focus on success	– a focus on failure and problems
– and performance	– permanent structure and roles
– flexible structures and roles	– no change in managers
– changes in managers	

Checklist for teambuilding

1. I understand the reasons why teams can help productivity and the quality of working life.

2. I understand that team building should not be pursued for its own sake.

3. I can use a number of theories about team building to understand what goes on.

4. I can communicate effectively within a team.

5. I can identify and select roles within a team.

6. I can develop a task focus for a team.

7. I can identify some of the behaviours which will assist the processes of team building.

8. I can relinquish control to the team.

Summary

- *Team building is a technique which can be used for a number of purposes – to improve work performance, communication, etc.*

- *Essentially, it is a manager's tool for facilitating and developing relationships with his or her employees.*

- *There are a number of theories as to what makes teams work. These can be divided into three groups: process models, role models and models involving group dynamics. Most of these models rely on the manager enhancing communication between team members.*

- *There are drawbacks to team building which should be considered. Enhancing relationships between employees may mean that a manager can be pushed out, or his/her role changed.*

- *True teams are effectively self-managing. It is difficult, if not impossible, to employ the old role of manager or leader within a team. Responsibility and authority are shared amongst team members.*

- *In a 'true' team, the role of leader is likely to shift amongst members. Improved communication will mean that levels of skill and knowledge are high.*

- *It is possible to identify a number of rules for effective team development from practical sources.*

- *These are broadly as follows:*
  - *Recruitment processes are important in team development.*
  - *Diversity gives a team competitive advantage provided that communication is good and conflict is managed.*
  - *Example, rather than command, holds a team together.*
  - *Specialised language helps to develop cohesion and commitment.*
  - *Ceremonies reinforce values within a team.*
  - *Humour and play release tension and encourage creativity.*
  - *Informal roles within a team can be more important than formal roles.*

- *The underpinning of all team building involves roles, relationships and communication.*

- *Team building can unblock energy within your organisation but it is not a partial process.*

14 LEADERSHIP

'The ancients, who wished to manifest illustrious virtue
throughout the world, first ordered well their own states.
Wishing to regulate their own families, they first cultivated
their own selves . . .

'Their selves being cultivated, only then did their families
become regulated. Their families being regulated, only then
did their states become rightly governed. Their states being
rightly governed, only then could the world be at peace.'

TZENG TZU

This chapter has been written to help you integrate the skills and resources,
which we looked at earlier in the book, into a whole package. Leadership
involves you in communicating, setting objectives, learning, recruiting and
selecting, developing people, appraising, motivating and delegating, as well as
team building.

This book as a whole has talked about managing and managers. Some people
believe that managing and leadership are two different things. This may be true
in larger organisations, where managers are employed to maintain the status quo
and keep the organisation running smoothly. Small organisations face constant
changes in their environments. Innovative strengths, resource weaknesses,
market opportunities, competitive threats mean that the manager in a small
organisation has to cope with these constant changes. Coping with change is
one of the characteristics of leadership.

The objectives of this chapter are:

► *to define leadership in a small organisation;*

► *to integrate the skills and resources in the other chapters of the book.*

As the speed of information transferral and processing increases, larger organisations are also having to cope with change and leadership skills are becoming more important here, too.

So far we've looked at a manager's basic skills of information processsing, communication and self-management in a variety of settings – recruitment, appraisal, etc. This chapter expands these settings to look at five leadership roles.

- leaders as designers and builders;
- leaders as visionaries;
- leaders as catalysts and facilitators;
- leaders as co-ordinators and navigators;
- leaders as energisers.

Each of these is one of the roles which a leader will fulfil at some time in his or her career. Leadership may involve holding two or more of these roles simultaneously and each role will involve some of the skills which we've looked at so far.

Before we go on to consider these five roles, it may be useful to consider what leadership is and what other writers have had to say about leadership.

The concept of leadership

The word 'leadership' is like many of the concepts in this book: when we seek to define terms, the actual meaning of the word can often escape us. Leadership is not a thing, it exists only in relationships and in the imagination and perception of parties to a relationship. When managers are asked what leadership is, they typically provide three or four common-sense answers:

- Leadership involves getting others to do what you want.
- Leaders motivate people to get things done.
- Leaders provide a vision, a sense of meaning and purpose.
- Leadership is about helping people, leadership in this view is not about leaders getting their own way, but *empowering* people to do what they what.

Within these broad definitions, there is an archetype. A leader for many people is someone who finds something new – a new movement, a new purpose, a new city. In order to found something new, this person leaves the old behind. The word leader stems from the old English work 'laedere', which means to lead someone upon a journey. To give the lead is defined as 'guidance given by going in front, example' or 'guidance by example'. The idea of change is implicit in leadership, as is the idea of example.

Faced with a multitude of threats and uncertainties, people will turn to those who offer assistance. Leaders offer plausible and attractive versions of what to think, feel or do. They help us discover new ways of looking at the world and new possibilities.

Leaders are, then, very powerful and useful figures. To be a leader is to have answers, to be feared and loved, to be attractive to other people. It is hardly surprising that so many books have been written which promise to vouchsafe the secret of leadership.

THE SECRETS OF LEADERSHIP

Within the wide field of writing on leadership, there are a number of themes. The first of these sees leadership as a natural focus of the processes within groups. Here the leader is a central or focal person who integrates the group.

Another theme involves issues around personality and tries to explain leadership as strength of personality or personality traits. In these models the leaders influence the group through force of personality, which also makes possible feats of leadership of which ordinary men and women are incapable.

The exercise of influence over other people is also considered to be the hallmark of leadership. Leaders here change other people's behaviour through modelling desirable behaviours or successfully communicating the need for change.

Power is also important in the exercise of leadership. We saw in Chapter 3 the exercise of power in relationships according to French and Raven's eight types of power. A leader here uses power to gain conformity to his or her will.

A further group of ideas see a leader as someone who initiates structure. The leader in this model is the person who comes up with ideas, who gives the group which they lead purpose and meaning.

Finally, leaders may be seen as people who act or behave in a particular way. Thus anyone who directs or co-ordinates the activities of other people is a leader.

Within these groups of definitions, we can see a number of powerful theories that have attempted to explain what leadership is. One of these is the grid devised by Jane Mouton and Robert Blake.[1] They saw the two most important dimensions of leadership as being concern for production and concern for people. Measured on the grid overleaf we can identify a number of positions, depending on levels of concern for people and production.

---

[1]R. Blake and J. Mouton, *Managerial Grid III*, Gulf, 1985.

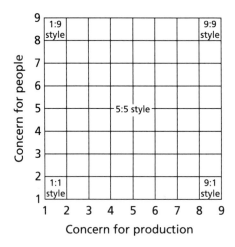

Fig. 14.1 The management grid

9:1 Style: The authoritarian manager concentrates on task, ignoring people.

1:9 Style: The indulgent manager looks after people, but neglects production.

1:1 Style: The minimal manager has little concern for either people or production.

5:5 Style: The compromise manager compromises – a reasonable day's work without upsetting anyone.

9:9 Style: The integrative manager develops commitment from people and creates high production.

How do you 'score' on this grid? Are you 9:1 manager, a 5:5 manager. What sort of manager, or what sort of leader do you want to be?

A similar model of leadership style is that advocated by Paul Hersey. He takes a similar two dimensions to Blake and Mouton – task and people – and combines task and people in a grid chart which illustrates four leadership styles. These styles depend on the situation in which the leader is working:

- When staff are unable and unwilling to carry out the task, the leader should presumably explain and tell or direct. Such people need to be directed.

- When staff are willing, but unable to do the job, the leader should 'sell' to staff, explaining their decisions and providing staff with the opportunity for clarification.

- Where staff are able but unwilling, the leader should invite staff to participate in order to increase motivation.

High Relationship – Low Task	High Relationship – High Task
Leadership through Participation	**Leadership through Selling**
Use when staff are 'able' but 'unwilling'	Use when staff are 'unable' but 'willing'
Low Relationship – Low Task	Low Relationship – High Task
Leadership through Delegation	**Leadership through Telling**
Use when staff are 'able' and 'willing'	Use when staff are 'unwilling' and 'unable'

Fig. 14.2 Situational leadership

- At the highest level, staff are 'willing' and 'able' and the leader should simply delegate.

Hersey claims that his situational leadership model is a training programme used by over 500 of American's top companies. In a complex real world situation these models, working with two dimensions of leadership, may be of limited use. They have the benefits of being simple to understand and to implement, but again focus on the group and neglect important elements of the leadership process.

Another, slightly more complex, method of looking at the leadership process is John Adair's[2] Action-Centred Leadership Adair suggests that leaders achieve the task, build the team and develop individuals. These stages are interlinked. Developing staff will achieve the task. Building the team develops staff.

ACTION-CENTRED LEADERSHIP

John Adair advances a theory of Action-Centred Leadership which involves three interlocking elements (Fig 14.3).

An owner-manager may be focused on achieving the task more than building the team or developing the individual. Look at yourself. Where is your primary focus? Adair offers a checklist for effective action-centred leadership:

Task

- Be quite clear about what the task is, put it over with enthusiasm, and remind people of it often.
- Understand how the task fits into the short- and long term objectives of the business.
- Plan how to accomplish it.

[2]John Adair, *Action Centred Leadership*, Talbot Adair, 1983.

- Define and provide the resources needed, including the time and the authority required.
- Do everything possible to ensure that the business management structure allows the task to be done efficiently.
- Pace progress towards the achievement of the task.
- Evaluate results and compare them with original plans.

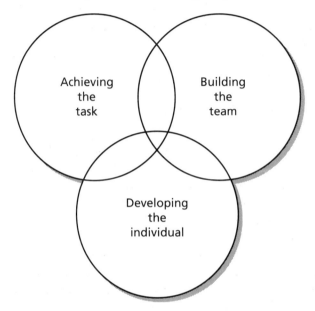

Fig. 14.3 Task, Team and individual

Team

- Set and maintain the team's objectives.
- Involve the team as a whole in the achievement of objectives.
- Maintain the unity of the team by coping effectively with conflict.
- Communicate regularly with the team face-to-face on matters of people, policy, progress and points for action.
- Consult with the team where possible before making decisions which affect them.
- Explain the business's results and achievements.
- Communicate changes in the business and how it will affect the team.

Individuals

Every leader must:

1. Provide a challenge and scope for development by:
   (a) setting targets after consulting, and reviewing them at regular intervals;
   (b) providing relevant training and, where appropriate, using employees to train each other in relevant skills;
   (c) arranging any necessary external and internal contacts;
   (d) restructuring or grouping tasks to use people skills to the fullest;
   (e) rotating jobs to broaden experience;
   (f) providing scope for individuals to take greater responsibility;
   (g) training at least one deputy thoroughly.

2. Make people feel valued by:
   (a) knowing their name, place of work, where appropriate, and interests outside of work;
   (b) regularly monitoring and appreciating individual effort;
   (c) sharing an interest in what they hold important;
   (d) creating a good working environment by being approachable;
   (e) ensuring that everyone understands the importance of their contribution to the team's objectives;
   (f) ensuring that everyone understands the function of the business.

3. Recognise achievements by:
   (a) praising and communicating individuals' successes;
   (b) holding regular meetings with each individual to monitor and counsel;
   (c) providing guidance for a personal development programme;
   (d) operating a fair and open policy linking salary to performance.

Adair offers a slightly more complex model than either Hersey's, or Blake and Mouton's. We may benefit, however, from looking for an even more complex model. We have looked elsewhere in the book at the idea of roles. The following model of leadership is one which takes the idea of the 'laedere' – the guide for the journey, and identifies the roles that this person will need to occupy and the relationships he or she will need to maintain to guide others on that journey.

Roles of the leader

THE LEADER AS DESIGNER AND BUILDER

The leader in this role caters to a follower's need for structure or rules. There are situations in which people need structure. Driving in today's traffic would be impossible without structure or rules. Drivers need to know that oncoming traffic will stay on the right side of the white lines and that other drivers will obey red lights and signs to give way .

Studies have shown that where employees do not have access to procedures and rules and are forced to learn by trial and error, they become dissatisfied. Need for structure and safety corresponds to the security needs which we saw in Maslow's hierarchy of needs.

The journey to new places may often be fraught with danger. It may take a long time and cross a great deal of territory. People cannot go alone and the leader, as designer and builder, is the person who designs and builds the vehicle in which his or her followers will travel.

This symbolic vehicle can be a rigid structure with fixed processes and clear 'laws' with suitable punishments for breaking them. On the other hand it may be a more flexible structure with its crew bound together by a shared vision rather than defined procedures. This vehicle needs to be appropriate for the journey. Leadership needs followership in order to exist. The leader as designer and builder answers the needs of followers who may ask questions such as:

- Who am I?
- What am I supposed to do?
- What is important and unimportant here?

Other followers may ask different questions such as:

- How can I best carry out the task?
- What can I contribute to the organisation?
- How can I develop within the organisation?

We saw earlier the archetypal role of leader as someone who offers people plausible visions of what to think, feel or do. The leader as designer and builder answers these questions by developing structures, roles, rules and procedures. The effective leader is the one who develops the right sort of structures, roles, rules and procedures.

An appropriate organisational structure can offer security. People working in the organisation can see what needs to be done. Rules and procedures can act to reduce uncertainty by building something which makes the external world seem unimportant. Such organisations may tend to look inward and ignore variables in the outside world.

The way in which you design and build an organisation will depend on the individual and collective nature of the people who need to live in the organisation. It will also depend upon the way in which information flows in the organisation and the way in which the organisation communicates with the outside world.

The design of an organisation may involve answering a number of questions. The first of these is, ***what sort of structure will suit the type of people who make up your organisation?*** Some people may prefer a tight structure within well defined positions and procedures; others may prefer a looser structure with less well defined roles and procedures. Other questions include the following:

- *How many tasks should a given position in the organisation contain and how specialised should each task be?* This will involve making decisions about who does what and telling people what they have to do.

- *To what extent can work be standarised for each position?* This will involve decisions about rules and procedures and the degree to which the work is controlled by the worker or by the manager.

- *What knowledge, skills and attitudes should be required for each position?* This involves using the recruitment skills we looked at earlier.

- *On what basis should work positions be grouped into units and units into larger units?* This involves the leader in decisions about whether people are grouped in specialised teams which carry out a complete job or whether they are grouped into units by function (all the milling machines or the word processing operators together). Units could also be created on the basis of geographic spread, customer type, etc.

- *How large should each unit be and how many individuals should report to a given manager?* In formally structured organisations, which are designed to ensure predictability, uniformity and reliability, this can be an important question because of the amount of attention and time which managing people can take up in a loosely structured organisation. Greater worker autonomy means that this is less important.

- *To what extent should the output of each position be standardised?* Standardisation involves decisions about measurement. Consider the benefit which measuring one position's work output can bring in terms of setting targets for motivation.

- *What mechanisms should be established to facilitate adjustment between positions and units?* This is more important as organisations become larger, but even in small organisations decisions need to be made about who sorts out the arguments.

- *Who makes the decisions?* We saw Tannenbaum and Schmidt's decision-making contained at the beginning of the book. This question involves decisions about trust and the capacity for accurate decision-making.

As well as answering those questions the leader as designer and builder will need to consider issues around communication. Information is the life blood of an organisation. Where information is accurately routed and shared, as well as captured from outside, an organisation will operate and flourish. Where information is held back, given to the wrong person or ignored, the organisation is likely to be blocked and fail.

Remember, however that leaders as designers and builders do not have to work on a large scale. Structuring an organisation can involve simple behaviours such as:

Telling people why they should carry out a task

Often we only tell people what they should do and not why they should do it. Knowing the underlying reasons for action is motivating in itself. So if you tell Danny that he should clean the floor of the workshop, he'll be likely to clean it much more effectively if he knows it's because you're expecting a customer to come round to look at the workshop before placing an order.

Employees need to know:

- the task in detail 'Could you clean up the workshop and make sure that all the old packing material is put in the skip?';

- the reason why the task has to be carried out 'We've got Mr Noakes coming round at 2.00 pm to have a look at the workshop. He's thinking about placing an order;

- what Danny might need to carry out the task 'You'll probably need . . . Do you think there's anything else?';

- the potential reward either for themselves or their organisation 'If we get this order, it'll be a feather in my cap'. Be honest about rewards: if there isn't anything in it for Danny, make sure that he knows what's in it for you or the company;

- potential problems if the task isn't done. 'If we don't clean up the workshop, Noakes probably won't give us the order and we'll all look bad'.

Being clear about the nature of the relationship between the employee and yourself is important. Clearly setting out responsibilities will help you realise what the task involves and help the employee to achieve it. It can be seen as the first step in the process of leadership.

Telling people how they should carry out a task

As we saw in the chapter on development, people hate admitting that they don't know how to do something. Consider how often you use the following phrases:

- 'Look, do I have to tell you everything? What am I paying you for?'
- 'Yes, sure, I'll help you, I'm just a bit busy right now.'
- 'Never mind, I'll do it.'
- 'Can't you think for yourself?'
- 'Look, it's obvious . . .'
- 'Do I have to hold your hand?'

Remember that telling isn't training.

Telling people what they should do

We saw in Chapter 11 on motivation that learned helplessness means that employees may not understand what they need to do to meet their needs within your organisation. If they have a responsibility to find out what they need to do themselves, let them know that. On the other hand, if you expect them to do what you tell them, you will need to tell.

It is a common human problem that once you know something everybody else knows it, too. At best, a new employee will be given a few hours' introduction to the job; at worst, he'll be given a staff handbook and told to get on with it. This means that there is a big discrepancy between what the manager imagines is the responsibility of the staff member and what the staff member thinks it is.

The only way you can close this gap is by communicating adequately and checking for understanding. Ask them if they know what to do and ask then to describe it – you may have some surprises. Remember also that consistency is an important quality in your relationship. If you are going to 'tell' someone what to do one minute, don't expect them to find out what to do the next minute. This will weaken the relationship.

THE LEADER AS VISIONARY

Once you've built the vehicle which will take the people on the journey, the next stage is to describe the outcome of the journey. This role is one which involves two sets of skills. The first is the ability to imagine a vision of possible features and the second is to communicate this to the people who follow.

In your role as designer/builder, you have offered guidelines which will fulfil people's needs for security. The role as designer builder involves fulfilling other needs.

J.M. Burns[3] offers the terms 'transactional' and 'transformational' leadership in his book *Leadership*. He studied leaders such as Gandhi and Martin Luther King, and saw transactional leaders as being those who approach followers with an eye to 'trading one thing for another: jobs for votes or subsidies for campaign contribution'. According to Burns, these are less powerful than transforming leaders who bring out the best in their followers and motivate them to produce goals which are for the good of all.

The visionary leader is one who can employ transformational processes by creating the vision of a likely possible future. A vision in this sense is not something mystical or intangible. It is a description of something in the future – possibly the distant future – in terms of what it can become. This 'something' can be as specific as the relationship between managers and workers or as general as a business or an activity. It can be mundane, such as a reference to the better quality of life given by the opening of a staff canteen, or electrifying, such as

[3]J.M. Burns, *Leadership*, Harper and Row, 1978.

being the best design company in Europe. Visions are specific enough to encourage initiative and general enough to remain relevant under changes in the operating conditions.

Basically, a vision must, in order to change people's behaviour, pass two tests. The first of these is the desirability test and the second the feasability test. The desirability test is how well the vision – the description of a future state – serves the interests of the people whose behaviours the leader is attempting to change. These people will be the 'stakeholders'. Stakeholders can be management, staff, equity holders, financial providers and customers.

The feasibility test is the degree to which the strategy can realistically achieve the vision. The creation of a vision which passes both the feasibility and the desirability test is one which involves the collection of accurate information in response to basic questions.

Consider these basic questions for your own organisation:

- What helps our competitors?
- What helps them succeed?
- Why are some succeeding more than others?
- Why are some succeeding more than us?
- Who are our customers and what helps them to succeed?
- How is all this changing?
- In this environment, what are our major strengths?
- What are our most important weaknesses?

People are involved in answering these questions because of the difficulty one person would have in answering them alone. This visionary process tends to take place over a period of time and is a dynamic, not a static, process. The vision will change slightly over time.

A classic example of the visionary approach to leadership was that of Lou Gerstner who, between 1978 and 1987, was the executive Vice-President of Travel Related Services, the core of the American Express operation. Gerstner joined TRS from the consultancy firm McKinsey, where he learnt to ask similar questions to the ones above. Gerstner challenged the accepted – and complacent – view that TRS had reached its peak position in the market. In its place he built a vision of an organisation that was dynamic, growing and diversifying into new markets. To bring the organisation into line with the vision, Gerstner developed the organisation with what John Kotter[4] called an 'almost obsessive focus on the customer'. To support this fixation, he raised the standards of recruitment and development, creating a challenging and entrepreneurial culture. Gerstner constantly talked about 'quality people' and discouraged unnecessary bureaucracy to foster this entrepreneurship. As people within the organisation

[4]John Kotter *The Leadership factor*, Free Press, 1988.

began to focus on the vision within a framework of basic managerial discipline, new product services and initiatives came on to the market and the market-place received these product services and initiatives well.

TRS expanded its operations dramatically. In 1978, American Express cards were issued in eleven currencies; in 1988, this rose to twenty-eight. In 1979, the firm focused on two market segments which were to prove extremely profitable, women and students. During the 1980s American Express moved into direct mail selling, and by 1988 had become the fifth largest direct mail selling organisation in the United States. Gerstner's vision and energy had created a direction for TRS and had shown it to be a realistic and desirable direction. This had aligned the workers within the organisation and had motivated them to create a business success.

The type of needs which the leader, as visionary, fulfils are the needs for achievement. In the same way that the leader as designer/builder needs to take the needs of his or her followers into account, so does the leader as visionary.

Need for achievement (NAch) is a motivator which was identified and developed by Henry Murray, John Atkinson and David McLelland[5]. NAch can be identified as the desire or need to accomplish something difficult; to master, manipulate or organise physical objects, human beings or ideas, and to do this as rapidly and independently as possible; to overcome obstacles and attain a high standard; to excel oneself; to rival and surpass others and to increase self-regard by the successful exercise of talent. By painting a convincing vision of a successful future, the leader as visionary fulfils the NAch needs of his or her followers.

The following quiz enables you to gain a picture of the strength of your own, or others', need to achieve.

QUIZ

Answer the questions below by ticking your preference.

		Greatly prefer	Rather prefer	In between	Rather prefer	Greatly prefer		
1(a)	I prefer work that I can be sure of doing well	1	2	3	4	5	1(b)	I prefer work that needs a lot of hard physical or mental effort
2(a)	I prefer to receive constant feedback on my progress.	1	2	3	4	5	2(b)	I prefer just getting along with the work
3(a)	I prefer to work at my own pace	1	2	3	4	5	3(b)	I prefer to work at the pace required of me

[5]David McClelland *The Achieving Society*, Von Notrand, 1961.

4(a) I prefer to know every detail about a task from the beginning	1	2	3	4	5	4(b) I prefer to work step by step through the task as information is given to me
5(a) I prefer clear detailed instructions	1	2	3	4	5	5(b) I prefer work which requires initiative and judgement
6(a) I prefer to do one job at a time and to hear about that job when I need to do it	1	2	3	4	5	6(b) I prefer to have several jobs going at once and to have information well ahead of time to allow for planning
7(a) I prefer to set my own targets and to alter them as and when necessary	1	2	3	4	5	7(b) I prefer stable targets which are worked out for the group and not chopped and changed
8(a) I prefer taking controllable risks about work	1	2	3	4	5	8(b) I prefer not taking risks with work

Score your questionnaire on the following grid.

1(a)	1	2	3	4	5	1(b)
2(a)	5	4	3	2	1	2(b)
3(a)	5	4	3	2	1	3(b)
4(a)	5	4	3	2	1	4(b)
5(a)	1	2	3	4	5	5(b)
6(a)	1	2	3	4	5	6(b)
7(a)	5	4	3	2	1	7(b)
8(a)	5	4	3	2	1	8(b)

Put down your score for each question

1 ☐ 2 ☐ 3 ☐ 4 ☐ 5 ☐ 6 ☐ 7 ☐ 8 ☐ and add the total score.

The total score shows the type of work which the respondent prefers. When NAch is high amongst employees, a looser vision-building style of leadership may be appropriate. Where NAch is low, a more structured and procedural leadership style might be appropriate.

Score: 31 or more	high levels of NAch may prefer work within a very loosely bounded framework motivated by vision.
Score: 26–30	Above average NAch. Also motivated by vision but needs some procedures and guidance.
Score 20–25	Average NAch. Prefers to work within a fairly structured setting. Vision less important.
Score 15–19	Slightly below average NAch. Prefers a tightly bounded setting with clear procedures. Vision unimportant.
Score below 15	Low NAch. Work fairly unimportant. Vision not relevant.

This NAch quiz is a fairly rough tool. People's levels of achievement motivation will vary at different times in their lives and with different tasks which they take on. It may be that the leader as visionary can inspire even those with low NAch, although he or she may not have the time to do so.

Again, creating a vision can be done in different ways. We saw in Chapter 11 on motivation the benefits which can come from 'painting the big picture'. Leaders as visionaries can be involved in developing challenging tasks for staff to complete.

A visionary leader will build his vision on the information – the learning that he or she does from within and outside the organisation. Visionary leaders pay attention to the vague ideas of the salesmen about what the customer really wants and the imperfect ideas in the service section about quality improvement. Visionary leadership is a two-way street, but the leader here will develop, focus and reinforce the vision by telling stories about the organisation – what 'we' can do. 'We' here can be an organisation, a work team or an individual. The story can be about running an order, finishing a job ahead of schedule or being the best.

THE LEADER AS CATALYST AND FACILITATOR

The next role for the leader to play in helping his or her followers in their journey is actually to get the vehicle – the organisation – moving. This involves providing the jump start for change by acting as a catalyst and facilitator.

Another approach to the role of leader is that of catalyst and facilitator. As we've seen in considering the leader as visionary, part of a leader's role is about change; part of this role is that of catalyst and facilitator. A catalyst is something which provokes change or releases a force for change which is potentially already in existence, and a facilitator is someone who helps focus that force to achieve realistic objectives.

We have already seen elsewhere in this book that the major resource of an organisation, particularly a smaller organisation, is its people. People have wide ranges of knowledge, skill and attitudes which can be mobilised to help an organisation reach its goals. There are two main areas in which leaders in this role employ their skills. The first of these is in the area of delegation, where the leader will clearly communicate responsibilities and accountabilities to staff in order to allow them to bring energy to bear on the task. The second is in the level of communication which takes place, communicating information throughout the organisation to share the vision and to help people learn when they should carry out the task.

In this role, the leader is sociable and makes use of his or her communicative skills. For Robert Merton, leadership was 'an interpersonal relationship in which others comply because they want to, not because they have to'. He or she will also capitalise on the differences within the organisation which they lead, by building roles and jobs around interpersonal differences to demonstrate concern for people.

Peter Greenleaf, an American humanist, argues that followers 'will freely respond only to individuals who are chosen as leaders because they are proven and trusted as servants' and that the best test of leadership is: do those 'served' grow as persons and do they, while being served, become healthier, wiser, freer, more autonomous, more likely to become servants?

This leadership through service should not be an excuse not to lead. Organisations are full of managers who use participation and caring as an excuse not to lead. Used properly, however the leader as catalyst can produce extraordinary results by channelling people's energy.

We have already seen that this type of leader will tend to communicate. They do not, however only communicate the vision, they also communicate their belief in people. Catalytic leaders believe profoundly in 'productivity through people' and demonstrate this in words and actions. Leaders as catalysts and facilitators do not see communication as a one way process.

Nowhere is this emphasis more clearly seen than in the work of a corporation quoted by Peters and Waterman. When Ron McPherson became the Chief Executive of Dana, he eliminated reams of policy manuals and put in their place a one-page philosophy statement that stressed the need for more training and opportunities for employment. McPherson once ran the ad below in a number of leading American business publications.

TALK BACK TO THE BOSS

It's one of Dana's principles of productivity: bosses don't have all the answers. The worker who does the job always knows more about it than his boss. But all that he knows can't be used unless he's free to talk about it; especially to his boss.

At Dana, bosses listen. It's part of what we call humanistic management, giving people the freedom to work well, to grow and share in the rewards.

You can see the results in our productivity. It's more than doubled in the last seven years.

Productivity alone does not produce profits. But we're balancing our output of parts for the vehicular, service and industrial equipment markets we manufacture for. So, as well as increasing productivity, we've improved our earnings year after year.

And that's not bad for a bunch of people who talk back to their bosses!

Perhaps because of the amount of listening that they have to do, leaders as facilitators tend to be visible and accessible. Peters and Waterman[6] popularised the idea of 'management by wandering about' – the idea that managers needed to get out of the office and interact with customers and employees. Under pressure, managers in smaller organisations can sometimes find this difficult and either avoid employees and colleagues or interact in a very structured manner by giving orders or by telling.

One way of overcoming this problem is to develop vehicles through which communication can be carried out. One example of this is the management turnaround of Robert Crandall in Kodak copiers' design and manufacturing division. Crandall met all supervisors every three months to talk about new projects and how things had improved. He established something called 'copy product forum', at which a different member of each department would meet with him as a group once a month, just to talk. He introduced a monthly journal for the division and a scheme called 'dialogue letters' which allowed employees to ask Crandall and other managers anything they wanted, anonymously, and be guaranteed a reply.

[6]Tom Peters and Robert Waterman. *In Search of Excellence*, Harper and Row, 1982.

Crandall instituted regular business lunches every Thursday with their biggest supplier to communicate the message that design and manufacturing increased production. This increase was reflected by the powerful use of large charts in the workplace to give staff the message that they were succeeding. These images showing a dramatic drop in defects per unit, production costs and inventory levels with an increase in volume and productivity per employee. They were simple and easy to understand, but communicated powerful messages which did not clog already over-used communication channels or require scarce managerial time.

Leaders as facilitators empower people in two useful ways. The first of these is through communicating a clear sense of direction which unlocks lower level employees and allows them to take initiative with a degree of freedom. If their behaviour is consistent with the direction, it is difficult to punish them. Second, because everyone has a clear idea of the direction in which the organisation is going it is less likely that a single person's initiative will be stalled when it comes into contact with someone else.

In a small organisation, it is essential to make use of the maximum capacity of the human resources available. Failing to do this is like tying a stone around the neck of the organisation. An additional benefit of the communication process is that it tells people what to do and gives them clear targets to aim for. This introduces us to the fourth leader role.

LEADERS AS CO-ORDINATORS AND NAVIGATORS

The next stage in the journey involves the leader developing a role as co-ordinator and navigator. Once the vehicle has been built, the destination decided and the energy released, there still remains the issue of how to get there. Again, this may involve the leader in delegating the leadership task while retaining overall control within the vision that he or she has created.

The leader as navigator also uses relationships, but is concerned about the day-to-day running of the organisational vehicle and ensuring that it maintains a course towards the vision. Often, it may not be enough simply to share the vision and release and focus energy. Followers may need a road map for the journey. Each organisation's and each leader's road map will be unique, but there are a number of behaviours which the navigator can demonstrate which will help steer the group.

Apart from delegation, the leader nagivator will deploy a range of skills which relate to both communication and power in relationships. He or she will demonstrate a range of persuasive and influence skills to deal with the conflict which may arise because of change.

Leaders as navigators will also draw upon the whole range of power types that we saw in Chapter 3 to increase their influence with the group, and will be heavily involved in the sort of problem-solving learning on behalf of the group which we saw in Chapter 2.

Finally, leaders as navigators will tend to embody the values which underpin the vision painted or focused by the leader as visionary. These values will be underpinned by their attitude towards risk and their need for development in themselves and in their followers, as well as their need for independence and autonomy. Independence indicates a high power since, as we saw in Chapter 3, power is about dependence.

The leader as co-ordinator is similar to the leader as navigator in that he or she takes direction from the world outside the organisational vehicle. The leader as co-ordinator actively manages a network of relationships both inside and outside the limits of the organisational vehicle. These relationships will give the leader as co-ordinator information and power, through which to make the adjustments necessary throughout the journey.

Thus the leader plays a mediating and connecting role between his or her followers and the outside world. They may often create cohesion within the group in this role. External threats tend to pull groups together as they focus on the perceived danger, and a co-ordinator will offer a structure or potential plan for meeting this danger.

At times like this, the group which you lead will experience stress. Energy within the group may be lost or diffused and the leader as energiser may need to replace that lost energy or refocus it. Group stress can come about from a variety of sources. Groups may be frustrated by apparently unattainable goals. The leader here will need to demonstrate that the goals are attainable; this may involve identifying the types of obstacle which will block the attainment of goals. Obstacles may be lack of resources, quality of resources or conflicting or ambiguous situations. The leader as energiser needs to identify what type of obstacle is likely to block objectives and remove it, or else clarify difficulties or ambiguous situations.

Groups may be afraid of impending danger. The leader as energiser here will use information gained in his or her role as co-ordinator to avoid or minimise these dangers by learning and encouraging followers to learn also.

Groups may also be in a state of inertia, which they perceive as less risky and costly than actively responding to warnings of danger. The leader here will re-enthuse the followers with vision and demonstrate by personal example, showing followers the inadequacy of simple solutions or defensive avoidance.

Overall, the leader as energiser is the tactical consort of the leader as navigator and co-ordinator. These roles are involved in the day-to-day maintenance of the organisation on its journey to the future, which has been painted by the leader as visionary and fuelled by the leader as catalyst within the vehicle built by the leader as designer.

LEADERSHIP AS A PERSONAL ISSUE

We have written throughout this chapter about the leader's roles in taking his or her followers on a journey. These roles will not follow each other sequentially, and are likely to overlap.

The key issue which supports all these roles is the *personal* nature of leadership. Leadership is specific to situation and people, it has no existence as a set of rules or laws. This is true of all people management. There are no right answers. This chapter, and indeed, the whole book, has attempted to offer a number of frameworks through which you can understand the management of people: some ways of behaving which seem to be appropriate in many situations and some roles which may help develop relationships for people management.

Leadership is dependent upon the survival of a group of followers. The survival of a group is dependent upon a type of leadership which is able to keep group members and subgroups working together to a common purpose, maintain productivity at a level sufficient to sustain the group and satisfy the expectations of the members regarding the group and the leader. This means that the leader must manage the expectations of the members through his or her relationships with those members.

The tools of managing relationships are those which we examined at the beginning of this book: self-management, communication, negotiation, etc. The real test of leadership doesn't lie in the personality or the behaviour of a leader, but in the performance of the group which he leads. Because groups have situational needs, leadership must be tailored to the group – the organisation which the leaders want to lead.

Generally, when groups are free to choose their own leaders, they tend to choose group members who will be able to maintain direction towards a goal, facilitate the achievements of tasks and ensure that the group stays together. Leaders may find that the short-term objective of measuring performance may conflict with the longer-term objectives of developing the group. Behaviours which foster the accomplishment of the task may be different from those which foster and develop the group. Some leaders are extremely effective in getting the job done, whereas others are exceptionally skilled in the art of building satisfaction with, and loyalty between, members of the group.

The most valued leaders are those which are able to do both and these can be done by maintaining an honest relationship with followers – employees in all of the situations which we have identified in this book. The overall emphasis of this book has been about developing an honest performance-orientated relationship. In small organisations, which are often fragile because of the nature of resource constraints in time, experience, effort, finance, etc., a performance orientation is essential to avoid the destruction of the organisation and to ensure its survival and development.

Conclusion

Overall, this book has described a performance cycle which first stems from the manager's ability to manage himself or herself. This goes on to a manager's ability to manage his or her relationships with other individuals in situations such as recruitment and selection, appraisal, motivation, etc. The final part of the cycle is the manager's ability to manage himself or herself as part of a group, and as a leader within that group.

All of the tools and behaviours within this book will depend on the nature of the individuals with whom you work. In order to use these behaviours effectively, you will need to carry out the following steps:

■ *Know yourself. What are your own attitudes, values and preferences? Where are your personal strengths and weaknesses? How can you develop?*

■ *Know the people you want to manage. What are their attitudes, values and preferences? What are their needs? What are their strengths and weaknesses? How can they develop?*

■ *Know what you want from the relationship. What are your criteria for a successful relationship? How do you define success? Is it money, friendship, security, fame and praise, power? What are your objectives? Be as clear as possible, and be sure.*

■ *Decide what purpose your existing behaviour fulfils in meeting these objectives.*

■ *Decide whether the behaviours suggested in this book will better fulfil your purposes.*

If you follow these steps, you may find that this book will help you to manage your relationships effectively to satisfy your own needs and to satisfy the needs of the people with whom your relationship exist.

Managing people through relationships will help you to develop performance within your own organisation and help you take it forward on its journey to success through the challenges which will help it, and you, develop.

Good luck and good people management!

INDEX